BF 28-50

ERALD

STATE
AND DIPLOMATIC
IMMUNITY

STATE
AND DIPLOMATIC
IMMUNITY

By

CHARLES J. LEWIS, M.A.

Of the Middle Temple, Barrister
quondam Open Scholar of
Oriel College, Oxford

SECOND EDITION

LONDON   NEW YORK   HAMBURG   HONG KONG
LLOYD'S OF LONDON PRESS LTD
1985

Lloyd's of London Press Ltd.
Legal Publishing and Conferences Division
26–30 Artillery Lane, London E1 7LX
Great Britain

U.S.A. AND CANADA
Lloyd's of London Press Inc.
87 Terminal Drive, Plainview
New York, N.Y. 10003 U.S.A.

GERMANY
Lloyd's of London Press
P.O. Box 11 23 47, Diechstrasse 41
2000 Hamburg 11
West Germany

SOUTH-EAST ASIA
Lloyd's of London Press (Far East) Ltd.
1502 Chung Nam Building
1 Lockhart Road, Wanchai
Hong Kong

©

CHARLES J. LEWIS
1980, 1985

First published 1980
Second edition 1985

British Library Cataloguing in Publication Data
Lewis, Charles
State and diplomatic immunity.—2nd ed.
1. Diplomatic and consular service in Great Britain
2. Law—Great Britain   3. Immunities of foreign states
I. Title
341.3'3   JX1672

ISBN 1–85044–047–6

Typeset in Linotron 202 Garamond by
Wessex Typesetters, Frome, Somerset

Printed in Great Britain by
The Eastern Press Ltd,
London and Reading

To my children
Benjamin and Janet
and my parents

ACKNOWLEDGMENTS

I should like to acknowledge with thanks the considerable assistance I have received on the international aspect of this subject from Sir Ian Sinclair, K.C.M.G., Q.C., Legal Adviser to the Foreign and Commonwealth Office. The responsibility for what I have written, however, is mine alone.

CHARLES J. LEWIS

ACKNOWLEDGMENTS TO THE SECOND EDITION

For the expansion of the text on diplomatic immunity I acknowledge a debt to Eileen Denza of the Foreign and Commonwealth Office and her authoritative volume *Diplomatic Law* (New York, 1976), at the moment regrettably out of print.

CHARLES J. LEWIS

PREFACE TO THE
FIRST EDITION

Until November 1978 the immunity of foreign governments in our courts in civil litigation was governed by the common law. Since the end of the Second World War the United Kingdom had become increasingly isolated in its adherence under the common law to the doctrine of absolute immunity. Most of the Continental jurisdictions had since adopted the restrictive view, which denies immunity in respect of commercial activities, though France had been something of a laggard in this respect. The United States had, under the lead of the State Department, followed the restrictive doctrine since 1952, and among civilized nations this country, thanks to the inherent conservatism of the common law, and the Soviet Union, for reasons which are not hard to seek, stood virtually alone in adhering to the absolute doctrine.

Then in 1975 the Privy Council adopted the restrictive doctrine for maritime law (actions *in rem*) in *The Philippine Admiral* [1977] A.C. 373. The United Kingdom had signed, but not yet ratified, the European Convention on State Immunity (May, 1972) embodying the restrictive view over a wider field. Then in January 1977 the Court of Appeal had, under the leadership of Lord Denning, M.R., purported to alter the common law into line with their view of current international law, and had held that the restrictive doctrine applied to all actions (the *Trendtex* case [1977] Q.B. 529).

This decision has aroused controversy, and one judge at first instance has declined to follow it (Donaldson, J., as he then was, in the *Uganda* case [1979] 1 Lloyd's Rep. 481).

With the advent of the State Immunity Act the law has been codified and the common law rules to a large extent abolished. The Act lays down specific rules for the granting or withholding of immunity, and it is the purpose of this book to provide a detailed analysis of those rules. At the same time, the old régime of the common law remains relevant, particularly in respect of matters arising before the Act came into force. In addition, the two important treaties in this field, the European Convention and the Brussels Convention, though operating within the narrow compass of signatory States, provide a useful comparison with the Act, and are indeed the source of many of its provisions.

For that reason I have adopted by and large a threefold treatment of the material, under the common law, under the Act, and under the treaties.

It has also been thought convenient to deal in Book II with diplomatic and consular immunity. In most respects this topic, concerned as it is with the personal immunity of government staff, and the protection of embassies, has little connection with State immunity. Yet in two respects the two topics come together, in their history and in the personal immunity of the sovereign himself. Although the details of the diplomatic immunities are likely to be studied only seldom, when, for example, embassy staff are seized as hostages by a "government" that cares nothing for the rules of international law, it is thought that a general understanding of the law of diplomatic privilege will be useful in studying the more complicated, and more interesting, question of State immunity.

PREFACE TO THE
SECOND EDITION

A lot has happened since 1980. The House of Lords gave judgment in *The I Congreso del Partido* case in July 1981, extending the restrictive doctrine at common law to all actions involving State-owned trading vessels, and probably beyond, at the same time illustrating by their conflicting views the difficulty of applying that doctrine to a given set of facts. Meanwhile the importance of the common law in this field lessens with the passing of time as the relevant date for current disputes tends more and more to fall after November 1978 when the Act came into force.

State bank accounts have been the subject of litigation both in West Germany and up to the House of Lords in this country (the *Alcom* case), and some light has been thrown on the workings of s. 6(1) and s. 16 of the Act in the context of premises leased for diplomatic purposes (*Intpro Properties* v. *Sauvel*). In addition public interest in diplomatic immunity has been aroused to an unprecedented degree in the aftermath of the murder of the woman police constable outside the "Libyan People's Bureau" in St. James's Square in April 1984 and the discovery of the crated Nigerian en route through Stansted airport. When I wrote the short chapter on diplomatic immunity for the first edition my intention was only to provide a short guide to the more important provisions of the Act of 1964, but in the light of subsequent events I have decided to expand it to give a more thorough treatment.

I have also made full use of the recent three volumes of the outstanding International Law Reports that provide a thesaurus of case law on State immunity (Vols. 63–5). In this way I have been able to avoid to a considerable extent references to abstruse foreign law reports, and for readers who do not have the English reports I have given in the table of cases by way of alternative the ILR reference where available. I have included references to United States and European decisions

PREFACE TO THE SECOND EDITION

where I thought this could prove of interest. Some of these cases will be no more than informative, others may be actually helpful.

Finally, the only English case on employment and State immunity has been heard in the Employment Appeal Tribunal, providing considerable guidance to the attitude and approach of our courts to the non-justiciable nature of sovereign functions (*Sengupta* v. *Republic of India*).

10 King's Bench Walk   CHARLES J. LEWIS
London
June 1985

CONTENTS

CONTENTS

BOOK 2: DIPLOMATIC IMMUNITY

CONTENTS

APPENDICES

xv

TABLE OF CASES

References are to paragraph number
The year given in apposition to the International Law Reports reference
(I.L.R.) is the year in which the decision of the Court was given

TABLE OF LEGISLATION

References are to paragraph number

CHAPTER 1

GENERAL INTRODUCTION

1.1   The scope of the book

This book is concerned, as its title suggests, with two topics:

(i) State immunity and
(ii) diplomatic immunity.

It is possible to a great extent to keep these two topics apart. But to do so one has first to recognize that at root they arise from the same consideration, namely that it is inconsistent with the dignity and independence of sovereigns if they are made subject to foreign jurisdictions. The immunity of States, like the immunity of diplomatic agents, grew out of the personal immunity of sovereigns. It seemed a natural extension at the time, though now, with the enthusiastic participation of governments in the commercial arena, and the proliferation of State-organized or State-controlled enterprises, the considerations that arise on the immunity of States seem a far cry from those relevant to a sovereign's personal immunity.

While the connection is still there (for example, a sovereign's personal immunities in his private capacity are transferred by the State Immunity Act from the common law to the umbrella of the Diplomatic Privileges Act 1964), it is important to be aware of the distinction between governmental immunities (which will apply to the sovereign or head of State himself only when acting in his public capacity—s. 14(1) of the Act of 1978) and the purely personal immunities of the sovereign and his household as private persons, and of those who claim diplomatic immunity through the sovereign as his accredited representatives. In this, as in any discussion, it makes for clarity if one attempts to define one's terms—

1

1.2   Terms

"State immunity" means the immunity from civil suit afforded to entities of sovereign status, including the sovereign or head of State when acting in a public capacity. The suit may be one brought directly against such an entity or head of State as defendant, it may be directed by an action *in rem* against property in which the sovereign has an interest, or it may be an *inter partes* action which imperils property in which the sovereign claims an interest. Due to the commercial significance and universality of marine trade, claims against property most frequently involve a ship in the ownership or possession of a State, and, as we shall see, a special body of law has arisen, both at common law and under statute, as well as internationally by treaty, that is applicable to shipping cases. The term "sovereign immunity" may be used to cover this immunity from civil suit, but as that term is also used to cover the personal immunities of the sovereign, I, like the Act, have preferred the term "State immunity". It follows that the sovereign's immunity from civil suit when acting in his public capacity falls within the term "State immunity".

It is then possible, and even appropriate, to place the sovereign's immunities when not acting in his public capacity, from suits both civil and criminal, under the head of "diplomatic immunity", along with the similar immunities enjoyed by his family and staff, and those immunities which perhaps more naturally attract the epithet "diplomatic", namely those afforded to diplomatic agents under the Diplomatic Privileges Act 1964 (and consular officials under the Consular Relations Act 1968), immunities which stem from the sovereign's own immunity, and which now share a common statutory basis under the Act of 1964.

1.3   Conclusion

In this book, therefore,

(i)   "State immunity" is used for the immunity from civil process of entities of sovereign status (including the head of State in his public capacity);

(ii) "diplomatic immunity' is used for the personal immunities of diplomatic and consular officers, and heads of State in their private capacity;

(iii) "sovereign immunity" is not used, save in a very general sense, as in the expressions "the absolute doctrine of sovereign immunity" and "the restrictive doctrine of sovereign immunity", which have by constant usage effectively become terms of art.

1.4   Abbreviations

In the book the following short forms are used:—

"The Act" and "The Act of 1978" mean the State Immunity Act 1978.

"The Convention" and "The European Convention" mean the European Convention on State Immunity signed at Basle on 16 May 1972 (Cmnd. 5081).

"The Brussels Convention" means the International Convention for the Unification of Certain Rules Concerning the Immunity of State-Owned Ships signed at Brussels on 10 April 1926 (together with the Protocol of 24 May 1934) (Cmnd. 5672).

1.5

State immunity should not be confused with the act of State doctrine, neither the English one nor the totally different American one, nor with the principle of English law that our courts will not normally sit in judgment on the transactions abroad of foreign States.

In English law act of State refers to a prerogative act of policy in the field of foreign affairs performed by the United Kingdom Government in the course of its relationship with another State or its subjects, for example the making and performance of treaties, annexation of foreign territory, seizure of land or goods in rights of conquest, and declarations of war. These, being essentially exercises of sovereign power, cannot be challenged, controlled or interfered with by municipal courts. But what the United States courts mean by the act of State doctrine is that they will not pass judgment upon the validity of the sovereign acts of *foreign* governments where that would hinder rather than further the United States' pursuit of goals both for itself and for the community of nations as a whole in the international sphere. So their courts will not examine, for example, the taking of property *within* its own territory by a foreign sovereign government, even if the taking were alleged to be in violation of customary international law. Acts of State affecting property situate outside the United States will only be given effect to if consistent with the policy and law of the United States (see the recent case of *Libra Bank* v. *Banco Nacional de Costa Rica*.[1]

There is, on the other hand, in English law no established doctrine according to which the courts will in no circumstances sit in judgment on acts of foreign States. In practice the courts decide whether or not to assume jurisdiction in each case on an *ad hoc* basis. A helpful treatment of the subject is to be found in Lord Wilberforce's judgment in *Buttes Gas and Oil Co.* v. *Hammer*,[2] which fundamentally concerned disputed territorial claims of States in and around the Persian Gulf. The case called for adjudication on the validity, meaning and effect of transactions of foreign sovereign States, which were not, however, confined within the territorial jurisdiction of such States. The relevant principle, the learned judge said, was not a form of the act of State doctrine but a matter of the need for judicial restraint or abstention in the light of the exigencies of foreign relations. In that particular case most of the claim was held to be non-justiciable: the court would be entering a judicial no-man's land, asked to review transactions in which a number of foreign States had been involved, transactions brought to a precarious settlement after diplomacy and the use of force, and to say that part at least of those transactions were "unlawful" under international law.

It remains to be seen how far this principle of non-justiciability will be invoked so as to interrelate with the

1. 676 F. 2d 47 (2nd Cir. 1982).
2. [1982] A.C. 888; 64 I.L.R. 331 (1981).

doctrine of State immunity in our law, as the act of State doctrine has so often been used in United States cases on State immunity. It is at least imaginable that it could provide some sort of long-stop for foreign States in claims where for one reason or another, perhaps due to waiver or the commercial nature of the transaction involved, the defence of State immunity is not available.

BOOK 1
STATE IMMUNITY

CHAPTER 2

INTRODUCTION TO BOOK 1

2.1   The régimes

Three different régimes govern the issue of State immunity.
They are
  (i) the common law
  (ii) statute
  (iii) treaty.

2.2   (i) The common law

Until comparatively recently all questions of State immunity
were solved by reference to the common law. As happens from
time to time, the common law, by an unhappy combination of
respect for precedent on the one hand and judicial activism on
the other (on the part of those judges who saw the need for
change and did their best according to their own lights to
promote it) had, largely due to the efforts of Lord Denning,
M.R., to constrain the law into something approaching a
contemporary image, got itself into a tangle, from which to
extricate our jurisprudence the *deus ex machina* of legislative
intervention was required.

2.3 The State Immunity Act 1978 came into force on 22
November 1978. It enabled this country to ratify both the
Brussels Convention of 1926 and the European Convention of
May 1972. It codifies the law on State immunity, and
represents a radical departure from the position at common
law (at least, as understood by most commentators). But the
common law continues to play an important part in this field
for the following reasons:

2.4 (a) the Act is not retrospective (see Chapter 11). Matters occurring before it came into force are still governed by the common law. As disputes may not arise until years after the formation of a contract, and may not then reach the courts for several more years, it was to be expected that for some time a considerable number—the majority at first, and thereafter a steadily decreasing number—of the disputes arising in the field of State immunity would fall to be decided under the common law.

How far the courts will bend, or constrain, the common law, while it is still relevant on the issue, to tally with the statute remains to be seen. There is no jurisprudential reason why they should, and it is unlikely that the more conservative judges will make any effort to do so. In *Hispano Americana Mercantil S.A.* v. *Central Bank of Nigeria*[1] the Court of Appeal applied the law as it stood in 1975 at the time the relevant contract was made, and were not influenced by the contrary provisions of the Act, which had come into force by the date of the hearing.

The Act provides by s. 23(3) that the provisions of Part 1 do not apply to "proceedings in respect of matters that occurred before the date of the coming into force of this Act", and in particular the statutory rules as to immunity in contractual actions do not apply to contracts entered into before that date.

The Act provides by the combined effect of s. 14(4) with s. 13(2) and (4) that property of a State's central bank shall not be subject to any process for the enforcement of a judgment. The defendants in this case were indebted to the plaintiffs for a quantity of cement supplied to the Nigerian Ministry of Defence. A subsequent administration found that it no longer needed the cement (far too much had been ordered) and refused to pay for it. A letter of credit had been opened by the defendants on account of the Ministry of Defence at the Midland Bank. The plaintiffs obtained an injunction from Donaldson, J., in March 1976 restraining the defendants from disposing of the funds deposited with the Midland Bank. In April 1979 the Court of Appeal held that the injunction should be continued to trial of the action, and that the provisions of the Act which would give such funds immunity from such an order were not in point, neither as a matter of law nor as being

1. [1979] 2 Lloyd's Rep. 277; 64 I.L.R. 221 (1979).

of persuasive effect, as they applied only to matters arising after the Act came into operation.

One may be forgiven for wondering whether this Court of Appeal, presided over by Lord Denning, M.R., had it considered it desirable to grant immunity in the case, might not have held that the common law should be interpreted in the light of the later, and current, statutory provisions.

Another example may be found in *Uganda Co. (Holdings) Ltd.* v. *Government of Uganda*[2] where Donaldson, J., said briefly (page 483): "This application is not affected by the State Immunity Act 1978, which has only just come into force and is not retrospective in its operation". Lloyd, J., took a similar view in *Planmount Ltd.* v. *Republic of Zaire*,[3] a claim for the cost of building works carried out at the ambassador's official London residence, the contract having been made some 10 months before the Act came into force. And in *The I Congreso del Partido*[4] Lord Wilberforce expressly declined to use the Act as a guide to what international law was at the time.

2.5 (b) The common law is also still of importance, and will continue to remain so, in those areas not covered by the Act (see Chapter 10). Section 16 of the Act excludes its operation from criminal proceedings. Although the immunities of the sovereign or head of State himself and his household are transferred by s. 20 of the Act from the common law to the protection of the Diplomatic Privileges Act 1964, the immunity from criminal jurisdiction of foreign governments and entities of sovereign status, which might be a matter for consideration under, for example, consumer legislation, or possibly health and safety at work legislation, would be decided at common law. (It may, however, be presumed that the question would be quickly resolved in favour of that complete immunity which has always been enjoyed at common law by the foreign potentate.) The Act is inapplicable also to proceedings relating to taxation other than those specified in s. 11 (see Chapter 6, H), so that immunity in such proceedings would fall to be considered at common law, in so

2. [1979] 1 Lloyd's Rep. 481; 64 I.L.R. 209 (1978).
3. [1981] 1 All E.R. 1110; 64 I.L.R. 268 (1980).
4. [1983] 1 A.C. 244; 64 I.L.R. 307 (1981).

far as unaffected by any other statutory provision. The Act is also inapplicable to proceedings relating to anything done by or to the armed forces of a State while present in the United Kingdom, so that the issue would be debated at common law, subject to the operation of the Visiting Forces Act 1952.

2.6 (c) The common law is likely also to be relevant to assist interpretation of the Act where the point does not appear completely settled by the text of the statute. In many cases a statute has been clarified by reference to decided case law. Although the Act is certainly not declaratory of the common law, and one must therefore be careful in attributing any weight to common law precedents upon issues covered by the statute, nevertheless, where the Act appears to embody the common law rule, for example on the question of immunity on counterclaims (s. 2(6)) or a State's claim to be interested in property (s. 6(4)), common law precedents may be a proper subject for consideration.

Also, if the Act should appear unclear in its effect, reference may be had to common law precedent to clarify the ambiguity, where the presumption that the Act was not intended in that particular connection to alter the common law may be made. For example, the precedents on what entities are of sovereign status may be useful in a particular case to assess the operation of s. 14 (see Chapter 4, paragraph 4.8), and those on submission by taking a step in the proceedings may assist a decision on s. 2 (see Chapter 8).

2.7 (d) It may also be the case that parties agree that the Act shall not apply to a particular transaction (this is not prohibited by the Act); if that is done it would seem that the common law rules would apply.

2.8 (e) Finally, the common law remains of significance from the historical and the jurisprudential point of view. A knowledge of it will assist understanding of the source, the creation, the purpose and the effect of both the Act and the treaties.

2.9 In applying the common law to disputes governed by it, one should briefly consider the effect of the European Convention on State Immunity of 1972, and the Brussels Convention of 1926 with Protocol of 1934, which this country finally ratified on 6 July 1979. The European Convention, for those countries that had originally ratified it, had come into force on 11 June 1976. It has now been ratified by five countries only—Austria in 1974, Belgium in 1975, Cyprus in 1976, the United Kingdom in 1979 and Switzerland in 1982. It was important for the United Kingdom to adopt the Convention and embody it in the municipal law because after the coming into force of the United States' Foreign Sovereign Immunities Act of 1976 a lot of commercial work was about to be lost by the City of London to New York had the United Kingdom law on immunity remained unclear or unsatisfactory. But the comparative lack of interest in the Convention in Europe, in such marked contrast to the enthusiasm shown for the Vienna Convention on Diplomatic Immunity, is probably due to the fact that many countries are waiting to see what the International Law Commission (ILC) at the United Nations finally comes up with (see below at 2.16) before deciding which system to adopt. Many non-European countries are not attracted to the restrictive doctrine, at any rate in its wider form, and it is likely therefore that the ILC agreed draft will embody a less restrictive view than the European Convention.

Treaty obligations do not affect municipal law, for otherwise the Crown in the exercise of its prerogative would be legislating for Parliament; but municipal law, whether common law or statute, will always be construed, so far as possible, in such a way as not to conflict with this country's international obligations. Moreover, in so far as one accepts that rules of international law are *ipso facto* rules of municipal law by a process of automatic incorporation and do not need to be explicitly adopted by Act of Parliament or judicial precedent (the two theories have each their distinguished supporters), it may be argued that treaty obligations reflect contemporary rules of international law, and that therefore the common law necessarily incorporates those obligations. If in any particular case it be objected that the provisions of a treaty may represent a departure from the customary rules of international law, one may pray in aid the view of the majority of the Court of Appeal in *Trendtex Trading Corporation* v. *Central Bank of Nigeria*[5] that as international law within the municipal framework knows no rule of *stare decisis* the court is entitled, indeed bound, in each case to apply the contemporary rule of international law.

There is some scope for argument, therefore, that if the Act of 1976 is not in point, the common law should nevertheless be construed in the light of the provisions of the Conventions which have created international obligations for a number of States. In this connection reference may be made to the argument of plaintiff's counsel in *The I Congreso del Partido*[6] at first instance that the common law rule as to immunity in respect of State-owned trading ships should be considered in the light of the provisions of the Brussels Convention, even though at that time this country had not yet ratified it. Goff, J., though he did not find the reference helpful in the particular case, took pains to demonstrate that in his judgment the view he was taking was not in conflict with the effect of the Convention.

2.10 (ii) Statute

The State Immunity Act 1978, which came into force on 22 November 1978, brought the law of the United Kingdom into line with that of most other civilized countries. Judicial activism had sought to bend the tardy cripple-gaited common law back upon itself so that it should reflect the contemporary international scene, rather than the views of yesteryear, but the labour pains of the new doctrine were prolonged and disquieting to witness. Nor had they yet produced a healthy child, whose survival was assured (for an account of these travails see Chapter 3).

The conflict was between the absolute theory of sovereign immunity and the restrictive theory. Under the restrictive theory immunity is only afforded in respect of acts in exercise of sovereign authority (called, in Latin, *acta jure imperii*). No

5. [1977] Q.B. 529; 64 I.L.R. 111 (1977).
6. [1978] Q.B. 500; 64 I.L.R. 154 (1977).

immunity is granted in respect of commercial activities (*acta gestionis*).

It is inherent in this dichotomy that governmental acts are of either the one kind or the other. The restrictive theory, with variations, had by the 1950s been adopted by most civilized countries. It was clearly right that this country should follow suit, not merely because other countries had done so (although our role may no longer be to lead, it does not mean that it must be to follow), but because the restrictive theory manifestly suited the commercial realities. However, it proved difficult to free our law from the icy hand of precedent. The United Kingdom had signed the European Convention on State Immunity in Basle in May 1972 but had been unable to ratify it, as ratification would have put our municipal law in conflict with our international obligations.

2.11 The legislature therefore stepped in and provided by the State Immunity Act a complete code of law for all aspects of State immunity; in addition the Act affected the law of diplomatic immunity (in the sense of the terms given above in Chapter 1) by affording to the head of State and his retinue the immunities of the Diplomatic Privileges Act 1964.

That code of law embodies the theory of restrictive immunity. It is considerably more restrictive than the European Convention on which it is largely based. It states a basic rule of immunity for States which is then cut down by very considerable exceptions. These exceptions are all specifically spelt out, save for one catch-all provision (s. 3(3)(c)). On many questions, therefore, in respect of matters arising after the Act came into force, it will not be necessary to look further than the text of the Act. However, as already pointed out in paragraph 2.6, in the event of doubt or ambiguity the court may derive assistance from a consideration of the common law precedents. This is likely to be the case where the Act, despite its basic theme of radically altering the common law, echoes in some part a rule of the common law.

2.12 It is also to be expected that in some measure argument over the interpretation of the Act will be assisted by reference to the Conventions. The Act is intended to provide for ships a regime which harmonizes with the provisions of the Brussels Convention, and, even though the Act goes much further than the provisions of the European Convention (though not further than the Convention envisaged in the case of States making a declaration under Article 24 (see Chapter 9, paragraph 9.19)) in restricting immunity, it is nevertheless intended to be consistent with the Convention, and in many aspects effectively reproduces it.

Should the Act be difficult to interpret it may be that the corresponding provision in the Convention can clarify its meaning: for example, the obscurity of s. 4(4) may be clarified by reference to Article 5(2)(c) (see Chapter 6, paragraph 6.11).

2.13 Limited aspects of immunity are dealt with by other statutes, e.g. s. 17(6) of the Nuclear Installations Act 1965 and the Visiting Forces Act 1952 (see Chapter 10).

2.14   (iii) Treaty

Various attempts have been made at the international level to harmonize the law on State immunity between nations. In September 1891 the plenary assembly of the Institute of International Law considered draft international regulations on the subject. In April 1954 they adopted a set of new resolutions on the immunity of foreign States from jurisdiction and execution (Annuaire de L'Institut de Droit International Vol. 45 (II) 1954 pp. 293–4). The League of Nations, and more recently the United Nations, have considered State immunity, but without reaching any positive conclusions. The Brussels Convention, assimilating the position of State-owned trading vessels to that of private merchant ships, was signed in 1926, not long after this country had established by judicial precedent (*The Porto Alexandre*[7]) a quite contrary rule of absolute immunity for trading vessels, a rule which was not fully abrogated until 1977 (see Chapter 7).

By resolution of December 1963 the Committee of the Ministers of the Council of Europe included the subject of

7. [1920] P. 30; 1 I.L.R. 146 (1919).

State immunity in the Council of Europe Intergovernmental Work Programme, and then, pursuant to a resolution in May 1964 at the Third Conference of European Ministers of Justice, a committee of experts, meeting between 1965 and 1970, drew up the draft European Convention on State Immunity, which is the first international Convention of a general nature in the field of State immunity (the Brussels Convention, as noted, being concerned only with State-owned shipping).

2.15 The two Conventions were ratified by the United Kingdom on 6 July 1979. Before the Act of 1978 our municipal law, still clinging, although a trifle precariously, to the absolute theory of State immunity, had made it impossible for the United Kingdom to assume the international obligations of the Conventions. On the statutory endorsement of the restrictive theory ratification became possible.

As noted above, although these Conventions now impose legal obligations on this country vis-à-vis other parties to the treaty, they are not to be taken, short of a judicial decision, to affect municipal law, except in so far as they are adopted by Act of Parliament. Unlike in the field of diplomatic immunity, where the texts of the Vienna Conventions on diplomatic agents and consular officers have been largely adopted by statute by way of Schedules to the Diplomatic Privileges Act 1964 and the Consular Relations Act 1968, the texts of the Conventions of 1926 and 1972 have been nowhere embodied in statute. How far our international obligations under those Conventions have been put into statutory form is a matter for close comparison of the texts and for interpretation, and it will be discussed where appropriate throughout the book. Each aspect of the law of State immunity is examined not only from the standpoint of common law and statute, but also under the Conventions. In this way it is hoped to present a comprehensive picture of what is a radically new regime for English law. It should, of course, be borne in mind that whereas the Act creates rights and obligations under our law for all "States", the Conventions create international rights and obligations only as between the "Contracting" States that have ratified them. It is currently in force, as we have seen, between five States only (the United Kingdom, Austria,

Belgium, Cyprus and Switzerland), nor can it be confidently expected that that number will increase significantly in the immediate future as potential signatories await the alternative proposals of the ILC. Moreover, whatever importance may attach to the Convention as the precursor of the Act, it was intended only as a regional treaty, having been formed within the framework of the Council of Europe. It does not purport to be a comprehensive codification or restatement of any general rules of international law on sovereign immunity.

2.16 The International Law Commission of the United Nations put the question of "Jurisdictional Immunities of States and their Property" on its active agenda as part of its programme directed towards the progressive development and codification of international law. In 1978 the Commission appointed a Special Rapporteur on the topic, Professor Sompong Sucharitkul. It was clear from their Report for 1979 that the Commission were approaching the matter with caution. They discussed the Rapporteur's Preliminary Report in July 1979 and authorized him to continue with the study. The Sixth Report was produced by mid-1984 and the debate continues. One of the reasons, no doubt, why the Commission tread warily in this field is that the concept of absolute immunity, rooted as it is in an exaggerated notion of governmental authority, internally and externally, is particularly dear to both the People's Republic of China and the Soviet Union. In this connection one may do well to bear in mind the words of Professor Schreuer of Salzburg University: "An orderly judicial settlement of disputes is often more in the long term interest of States than a frustration of claims against them and the insecurity and suspicion engendered by the reckless invocation of immunities" (see *Comparative Law Yearbook*, 1978, p. 215).

CHAPTER 3

THE BASIC RULE

3.1   (i) The common law

Until comparatively recent times it was generally accepted that
English law afforded immunity to entities of sovereign status
regardless of whether the dispute arose from commercial
activity or the exercise of sovereign power. The high-water
mark of this absolute doctrine of immunity may be found in
the judgment of Lord Atkin in *Compania Naviera Vascongada*
v. *S.S. Cristina (The Cristina)*.[1]

The salient facts of that case were these. In June 1937 the
Government of the Spanish Republic, the ultimate losers of the
civil war, issued a decree requisitioning all vessels registered at
Bilbao, a port then occupied by the insurgents. The *Cristina*,
which was at that time on the high seas, came within this
decree, and when she arrived at Cardiff the Spanish consul
took control of her. The owners objected and claimed the
vessel. The Spanish Government asserted a claim to immunity
and sought to have the writ set aside.

The issue in dispute was whether the Spanish Government
had sufficient interest in the ship to sustain a claim to
immunity. It was unanimously decided by the five Law Lords
that the Government did have sufficient interest. But the case
was memorable for the following much-quoted passage in the
judgment of Lord Atkin on the general principles (at pages
490–1):

> "The foundation for the application to set aside the writ and arrest of the
> ship is to be found in two propositions of international law engrafted into
> our domestic law which seem to me well established and to be beyond
> dispute. The first is that the courts of this country will not implead a
> foreign sovereign, that is, they will not by their process make him against
> his will a party to legal proceedings whether the proceedings involve

1. [1938] A.C. 485; 9 I.L.R. 250 (1938).

19

process against his person or seek to recover from him specific property or damages.

The second is that they will not by their process, whether the sovereign is a party to the proceedings or not, seize or detain property which is his or of which he is in possession or control. There has been some difference in the practice of nations as to possible limitations of this second principle as to whether it extends to property only used for the commercial purposes of the sovereign or to personal private property. In this country it is in my opinion well settled that it applies to both.

I draw attention to the fact that there are two distinct immunities appertaining to foreign sovereigns: for at times they tend to become confused: and it is not always clear from the decisions whether the judges are dealing with the one or the other or both. It seems to me clear that, in a simple case of a writ *in rem* issued by our Admiralty court in a claim for collision damage against the owners of a public ship of a sovereign State in which the ship is arrested, both principles are broken. The sovereign is impleaded and his property is seized".

Lord Atkin there propounded the doctrine of absolute immunity, applicable in respect both of actions *in personam*, the ordinary action against a named defendant, and of actions *in rem*, actions in Admiralty to effect the arrest or detention of a ship or other property. This was to remain the law, as generally understood, until 1975.

Early Days

3.2 The doctrine of sovereign immunity found its earliest manifestation in the protection afforded to diplomatic agents. The immunity of the sovereign himself in his own person was not at first a recognized principle: if he fell into alien hands he might expect to be ransomed, mistreated, or killed. But the agent's immunity was recognized. It was based on pragmatic considerations. This is illustrated from the earliest times by the herald: parlies would fall into disrepute and the business of conquest and surrender impeded if terms could not be negotiated during or in contemplation of hostilities. Even then those leaders who returned the emissary to his king in small pieces were felt not to be playing the game. Similarly, if the diplomatic agent was to be liable to process the business of international relationships and communication between States would become more difficult. There would also in some cases be the temptation to prosecute the envoy to embarrass his master: that would then lead to reciprocal action of a similar nature. Even now that can happen where, for example, spying charges are fabricated, either as an excuse to banish the diplomatic agents from the realm, or, more often, as mere retaliation for an action that may well have been justified. But, human nature being what it is, and a State's "nature" being no more than the nature of the human beings that run it, that sort of unstatesmanlike behaviour is bound to occur from time to time.

3.3 It is perhaps surprising how recent is the emergence of the modern concept of sovereign immunity. Hugo Grotius, the Dutch jurist and polymath, who may be regarded as the father of international law, is silent on the matter. Vattel treats sovereign immunity as no more than an incidental aspect of immunity enjoyed by ambassadors, adding that if a sovereign has come to a foreign State not for the purpose of negotiating on public matters but rather as a traveller, it is his dignity alone and what is due to the State he represents and which he governs which entitles him not only to respect and honours but also to exemption from the local jurisdiction. The theoretical basis of the rule of sovereign immunity can be traced to a time when most States were ruled by personal sovereigns who, in a very real sense, personified the State ("L'Etat, c'est moi."). In time the diplomat's immunity came to be based on a formal view of the rightful demands of a king or other head of State. Even after the demise of the doctrine of the Divine Right of Kings and its last exponent, at least its last explicit one, on the block at Whitehall some three hundred and thirty years ago, kings and governments have felt that the law should accord them special treatment. Until 1949 it was possible to assert of this country that the Crown was above the law, and even now it retains at law some privileges irksome to those that seek to sue it. It was therefore strongly considered that it offended the dignity and independence of sovereigns, quite apart from the pragmatic considerations, if their representative was liable to legal process. It was thought to be an affront to the sovereign. It was also thought at this time (the 18th century) that, as a sort of vague principle of jurisprudence (and the 18th century was certainly a flourishing time for vague principles of jurisprudence), if two sovereigns were theoretically of equal rank, one could not exercise jurisdiction over the other. This hazy notion was sought to be dignified by the Latin tag *par in parem non habet imperium.*

Lord Denning, M.R., said in *Rahimtoola* v. *Nizam of Hyderabad*[2]:

> ". . . I think we should go back and look for the principles which lie behind the doctrine of sovereign immunity. Search as you will among the accepted principles of international law and you will search in vain for any set propositions. There is no agreed principle except this: that each State ought to have proper respect for the dignity and independence of other States".

3.4 The immunity of the diplomatic agent may be illustrated by *Barbuit's* case[3] which arose in 1737 from the trading activities of one Barbuit, a tallow chandler with a commission from the King of Prussia to deal in matters of trade on his behalf.

Lord Talbot said:

> ". . . the privilege of a public minister is to have his person sacred and free from arrests, not on his own account, but on account of those he represents . . . The foundation of this privilege is for the sake of the prince by whom an ambassador is sent".

The 19th Century

3.5 It was inherent in this thinking that, when in due course the time came to consider the immunity of the prince himself (not yet his government though), he be held to be immune from any sort of process. However, with the radical thinking of the 19th century, a sensible compromise began to emerge between on the one hand giving *carte blanche* to every head of State and, inevitably, every government representing a State, to act without regard to their responsibility at law (if they so chose), to the consequent impairment of justice and of the confidence of the general public in governments, and, on the other, imposing a fair and reasonable legal accountability. What is of particular interest is that the initial ideas outlined in

2. [1958] A.C. 379; 24 I.L.R. 175 (1957).
3. (1737) 25 E.R. 777.

England at that time, although cast into limbo for a hundred years or so while the common law followed a most unsatisfactory path, getting itself all the while into greater difficulties and not a little disrepute, emerged triumphant only recently, thanks to the radical action of the legislature.

Those initial ideas were prompted by the fact that towards the end of the 19th century States were beginning to play a considerable part in the commercial theatre. Lawyers, and some judges, faced with an ordinary commercial contract to which a State was a party, began to ask themselves what purpose was served by the obvious injustice of allowing a State to avoid the legal consequences of a contract into which it had, for its own commercial advantage, freely chosen to enter.

Although it had been recognized in the middle of the 19th century that a foreign sovereign enjoyed immunity in respect of his public acts, and was entitled to assert immunity in respect of State property destined to public uses, the position had been reserved in respect of private transactions. In this connection reference may be made to two cases. In *Duke of Brunswick* v. *King of Hanover*[4] the plaintiff, who had been deposed by a decree of the Germanic Diet in 1830, challenged the validity of an instrument signed in 1833 by King William IV and William, Duke of Brunswick (later King of Hanover) appointing a guardian of his fortune and property, the guardianship to be legally established in Brunswick. For the defendant it was argued that, as an independent sovereign prince, he was not liable to be sued in any English court. The House of Lords did not accept the broad proposition but rested their decision on the narrower ground that "the courts of this country cannot sit in judgment upon an act of a sovereign, effected by virtue of his sovereign authority abroad, an act not done as a British subject, but supposed to be done in the exercise of his authority vested in him as sovereign" and that ". . . the acts could not have been done, and were not done, in any private character, but . . . were done, whether right or wrong, in the character of the sovereign of a foreign state" (*per* Lord Cottenham).

In *de Haber* v. *Queen of Portugal*,[5] an action of debt

4. (1844) 6 Beav. 1.
5. (1851) 17 Q.B. 171.

brought against "Her Most Faithful Majesty Doña Maria da Glora, Queen of Portugal" Lord Campbell, C.J., had spoken of immunity for acts of a foreign potentate "in his public capacity as representative of the nation of which he is head", in respect of which he said ". . . to cite a foreign potentate in a municipal court . . . is contrary to the law of nations".

Reference may also be made by the historian to the earlier, somewhat ambivalent, judgments of United States Chief Justice Marshall in *The Schooner Exchange* v. *McFaddon*[6] and of Sir William Scott (later Lord Stowell) in *The Prins Frederik*.[7]

3.6 In *The Charkieh*[8], an action *in rem* for damages arising from a collision in the River Thames, where the vessel in question was a cargo-carrying vessel belonging to the Khedive of Egypt and under charter to a British subject to carry cargo to Alexandria, that great international lawyer, Sir Robert Phillimore, said in his judgment:

> "No principle of international law, and no decided case, and no dictum of jurists of which I am aware, has gone so far as to authorize a sovereign prince to assume the character of a trader, when it is for his benefit; and when he incurs an obligation to a private subject to throw off, if I may so speak, his disguise, and appear as a sovereign, claiming for his own benefit, and to the injury of a private person, for the first time, all the attributes of his character".

Sir Robert, then, had no doubt that if a trader chose to enter into a commercial contract, he became subject to the ordinary laws governing that transaction. His actual decision, however, was based on his finding that the Khedive of Egypt was not in law of sovereign status.

Sir Robert, of course, accepted that immunity should be granted in proper cases. He said:

> "The object of international law, in this as in other matters, is not to work injustice, not to prevent the enforcement of a just demand, but to substitute negotiations between governments, though they may be dilatory and the issue distant and uncertain, for the ordinary use of courts of justice in cases where such use would lessen the dignity or embarrass the functions of the representatives of a foreign state".

6. (1812) 7 Cranch 116. (U.S.).
7. (1820) 2 Dod. 451.
8. (1873) L.R. 4 A. & E. 59.

3.7 Why then was this excellent lead not followed? Other European jurisdictions were soon coming to a similar conclusion, whereby such acts of a sovereign as were no more than what an ordinary person could perform were denied immunity. Belgium drew the distinction between acts of trade and acts in exercise of sovereign power at the beginning of this century, while Italy had accepted the distinction as early as 1886. Other European jurisdictions followed later, and the United Kingdom was left increasingly isolated. Even the United States followed suit in 1952, as described below.

3.8 It was early in this century that the doctrine of absolute immunity, that accorded immunity not only to acts in exercise of the sovereign authority (*acta jure imperii, acta imperii*) but also to ordinary commercial activities (*acta gestionis*), began most clearly to assert itself.

In *The Parlement Belge*[9] the Court of Appeal reversed a decision of Sir Robert Phillimore. He had refused immunity in respect of a mail packet owned by the King of the Belgians and officered by Belgian naval officers, on the ground that, as he had said in *The Charkieh*[10], immunity would not be accorded in respect of vessels used for trade. The Court of Appeal said first that a foreign sovereign could not be sued *in personam* in the English courts (a proposition which was not in fact questioned thereafter by the courts until the judgment of Lord Denning, M.R., with which none of his brethren agreed, in *Rahimtoola* v. *Nizam of Hyderabad*,[11] and not departed from at any time until the judgments of Lord Denning, M.R., and Shaw, L.J., in *Trendtex Trading Corporation* v. *Central Bank of Nigeria*[12] (see below), though the proposition was to be statutorily negated by the State Immunity Act in 1978).

The Court of Appeal also held in *The Parlement Belge*[13] that an action *in rem* cannot be maintained against a ship owned by a foreign sovereign if she is being used substantially for public, i.e. State purposes.

This was the thin end of the wedge, the wedge of absolute

9. (1880) 5 P.D. 197.
10. *Supra*, fn. 8.
11. *Supra*, fn. 2.
12. [1977] Q.B. 529; 64 I.L.R. 111 (1977).
13. *Supra*, fn. 9.

immunity that was to be driven into our law until, years later, it threatened to split the fabric when men of business, dissatisfied with the privileged position accorded by our legal system to the innumerable commercial State enterprises with which they had to deal, began to look elsewhere than the City of London for the centre of their activities.

The 20th Century

3.9 In itself the decision in *The Parlement Belge*[14] was not an unequivocal assertion of the absolute doctrine because the vessel was indeed used largely for State purposes. However, the Court of Appeal went further in *The Porto Alexandre*[15] when they granted immunity in respect of a vessel owned by the Portuguese Government and used wholly or substantially for the carriage of freight in an action for salvage charges where the cargo owners had entered an unconditional appearance. The court seemed to think they were bound by *The Parlement Belge*[16] decision even though that ship had been employed substantially for *public* purposes. This decision was given shortly before the Brussels Convention was agreed by which the position of a trading ship owned by a State is assimilated to that of a private trader (see Chapter 7, paragraph 7.23). (That Convention has at last been ratified by the United Kingdom, consequent on the coming into force of the State Immunity Act.)

3.10 It was against the background of these cases that the judgments were given in *The Cristina*[17] (*supra*). It should be noted that in that case only Lord Wright agreed with Lord Atkin in applying the absolute doctrine of immunity to trading vessels. Lord Thankerton and Lord Macmillan had doubts about the decision in *The Porto Alexandre*,[18] though as *The Cristina* was found to be *publicis usibus destinata* they did not need to reach a decision on that point, while Lord Maugham

14. *Ibid.*
15. [1920] P. 30; 1 I.L.R. 146 (1919).
16. (1880) 5 P.D. 197.
17. *Supra*, fn. 1.
18. [1920] P. 30; 1 I.L.R. 146 (1919).

thought that decision was actually wrong. This divergence of opinion was not finally resolved until 1975 when the Privy Council declined to follow *The Porto Alexandre* and held, illogically, as the Privy Council itself admitted, that although the theory of absolute immunity was applicable to an action *in personam* against a foreign sovereign on a commercial contract it was inapplicable to an action *in rem* against a trading ship owned by a foreign sovereign (*The Philippine Admiral*,[19] see below Chapter 7, paragraph 7.13).

3.11 Limited exceptions to the absolute doctrine have arisen from time to time. They were conveniently listed by Lord Denning, M.R., in the *Thai-Europe* case[20]: a foreign sovereign has no immunity in respect of land situate in England, in respect of trust funds here or money lodged for the payment of creditors, in respect of debts incurred here for services rendered to his property here. Lord Denning's important fourth exception, in respect of commercial transactions with a trader here giving rise to a dispute which is properly within the territorial jurisdiction of the courts, has not yet established itself (see below).

The Privy Council said in *The Philippine Admiral*[21] that the only possible exceptions were an action relating to immovable property here and the trust fund cases

"in which the court has not been deterred from administering a trust subject to its jurisdiction by the fact that a sovereign claims an interest in it".

3.12 By the outbreak of the Second World War, then, this country's position was exemplified by the decision in *The Cristina*. Other countries took different views. The involvement of governments on the commercial scene, themselves or by departments or bodies they controlled, had grown apace, beyond anything foreseen in the previous century, when the function of governments had been exclusively to govern. The heavens, as well as the seas, were filled with commerce; the pilots of the purple twilight would

19. [1977] A.C. 373; 64 I.L.R. 90 (1975).
20. [1975] 1 W.L.R. 1485; 64 I.L.R. 81 (1975).
21. [1977] A.C. 373 at 392.

turn out often to be nothing more romantic than government employees and their costly bales of government merchandise. Italy and Belgium, as noted above, adopted, at an early date, the restrictive doctrine. Austria broke with the rule of absolute immunity in the *Dralle* case[21a] in 1950. The United States, which had hitherto accepted the absolute rule as exemplified in their own *Porto Alexandre* of the 1920s (*The Pesaro*[22]), adopted the restrictive view, when on 19 May 1952 J. B. Tate, the acting adviser of the State Department, wrote the so-called "Tate letter" to the then acting Attorney-General of the United States, notifying him of a change in the policy of the Department of State with regard to the granting of immunity to foreign governments. The letter pointed out that at that time countries were more or less equally divided on the absolute/ restrictive dichotomy, and that the Department, without wishing to control the courts, would be following the restrictive theory in future. It appears in fact that the United States courts hardly exercise their own discretion since then in the matter, but merely accept the view of the Department (though the United States statute transfers the responsibility to the courts). Lord Cross said in *The Philippine Admiral* (at page 399) a little drily, one may imagine:

> "It was not suggested by counsel on either side that their Lordships should seek the help of the Foreign and Commonwealth Office in deciding this appeal by ascertaining which theory of sovereign immunity it favours".

(The Foreign and Commonwealth Office's assistance is sought, of course, in other respects, for its certificate as to the status of a country, a sovereign, or a government is conclusive both at common law and under the Act.) See Appendix 4, part A.

The United States have now embodied the restrictive view in their Foreign Sovereign Immunities Act 1976.

West Germany's post-war adherence to the restrictive theory is exemplified by the decision of the Bundungsverfassungsgericht in 1963 in allowing a claim to proceed against Iran for repair costs to the embassy building,

21a. *Dralle v. Republic of Czechoslovakia*, 17 I.L.R. 155 (1950).
22. (1926) 271 U.S. 562; 31 I.L.R. 186 (1926).

and France has made it clear, at least since the 1960s, that she, too, accepts the restrictive theory (see Chapter 12).

3.13 Disquiet was already being felt in this country by the end of the war over our increasingly isolated position on this issue, and, following the case of *Krajina* v. *Tass Agency*,[23] in which immunity was accorded to the Soviet news agency in libel proceedings, a committee under Lord Somervell was appointed to report on whether United Kingdom law afforded to organs of foreign States a wider immunity than was desirable or strictly required by principles of international law; but the committee was unable to reach any final conclusions or make any recommendations as they said national divergencies made it impossible to establish the position in international law, and also their members differed as to the principles to be followed.

Recently

3.14 The most recent phase in the history of sovereign immunity in this country has been the most interesting of all. One may see in this how, as always when it is sought to turn the tardy, cripple-gaited progress of the common law into a radically new direction to meet the exigencies of the times, the movement has been attended with all sorts of difficulties, cries of outrage from the conservatives, dubious legal arguments from the radicals, and general confusion for the multitude, so that the ensuing morass can only be overcome by the intervention of the legislature.

The new movement was heralded by the judgment of Lord Denning, M.R., in the House of Lords in *Rahimtoola* v. *The Nizam of Hyderabad*.[24]

In that case the Nizam and the Government of Hyderabad sued the High Commissioner for Pakistan in the United Kingdom for the return of money which had been standing in the account of the Nizam and his Government at an English bank and which was transferred into the name of the High Commissioner without the Nizam's authority at the time in 1948 when Indian troops were invading Hyderabad.

23. [1949] 2 All E.R. 274; 16 I.L.R. 129 (1949).
24. [1958] A.C. 379; 24 I.L.R. 175 (1957).

Lord Denning, M.R., proposed a test which had not been argued by counsel and which he conceived out of his own researches: if a dispute concerned the commercial transactions of a foreign government (whether carried on by its own departments or agencies or by setting up separate legal entities) and

> "it arises properly within the territorial jurisdiction of our courts, there is no ground for granting immunity".

This owes a lot to the concept of *forum conveniens*, and not so much to the *acta imperii/gestionis* distinction, which he did not endorse ("Others have adopted a rule of immunity for public acts but not for private acts, which has turned out to be a most elusive test").

Applying his test, Lord Denning, M.R., agreed with the result proposed by his brethren, that immunity should be accorded to the High Commissioner, on the ground that, as the judge at first instance had said:

> "The present transaction was an inter-governmental transaction; let it be solved by inter-governmental negotiations".

However, Viscount Simonds, applying the doctrine of absolute immunity, said at the end of his judgment (and the other three Law Lords expressly associated themselves with his words):

> "My Lords, I must add, that, since writing this opinion, I have had the privilege of reading the opinion which my noble and learned friend, Lord Denning, is about to deliver. It is right that I should say that I must not be taken as assenting to his views upon a number of questions and authorities in regard to which the House has not had the benefit of the arguments of counsel or of the judgment of the courts below".

3.15 Lord Denning, M.R., returned to this theme when he was sitting as Master of the Rolls, in *Thai-Europe Tapioca Service Ltd.* v. *Government of Pakistan.*[25] In that case the plaintiffs were German shipowners who had let a vessel to Polish charterers for the carriage of fertilizer on behalf of a department of the Pakistan Government from Gdansk in Poland to Karachi in Pakistan. While the ship was waiting for a berth in

25. *Supra*, fn. 20.

Karachi in December 1971 the port was bombed by Indian aircraft and the ship damaged. As a result, the plaintiffs sued under the charter-party for demurrage or damages, discharge of the cargo having been finally completed some 67 days late.

The Court of Appeal unanimously dismissed the appeal, affirming the Government's right to immunity. Lord Denning, M.R., said that the exception to the rule of immunity he had formulated in *Rahimtoola* v. *Nizam of Hyderabad* was limited to

"commercial transactions that have a most close connection with England, such that, by the presence of the parties or the nature of the dispute, it is more properly cognizable here than elsewhere".

This test is not precise and would give scope for much argument. He said the present case did not come within that formulation:

"None of the transactions here occurred within the territorial jurisdiction of these courts. They are as far off as the moon".

He further reaffirmed the

"general principle . . . that, except by consent, courts of this country will not issue their process so as to entertain a claim against a foreign sovereign for debt or damages".

This statement was to be heavily relied on by Donaldson, J., in *Uganda Co. (Holdings)* v. *Government of Uganda*[26] when he refused to follow the later decision of the Court of Appeal in the *Trendtex* case (see below) on the ground that it was not consistent with the *Thai-Europe* case.

Lawton and Scarman, L.JJ., felt that it was quite impossible for them to ignore precedent: the rule of absolute immunity was far too well established to admit of Lord Denning's exception. Lawton, L.J., said:

"In my judgment it is most important that rules of this kind should not be altered save by the appropriate judicial or legislative body . . . Those who make agreements of this kind very often seek to embody in these the law of this country. They would be unlikely to do so if the law became like some Continental street names, changing every decade or so. I can see no reason at all for departing from rules which have been recognized by the commercial world now for nearly a hundred years".

26. [1979] 1 Lloyd's Rep. 481; 64 I.L.R. 209 (1978).

In fact, however, the commercial world was far from happy
with those rules, under which a State-owned trading enterprise
could be in breach of its contractual obligations with impunity.

Scarman, L.J., saw no exception to the absolute rule save in
relation to property within the jurisdiction. He said:

> "I think it is important to realize that a rule of international law, once
> incorporated into our law by decisions of a competent court, is not an
> inference of fact but a rule of law. It therefore becomes part of our
> municipal law and the doctrine of *stare decisis* applies as much to that as to
> a rule of law with a strictly municipal provenance".

To these words of caution Lord Denning, M.R., and Shaw,
L.J., were to pay no heed in the *Trendtex* case (see below).

The Philippine Admiral

3.16 However, the real beginning to the end of the absolute
doctrine of immunity in our law came in November 1975 when
the Privy Council gave judgment in the case of *The Philippine
Admiral*,[27] an appeal from the Full Court of the Supreme
Court of Hong Kong by the Government of the Republic of
the Philippines. The Privy Council held that, although the
absolute theory of immunity applied to actions *in personam*,
the restrictive view applied to actions *in rem*. Therefore, as the
Philippine Admiral was being operated as an ordinary trading
ship, no immunity attached to it. *The Porto Alexandre*[28] and
the wide words of Lord Atkin in *The Cristina*[29] were not
followed. The judgment traced the history of the topic and
referred to the European Convention which had been signed at
Basle on 16 May 1972. (For a fuller treatment of this and the
other shipping cases see Chapter 7.)

Their Lordships acknowledged that by reaffirming the
absolute rule for actions *in rem* they had now created an
anomalous situation, but said:

> "The rule that no action *in personam* can be brought against a foreign
> sovereign State on a commercial contract has been regularly accepted by
> the Court of Appeal in England and was assumed to be the law even by
> Lord Maugham in *The Cristina*. It is no doubt open to the House of Lords

27. [1977] A.C. 373; 64 I.L.R. 90 (1975).
28. [1920] P. 30; 1 I.L.R. 146 (1919).
29. [1938] A.C. 485; 9 I.L.R. 250 (1938).

to decide otherwise, but it may fairly be said to be at the least unlikely that it would do so".

One may certainly presume that the members of the Privy Council were far from ignorant of the feeling of the Law Lords in this connection! At the same time one may note with interest that in speaking to the International Law Association in November 1978 Lord Wilberforce said:

> "We were hoping to get the *Trendtex* case [see paragraph 3.18] and to revolutionize the law but the parties went and settled it before we could!"

3.17 Now the Convention, which embodied to a considerable extent the restrictive doctrine at the international level for actions *in personam* (the Brussels Convention having applied similar régime to shipping cases), was not national law for our courts. How then was the by now clearly and comprehensively accepted doctrine of restrictive immunity to be made part of our national law? By waiting for legislation? That was still some way off, and, as Lord Denning, M.R., had said in another connection, you never know what may happen to a Bill (*Levison* v. *Patent Carpet Cleaning Co.*[30]). By waiting for a decision of the House of Lords to extend the restrictive doctrine to actions *in personam*? But when might that be? They might in any event, even if the opportunity arose, decline to do so. However, Lord Denning, M.R., was around to give the law a push in, as he saw it, the right direction.

The Trendtex Case

3.18 On 13 January 1977 the Court of Appeal gave judgment in the case of *Trendtex Trading Corporation* v. *Central Bank of Nigeria.*[31]

The salient facts of the case were that Nigeria, for one reason or another, had ordered too much cement. This had been done by the Government in charge in early 1975. By July 1975 the port of Lagos was hopelessly congested with cement-bearing vessels. All berths were occupied and up to 400 ships were waiting outside. The Government had ordered ten times as much cement for the year as the port could handle. At the end

30. [1978] Q.B. 69.
31. [1977] Q.B. 529; 64 I.L.R. 111 (1977).

of July 1975 a new military administration took over the business of governing. They described the cement contracts as "unorthodox, imprudent or inequitable". The plaintiffs had delivered cement under one of the contracts, for use in the building of Government barracks, but, on instructions, the Central Bank refused to pay for it. An irrevocable letter of credit had been issued by the bank in favour of the plaintiffs on 24 July 1975, and it was upon that letter of credit that the plaintiffs sued.

Donaldson, J., acceded to the defendant's claim to immunity, finding that the bank was a Department of State and holding, as indeed he was bound to on the authorities, that the absolute doctrine of immunity was to be applied under the common law. The Court of Appeal unanimously reversed that decision and allowed the action to proceed. Lord Denning, M.R., said that international law clearly favoured the restrictive doctrine, and that as international law was automatically the law of this country (i.e. without the need for prior adoption by Parliament or precedent) the rule of *stare decisis*, the doctrine of precedent, did not apply. This was a highly ingenious approach, and contrary to the orthodox view propounded by Lord Scarman in the *Thai-Europe* case[32] (see *supra*). Both Lord Denning, M.R., and Shaw, L.J., said that a municipal decision was only authority on an issue of international law for the proposition that at the time of the decision such was the relevant rule of international law to be applied in the municipal courts. If international law changed thereafter, so automatically did the common law. This was a device to avoid the icy clutch of precedent (just as in the *Miliangos* case[33] Lord Denning, M.R., had slipped out of that grasp by invoking the maxim *cessante ratione legis cessat lex ipsa*, so that he was able to hold that, as the reason for the rule that forbade an English judgment to be given in any currency but sterling no longer obtained, the rule itself was no longer law, despite recent House of Lords authority reaffirming it).

In fact the argument of Lord Denning, M.R., which rejects in the context of international law one of the two corner-stones of our jurisprudence (the other being the doctrine of

32. [1975] 1 W.L.R. 1485; 64 I.L.R. 81 (1975).
33. [1975] Q.B. 487.

parliamentary sovereignty) makes it clear that the doctrine of automatic incorporation into the common law of new international rules as they arise cannot be right, for it accords to a decision of even the highest tribunal on a matter of international law no more than transient effect. The doctrine that rules of international law, though of great persuasive force, are not part of our law until adopted by statute or judicial decision seems therefore to be right. The terms used to describe the two doctrines are not always free from confusion, "adoption" or "transformation" being generally used for the latter, "incorporation" for the former.

When, from the point of view of jurisprudence, one adds to Lord Denning's argument the consideration that a judicial decision is supposed to declare the law, i.e. that the law propounded by a judgment has always been the law, any earlier contrary decisions having been wrong, one gets into an intellectual morass of almost metaphysical implications from which there is little hope of escape and into which therefore it is not proposed here to plunge.

Of the Privy Council's statement in *The Philippine Admiral*[34] that it was unlikely that the House of Lords would apply the restrictive doctrine to actions *in personam* Lord Denning, M.R., said:

"That is a dismal forecast. It is out of line with the good sense shown in the rest of the judgment of the Privy Council".

Lord Denning, M.R., and Shaw, L.J., gave as an additional ground for allowing the appeal, and Stephenson, L.J., as his only ground, that the bank was not an organ of the State of Nigeria and so would not in any event be entitled to immunity (see Chapter 4, paragraph 4.4). Stephenson, L.J., said that he felt bound to stand "loyally but reluctantly" on the old doctrine of absolute immunity and the old decisions. He was particularly influenced by the Court of Appeal decision in the *Thai-Europe* case, which in his view reaffirmed the absolute doctrine.

An appeal to the House of Lords was eagerly awaited but in the event the matter was settled. Whether or not the House of Lords might have changed the law and extended the restrictive

34. [1977] A.C. 373; 64 I.L.R. 90 (1975).

doctrine to actions *in personam*, it may be thought that they would hardly have approved of the lower court's cavalier treatment of the precedents.

The State Immunity Act came into force on 22 November 1978, thus validating, one may say, the approach of the Court of Appeal in the *Trendtex* case if not their procedure.

3.19 Robert Goff, J., gave judgment at first instance in January 1977 in the case of *The I Congreso del Partido*.[35] A Chilean company brought an action *in rem* against a ship owned by Cuba on the ground that Cuba was liable to them for breach of a contract to deliver sugar to Chile (see Chapter 7, paragraph 7.16). The main point at issue, apart from the question of ownership, was, granted the original contract was *acta gestionis*, whether the fact that the breach itself was *actus imperii* (being due to Cuba breaking off diplomatic relations with Chile after a military coup in Chile) meant that even under the doctrine of restrictive immunity Cuba's claim to immunity was to be allowed. This question, whether the *acta gestionis* are limited to the original transaction or involve also the act that constituted the breach of contract, is considered below in Chapter 12. What is relevant for our present purpose is that the trial judge considered himself bound by the Court of Appeal decision in the *Trendtex* case. That consideration was not necessary, however, to his decision, as he was dealing not with an action *in personam* but an action *in rem*, in respect of which the doctrine of restrictive immunity could be said to have been persuasively established by the decision of the Privy Council in *The Philippine Admiral*.[36] Moreover, the learned judge held that, even applying the restrictive doctrine, it did not debar the States from immunity as one had to consider the manner of the breach, and that was clearly *actus imperii*.

3.20 As a linguistic note, it is worth observing that although the singular of "acta" is of course "actum" the alternative substantive "actus" is usually used in this connection.

35. [1977] 3 W.L.R. 778.
36. *Supra*, fn. 34.

3.21 However, acceptance of the *Trendtex* decision[37] was not forthcoming from Donaldson, J., in *Uganda Co. (Holdings) Ltd v. Government of Uganda.*[38] He had been the judge at first instance in the *Trendtex* case and had (understandably) allowed Nigeria's claim to immunity on behalf of the Central Bank. In the *Uganda* case the facts were that the plaintiffs, claiming an indemnity in respect of nearly a quarter of a million pounds paid by them as guarantors of the obligations of a Ugandan company, had obtained a *Mareva* injunction in May 1977 restraining the defendants from disposing of a quantity of tea warehoused in London. The latter entered a conditional appearance and sought immunity.

Donaldson, J., on 30 November 1978 said that the *Trendtex* case could not be reconciled with the *Thai-Europe* case[39] and the established position of the absolute doctrine of immunity for actions *in personam*. He felt he should not follow the *Trendtex* case as that decision was too novel, both in applying the restrictive doctrine to actions *in personam* and in holding that the doctrine of precedent did not apply where the court was deciding questions of international law. He pointed out that the *Thai-Europe* case was in line with the long history of precedent asserting the absolute rule of immunity, and that, if precedent did not apply to rules of law in international contexts, an enquiry would be necessary in each case to establish the contemporary position.

He also said that, even applying the restrictive doctrine, he would grant the defendants immunity, as deciding the case would mean expressing an opinion on the meaning and effect of Ugandan legislation in a suit to which the Government of Uganda was a party, and in his view the restrictive doctrine did not extend so far.

3.22 However, Lord Denning, M.R., said, in the case of *Hispano Americana Mercantil S.A. v. Central Bank of Nigeria,*[40] that the *Trendtex* case had not been decided *per incuriam* and should be followed by the Court of Appeal and

37. [1977] Q.B. 529; 64 I.L.R. 111 (1977).
38. [1979] 1 Lloyd's Rep. 481; 64 I.L.R. 209 (1978).
39. *Supra*, fn. 32.
40. [1979] 2 Lloyd's Rep. 277; 64 I.L.R. 221 (1979).

the instant case was on all fours with the *Trendtex* case. (It may perhaps be observed without impropriety that once Lord Denning, M.R., had made a new rule of law in a given case, he was in favour, in similar cases thereafter, of the Court of Appeal being bound by its previous decision.) The defendants appealed against the granting by Donaldson, J., in March 1976 of an interlocutory injunction restraining them from removing funds out of the jurisdiction. The court took the view that the injunction should remain pending an appeal to the House of Lords, and that the provisions of the State Immunity Act making the funds of central banks immune from such jurisdiction (see Chapter 9, paragraph 9.20) were not in point as the Act, although in force at the time of the hearing, did not apply to the case, the cause of action having arisen before the operative date of the statute. The court was not prepared to find the provisions of the Act of sufficient persuasive force to lead it to exercise its discretion in favour of the Central Bank.

3.23 *The I Congreso del Partido*[41] came before the Court of Appeal on 1 October 1979. The point at issue, whether the fact that a breach of a commercial contract may itself be an exercise of sovereign authority can be a ground for affording immunity, is considered below in Chapter 12. We may note here that Lord Denning, M.R., said in that case:

> "The restrictive theory holds the field in international law: and by reason of the doctrine of incorporation it should be applied by the English courts, not only in actions *in rem* but also in actions *in personam*".

Waller, J., did not comment on the *Trendtex* decision, nor was there any need to do so as the instant case was an action *in rem*.

In addition, Lord Denning, M.R., once again described the *acta imperii/gestionis* distinction as a very elusive test.

> "As to what acts fall within it is anyone's guess. As Terence says: *Quot homines, tot sententiae. Sua cuique mos* (So many men, so many opinions. His own a law to each)".

3.24 In *Planmount Ltd.* v. *Republic of Zaire*[42] Lloyd, J., dealing with an ordinary building contract, said: ". . . it seems

41. [1980] 1 Lloyd's Rep. 23.
42. [1981] 1 All E.R. 1110; 64 I.L.R. 268 (1980).

to me to have been clearly established by successive decisions in the Court of Appeal that, prior to the passing of the State Immunity Act 1978, a foreign State had no absolute immunity in the English courts, whether the action be *in rem* or *in personam*".

3.25 The House of Lords gave judgment in *The I Congreso del Partido*[43] in July 1981. They were unanimously of the view that the restrictive doctrine applied at common law in respect of actions over trading vessels regardless of whether the action was *in rem* or *in personam*. Lord Wilberforce said: "Sitting in this House I would unhesitatingly affirm as part of English law the advance made by *The Philippine Admiral* with the reservation that the decision was perhaps unnecessarily restrictive in, apparently, confining the departure made to actions *in rem*. In truth, an action *in rem* as regards a ship, if it proceeds beyond the initial stages, is itself in addition an action *in personam*—viz. the owner of the ship, the description *in rem* denoting the procedural advantages available as regards service, arrest and enforcement. It should be borne in mind that no distinction between actions *in rem* and actions *in personam* is generally recognized elsewhere so that it would in any event be desirable to liberate English law from an anomaly if that existed. In fact, there is no anomaly and no distinction. The effect of *The Philippine Admiral* if accepted, as I would accept it, is that as regards State-owned vessels, actions, whether commenced *in rem* or not, are to be decided according to the restrictive theory".

3.26 In *Sengupta* v. *Republic of India*[44] the Employment Appeal Tribunal applied the restrictive doctrine to an unfair dismissal claim (see below at 6.8).

3.27 The present position is therefore that, for any case arising still under the common law rather than the Act, the restrictive doctrine will certainly be applied if it concerns State-owned trading vessels and almost certainly if it concerns anything else.

---

43. [1983] 1 A.C. 244; 64 I.L.R. 307 (1981).
44. (1983) I.C.R. 221; 64 I.L.R. 352 (1982).

3.28   **(ii) Statute:**

The State Immunity Act 1978 provides by s. 1(1):

> "A State is immune from the jurisdiction of the courts of the United Kingdom except as provided in the following provisions of this Act".

Just as the European Convention states the absolute rule of immunity, listing (though in preceding paragraphs) the exceptions to it, so here the draftsman of the Act has chosen (as his first section) to endorse the absolute doctrine. The Act goes on in subsequent sections to specify the considerable exceptions to it. It would have been possible, though not necessarily better, to have provided that there should be no immunity except in specified cases. The effect of that would have been to place on the State the burden of showing that the case fell within one of the listed exceptions. As it is, the effect will be that immunity will be accorded unless the other party shows that the matter falls within one of the specified cases where immunity is not to be granted.

The privileged position accorded the State in this respect is emphasized by s. 1(2), which provides:

> "A court shall give effect to the immunity conferred by this section even though the State does not appear in the proceedings in question".

The effect of this provision is that there can be no summary judgment in the usual way against a State. The plaintiff will have to show (by affidavit in support of an application to enter judgment possibly, or upon application for leave to serve the writ out of the jurisdiction (Chapter 9, paragraphs 9.5 *et seq.*)) that the matter is such that it does not attract "the immunity conferred by this section".

By s. 22(1) " 'court' includes any tribunal or body exercising judicial functions".

It should be noted that this Act, unlike the Diplomatic Privileges Act 1964, s. 1, does not expressly abrogate the common law rules on the topic, so that, where the Act does not apply, the common law still has to be consulted (see Chapter 10).

3.29   (iii) Treaty

The Convention provides by Article 15:

> "A Contracting State shall be entitled to immunity from the jurisdiction of the courts of another Contracting State if the proceedings do not fall within Arts. 1-14. The court shall decline to entertain such proceedings even if the State does not appear".

The phrasing here suggests that it is up to the State to show that the proceedings do not fall within the exceptions to immunity set out earlier in Articles 1–14. By English canons of construction one would expect the text to read "shall be entitled to immunity unless the proceedings fall within Arts. 1-14" if it was intended that the other party have the burden of showing that the proceedings did fall within the exceptions. However, it is probably unhelpful, if not actually wrong, to construe a Convention with the nicety that our jurisprudence teaches us to employ in the construction of an Act of Parliament. Nor can one easily think that the draftsman of the Act intended that the evidential effect of s. 1(1), which is unambiguously expressed, should be the reverse of that produced by the corresponding provision of the Convention.

CHAPTER 4

"STATE"

4.1 (i) The common law

The most vexed question at common law, apart from the recent uncertainties about the basic rule, has been what entities are entitled to the protective mantle of immunity. The question may be phrased thus: what is the test of "sovereign status?"

The head of the State, himself or herself, is obviously of sovereign status. The government of a State is of sovereign status, as is the State itself (both of which are competent parties in an action in the English courts). But, as Lord Denning, M.R., said in the *Trendtex* case[1]:

> "The doctrine grants immunity to a foreign government or its department of state, or any body which can be regarded as its 'alter ego or organ' of the government. But how are we to discover whether a body is an 'alter ego or organ' of the government?
>
> The cases on this subject are difficult to follow . . .
>
> I confess that I can think of no satisfactory test except that of looking to the functions and control of the organization. I do not think that it should depend on the foreign law alone. I would look to all the evidence to see whether the organization was under government control and exercised governmental functions".

4.2 In *Krajina* v. *Tass Agency*[2] it was said that the certificate from the Soviet ambassador that the defendant body was a Department of State was weighty evidence, though not in itself conclusive. A writ for libel had been issued in respect of material published by Tass, a body that enjoyed all the rights of a juridical person under Soviet law. The court, however, did not appear to think that the test was whether the defendant agency had a separate legal existence under its domestic law. It held that even if the agency was a State Department having a separate entity it was not thereby disentitled to immunity.

1. *Trendtex Trading Corporation* v. *Central Bank of Nigeria* [1977] Q.B. 529; 64 I.L.R. 111 (1977).
2. [1949] 2 All E.R. 274; 16 I.L.R. 129 (1949).

Then in *Baccus S.R.L.* v. *Servicio Nacional del Trigo*[3] the Court of Appeal by a majority (Singleton, L.J., dissenting) accorded immunity to the defendant entity as being a Department of State, although under Spanish law it had both separate legal personality and the right to enter into contracts on its own behalf. This seemed to open the door to almost unlimited immunity for any entity the status of which was in some measure connected with the government.

4.3 However, in *Mellenger* v. *New Brunswick Development Corporation*[4] where two industrial consultants were claiming £250,000 commission alleged to be payable for effecting a business introduction leading to the establishment of a chipboard plant in New Brunswick, Lord Denning, M.R., in the Court of Appeal, commended the judgment of Singleton, L.J., in the *Baccus* case:

> "I have always felt that the dissenting judgment of Singleton, L.J., was very convincing, and that, if the case is to be upheld at all, it must be because of the very special evidence which was given there about the Spanish corporation. I adhere to the view which I expressed in the *Rahimtoola* case ([1958] A.C. 379) at page 417, that:
> '. . . a separate legal entity which carried on commercial transactions for a State was an agent, and not an organ, of the government, . . .' ".

Giving reasons for the court's decision to accord immunity to the New Brunswick Corporation, Lord Denning, M.R., considered both the status of the corporation under the establishing statute and its functions.

> "It has never pursued any ordinary trade or commerce. All that it has done is to promote the industrial development of the province in the way that a government department does, such as the Board of Trade in England. In the circumstances it seems to me that the corporation is really part and parcel of the Government of New Brunswick.
> . . . Apart, however, from the statute, the functions of the corporation, as carried out in practice, show that it is carrying out the policy of the Government of New Brunswick itself. It is its alter ego".

4.4 The Court of Appeal again considered the topic in

3. [1957] 1 Q.B. 438; 23 I.L.R. 160 (1956).
4. [1971] 1 W.L.R. 604; 52 I.L.R. 322 (1971).

Trendtex Trading Corporation v. *Central Bank of Nigeria.*[5]
Lord Denning, M.R., found it

> "difficult to decide whether or no the Central Bank of Nigeria should be considered in international law a department of the Federation of Nigeria, even though it is a separate legal entity. But on the whole, I do not think it should be".

Stephenson, L.J., said:

> "I am not satisfied that the bank was created by the Act [the Central Bank of Nigeria Act 1958] a department of the Nigerian Government or has been changed into one by any of the eleven amending decrees which it was contended for the bank had dramatically eroded its independence. A hobbled horse is still a horse".

Shaw, L.J., said:

> "I propose only to indicate what are the features which lead me to the conclusion that the Central Bank of Nigeria ought not to be accorded the status of a department of the government of that country. It is, in the first place, a statutory corporation whose personality, powers and legal attributes are determined by the Central Bank of Nigeria Act 1958 and the amending enactments which followed. The totality of that legislation represents the intention and objectives of those who created and moulded it for the performance of its contemplated functions. If it was designed as a Department of State, many titles indicative of that status come readily to mind. What was conferred upon it was the title of a bank. Nowhere in that legislation is it called anything but a bank; and not a 'Federal' or 'National' or 'State' bank but a 'Central' bank. The 52 sections of the principal Act and the several amending orders and enactments contain no direct indication that the bank is a department of the government and there are many indications which deny it that status. The very name has a commercial ring. Its powers do not identify it with the government and in some respects preclude identification with the government".

4.5 In *Czarnikow Ltd.* v. *Rolimpex*[6] the defendants were a Polish State enterprise who, as it happened, were anxious to show they were *not* an organ of the Polish Government, so that they might plead that their contractual obligations had been frustrated by the action of the Polish Government. The House of Lords endorsed the effect of the arbitrators' finding that Rolimpex, though set up and controlled by the Polish State, was not so closely connected with the government as to be an

5. *Supra*, fn. 1.
6. [1979] A.C. 351; 64 I.L.R. 195 (1978).

organ or Department of the State. Viscount Dilhorne said:

"The respondents are an organization of the State. Under Polish law they have a legal personality. Though subject to directions by the appropriate minister who can tell them 'what to do and how to do it'—as a State enterprise they make their own decisions about their commercial activities. They decide with whom they will do business and on what terms and they have considerable freedom in their day-to-day activities. They are managed on the basis of economic accountability and are expected to make a profit. The arbitrators in my opinion rightly found as a fact that the respondents were not so closely connected with the Government of Poland as to be precluded from relying on the ban imposed by the decree [of the Polish Government] as government intervention".

4.6 The immunity accorded to Departments of State extends in the case of composite States, to the government of a province of a State. In *Swiss-Israel Trade Bank* v. *Government of Salta and Banco Provincial de Salta*[7] the provincial government in Argentina was treated as the Government of Argentina or as a Department of that government.

The immunity also extends to independent countries of the Commonwealth (*Kahan* v. *Pakistan Federation*,[8] *Rahimtoola* v. *Nizam of Hyderabad*);[9] to their sub-divisions (e.g. a Canadian province in a Federal constitution—*Mellenger* v. *New Brunswick Development Corporation*);[10] and to States under British protection (*Mighell* v. *Sultan of Johore*,[11] *Duff Development Co. Ltd.* v. *Kelantan Government*).[12]

4.7 The question of the status of a foreign sovereign, government or State (i.e. who the head of State is, who the government is, whether the country is a sovereign State) is not a difficult one at common law, however vexed it may be in diplomatic circles.

"Once there is the authoritative certificate of the Queen through her minister of State as to the status of another sovereign, that in the courts of this country is decisive"

7. [1972] 1 Lloyd's Rep. 497; 55 I.L.R. 411 (1972).
8. [1951] 2 K.B. 1003; 18 I.L.R. 210 (1951).
9. [1958] A.C. 379; 24 I.L.R. 175 (1957).
10. *Supra*, fn. 4.
11. [1894] 1 Q.B. 149.
12. [1924] A.C. 797; 2 I.L.R. 124 (1924).

(*per* Lord Esher in *Mighell* v. *Sultan of Johore, supra*).

"... it is the duty of the court to accept the statement of the Secretary of State thus clearly and positively made as conclusive upon the point"

(*per* Lord Cave in *Duff Development Co. Ltd., supra*). See Appendix 4, part A.

4.8 (ii) Statute

Section 14(1) provides that references to a State include references to
- (a) the sovereign or other head of that State in his public capacity;
- (b) the government of that State;
- (c) any department of that government.

4.9 It is to be noted that where a head of State acts otherwise than in his public capacity the Act will not apply. His immunity will then be decided under the Diplomatic Privileges Act 1964 (see Chapter 13), for s. 20(1) of the Act of 1978 gives him, in place of his common law privileges, the immunities hitherto afforded to diplomatic agents under the Act of 1964. The division between the public and private acts of a sovereign or head of State is emphasized by s. 20(5) which provides that that section (s. 20) applies to the sovereign or other head of any State on which immunities and privileges are conferred by Part 1 of the Act and is without prejudice to the application of that Part to any such sovereign or head of State in his public capacity.

It will therefore be necessary to decide in any claim against a head of State personally whether he is being sued in his public or private capacity. One has to ask if he was acting as a private person or on behalf of the State. For example, if the sovereign's car runs over a pedestrian one may ask, upon a submission by the plaintiff that s. 5 of the Act of 1978 (see Chapter 6, D) denies immunity in such a case, what the purpose of the driving was. If it was a shopping expedition the sovereign would be able to claim immunity under the Diplomatic Privileges Act as acting in a private capacity (see Chapter 14), but if he was on his way to attend a conference of heads of State he would have been acting in his public capacity, the Act of 1978 would apply to him, and immunity would be denied accordingly under s. 5.

Similarly, in contract, if he purchases household items for his palace one will have to consider the precise nature and purpose of the goods in order to decide whether it was a public or private purchase. If it was a public purchase, perhaps of lighting equipment for the whole palace complex, immunity will be denied under s. 3(1)(*a*) (see Chapter 6, A), but if it is a private purchase, such as personal cosmetics for his immediate family, he will be able to claim immunity under the Act of 1964.

4.10 By s. 21 the certificate of the Secretary of State is conclusive evidence as to (i) whether a country is a State within the meaning of the Act; (ii) who is the head of State; and (iii) who is the government. See Appendix 4, part A.

4.11 In order to clarify what bodies may be regarded as Departments of State, s. 14 introduces the concept of the "separate entity". The references to "State" in the Act do not include a separate entity, which means an entity which is

(i) distinct from the executive organs of the government of the State; and
(ii) capable of suing or being sued.

A test merely of a separate legal personality was not considered sufficient by Parliament; the body must also be divorced functionally from the government. Whereas it should be easy to establish whether under the foreign law the body is capable of suing or being sued, it will no doubt be a matter for careful consideration whether the body is sufficiently distinct from the executive not to be a Department of State. In this connection consideration of the approach of the courts under the common law (see above Chapter 4, paragraphs 4.1–6) may be useful. The court is likely to consider the status of the entity under the establishing legislation, its role and functions.

Once it is established that an entity is a "separate entity" (the burden of which would seem to fall on the plaintiff) the provisions of s. 14(2) operate, by which the separate entity can gain immunity provided that (and the burden of showing this would seem to fall on the entity)

(a) "the proceedings relate to anything done by it in the exercise of sovereign authority"; and
(b) if it had been a State it would have been immune (or, where s. 10 applies, it would have been immune if it were a party to the Brussels Convention—see Chapter 7, paragraphs 7.18, *et seq.*).

Thus the separate entity's task is to show that it was acting as the sovereign's agent in the performance of *acta imperii*. This is another context in which the distinction, new to our law but not to many European jurisdictions, between *acta imperii* and *acta gestionis*, is likely to exercise the minds of our courts. The matter is discussed below in Chapter 12.

It follows that, if a separate entity, though entitled to immunity in respect of a particular suit, nevertheless submits to the jurisdiction, it has, by s. 14(3) the same procedural privileges as a State (see Chapter 9).

4.12 A State's central bank or similar monetary authority may or may not be a separate entity, depending on whether it satisfies the test set out above. If it is shown to be a separate entity, it has then, to gain immunity, to satisfy the test of *acta imperii*. If it is entitled to immunity but waives it, it is entitled, by s. 14(4), to the same procedural privileges as a State. In the case of a central bank or other monetary authority its property, by s. 14(4), is not to be regarded as in use or intended for use for commercial purposes, so that such property will never become liable to process of execution under s. 13(4) (see Chapter 9, paragraph 9.20).

4.13 **Constituent territories**

Under s. 14(5) there is now power to provide by Order in Council for a constituent territory to qualify as a "State". Until a constituent territory is given such status by Order it is to be treated as a separate entity (s. 14(6)). To gain immunity it will therefore have to show that the particular proceedings relate to *acta imperii*.

4.14 It may be of interest to note the corresponding United States provisions, where a considerable body of case law has already accumulated on this issue. The Foreign Sovereign Immunities Act defines "foreign State" by s. 1603 as follows:

(a) A "foreign State" . . . includes a political subdivision of a foreign State or an agency or instrumentality of a foreign State. . . .
An "agency or instrumentality of a foreign State" means any entity
  (i) which is a separate legal person, corporate or otherwise, and
  (ii) which is an organ of a foreign State or political subdivision thereof, or a majority of whose shares or other ownership interest is owned by a foreign State or political subdivision thereof, and
  (iii) which is neither a citizen of a State of the United States . . . nor created under the laws of any third country.

It has already been judicially decided, for example, that the expression "foreign State" includes the German Information Centre, which is "a section of the Consulate General of the Federal Republic of Germany" in New York City; the Libyan National Oil Company; the Permanent Mission of the People's Republic of the Congo to the United Nations. Within the meaning of "agency or instrumentality of a foreign State" it has been decided that a Chilean company is included which was 95 per cent owned by CORFO, a wholly-owned Chilean State entity. Also the Novosti Press Agency and the Tass Agency, as Socialist entities owned by the Soviet State. It is perhaps fortunate that similar complexities of analysis do not seem to be engendered by litigation in the United Kingdom.

4.15 (iii) Treaty

The Act follows the Convention as to separate entities. Article 27, the overall effect of which is to deny to entities, when they are not exercising public functions, any right to treatment different from that accorded to a private person, provides that "State" shall not include any legal entity of a State

"which is distinct therefrom and is capable of suing or being sued, even if that entity has been entrusted with public functions".

However, there is immunity for such an entity

"in respect of acts performed by the entity in the exercise of sovereign authority (*acta jure imperii*)".

It is also provided that if in similar circumstances the State if sued would not have been immune, then the entity shall not be immune.

Article 28 provides that

"the constituent States of a Federal State do not enjoy immunity".

However, a Federal State may make a declaration that its constituent States shall enjoy the same immunity as the Federal State.

CHAPTER 5

THE EXCEPTIONS TO THE BASIC RULE

5.1 (i) The common law

General exceptions

Until 1975 it was commonly thought that there were no general exceptions to the absolute rule of sovereign immunity but only a very few specialized cases. As noted elsewhere (Chapter 3, paragraph 3.14) Lord Denning, M.R., suggested in the case of *Rahimtoola* v. *Nizam of Hyderabad*[1] that immunity was not available where the dispute concerned the commercial transactions of a foreign government and arose "properly within the territorial jurisdiction of our courts", but his brethren disassociated themselves from this radical approach. Lord Denning, M.R., re-stated this view in the *Thai-Europe* case,[2] where he said that the grounds for not granting immunity were limited to

> "commercial transactions that have a most close connection with England, such that, by the presence of the parties or the nature of the dispute, it is more properly cognizable here than elsewhere".

5.2 In 1975 the Privy Council, not following earlier authorities, held that a ship used for trading purposes could not be the subject of a successful claim to immunity. In other words it applied the restrictive doctrine to actions *in rem* (*The Philippine Admiral*[3]—see Chapter 7, paragraph 7.13). Despite the assertion of the Privy Council that, anomalously, the absolute doctrine of sovereign immunity still applied to ordinary actions (*in personam*), the Court of Appeal in the *Trendtex* case[4] held by a majority (Lord Denning, M.R., Shaw,

1. [1958] A.C. 379; 24 I.L.R. 175 (1957).
2. *Thai-Europe Tapioca Service Ltd.* v. *Government of Pakistan* [1975] 1 W.L.R. 1485; 64 I.L.R. 81 (1975).
3. [1977] A.C. 373; 64 I.L.R. 90 (1975).
4. *Trendtex Trading Corporation* v. *Central Bank of Nigeria* [1977] Q.B. 529; 64 I.L.R. 111 (1977).

L.J.) that the common law position had automatically altered, in line with the contemporary rule of international law, so that the restrictive view applied to actions *in personam* too. Donaldson, J., felt unable to accept this in the *Uganda* case,[5] while Goff, J., accepted it in *The I Congreso del Partido*.[6] Lord Denning, M.R., reiterated his view on appeal in the latter case[7] and in the *Hispano Americana* case,[8] and the House of Lords in *The I Congreso del Partido*[9] endorsed this view, certainly for trading ships, not so clearly for other contexts. This topic is fully treated above in Chapter 3.

5.3   Conclusion

It is probable that, should any future issue fall to be decided at common law, which becomes less likely as time goes on, both the Court of Appeal and the House of Lords would accept Lord Denning's view as propounded in the *Trendtex* case,[10] that commercial activities in whatever context cannot attract immunity, not merely in the context of trading vessels.

5.4   Specialized exceptions

A survey of decided cases suggests the following exceptions to absolute immunity. In the administration of a trust fund a sovereign or State has been made a formal party to proceedings to give the opportunity to defend (*Duke of Brunswick* v. *King of Hanover*).[11] An order for winding up a company may be made notwithstanding any interest in the surplus assets that a State may have (*Re Russian Bank for Foreign Trade*).[12] An action against a foreign sovereign in respect of immovable

5. *Uganda Co. (Holdings) Ltd.* v. *Government of Uganda* [1979] 1 Lloyd's Rep. 481; 64 I.L.R. 209 (1978).
6. [1978] Q.B. 500; 64 I.L.R. 154 (1977).
7. [1980] 1 Lloyd's Rep. 23 (C.A.)
8. *Hispano Americana Mercantil S.A.* v. *Central Bank of Nigeria* [1979] 2 Lloyd's Rep. 277; 64 I.L.R. 221 (1979).
9. [1983] 1 A.C. 244; 64 I.L.R. 307 (1981).
10. *Supra*, fn. 4.
11. (1844) 6 Beav. 1.
12. [1933] Ch. 745; 7 I.L.R. 151 (1933).

property owned in a private capacity would seem another exception.

In *The Philippine Admiral*[13] Lord Cross, giving the judgment of the Privy Council, said:

"The only possible exceptions to the generality of the rule that no proceedings *in personam* can be brought against a sovereign or a sovereign State or a body which is a department (or equivalent to a department) of a sovereign State of which there is any trace in the English authorities brought to their Lordship's attention are (a) the case of an action relating to immovable property in the jurisdiction of the State in which the action is brought which was left open in *Sultan of Johore* v. *Abubakar Tunku Aris Bendahar* ([1952] A.C. 318, 343) and (b) the 'trust fund cases', in which the court has not been deterred from administering a trust subject to its jurisdiction by the fact that a sovereign claims an interest in it. If the sovereign does not choose to appear and argue its case the court will decide on the conflicting claims as best it can in its absence".

In the *Thai-Europe* case[14] Lord Denning, M.R., listed exceptions which included, as well as his highly contentious reference to commercial transactions (see Chapter 3, paragraph 3.15), proceedings in respect of land situate in England, proceedings in respect of trust funds here or money lodged for payment of creditors, and proceedings in respect of debts incurred here for services rendered to a State's property here.

5.5 (ii) Statute

The Act was intended to apply the restrictive view of sovereign immunity to the law of this country. It does not merely create for our law the dichotomy of *acta imperii* and *acta gestionis* leaving the courts to interpret those terms in the light of the various differing approaches of the European jurisdictions and the American courts (see Chapter 12), but sets out a detailed list of the types of proceedings in which immunity will not be granted. In case that list should not cover all *acta gestionis* a catch-all provision is inserted (s. 3(3)(c)) whereby immunity is denied to any activity in which a State engages "otherwise than in the exercise of sovereign authority".

The cases in which immunity is denied are set out in the

13. *Supra*, fn. 3.
14. *Supra*, fn. 2.

following paragraphs A to H, of Chapter 6, with a separate chapter on shipping. A comparison with each corresponding provision of the Convention is made. There is not a complete correspondence as the exceptions in the Convention to the absolute doctrine are much narrower than in the Act. However, it should be noted that Article 24 of the Convention permits a State, where that State under its domestic law applies a more restrictive doctrine of immunity than that contained in the Convention, to make a declaration to the effect that it will be applying to Contracting States also that more restrictive approach (but it is not permitted to derogate from the immunity from jurisdiction "which foreign States enjoy in respect of acts performed in the exercise of sovereign authority (*acta jure imperii*)"). The United Kingdom has made such a declaration as the Act's régime is more restrictive than the Convention's.

CHAPTER 6

THE STATUTORY
EXCEPTIONS

A: Commercial transactions (s. 3)

6.1 There is no immunity in proceedings relating to a commercial transaction entered into by a State. This exception does not apply where the parties to the dispute are all States, nor where the parties have otherwise agreed in writing. The parties are thus free to agree that there shall be immunity in any particular transaction. It would also appear that they are free to agree that the Act as a whole should not apply, in which case it seems the common law rules would govern the transaction with all their attendant difficulties (see Chapter 3).

6.2 "Commercial transaction" is the English equivalent of *acta gestionis*. As explained below in Chapter 12 the test of *acta gestionis* has proved difficult to apply in those jurisdictions that have hitherto subscribed to it. However, the Act provides a statutory definition which goes a long way towards clarifying the scope of the exception. "Commercial transaction" is defined to mean (by s. 3(3)):

(*a*) *any contract for the supply of goods or services* (but not contracts of employment, which have a section to themselves—see below Exception C).

It is unlikely to be difficult to decide whether or not a contract falls within this provision. There are two points to note:

(i) It is irrelevant what the purpose of the contract is. Thus the purchase of cement for a naval base or an army barracks is as much a commercial transaction within the meaning of the section as the purchase of paper to print books. The best view upon the dichotomy of *acta gestionis* and *acta imperii* has been that it is the nature

55

and not the purpose of the transaction that must be regarded (see below Chapter 12) and this section endorses that view. Similarly a contract for services, whether the services of a builder to construct a naval base, or a weapon instructor, or an accountant to advise on tax or insurance liability, falls within the definition in the section.

(ii) It would be irrelevant in an action for breach of contract, where the contract is a commercial transaction, that the act constituting the breach could be described as *actus imperii*. Thus the decision of Goff, J., in *The I Congreso del Partido*,[1] which was decided at common law, and the judgment of Waller, L.J., on appeal,[2] that there can be immunity where the breach is *actus imperii* even though the contract is *actus gestionis*, a principle accepted by Lord Wilberforce on appeal,[3] would not be good law under the Act. That case is fully considered below in Chapter 12. It is submitted that to read any such exemption into the words of the Act, so as to curtail the operation of the statutory exception, would not only be flying in the face of the clear words of the section, but would also be quite contrary to the intention of the legislature. Had they wished so to restrict the operation of the section they could have clearly provided for that. The school of thought that reads such an exception into the words of the Brussels Convention might put forward a similar argument in this context, but if it did one would hope to see it fail (see *The Charente*,[4] the reference to that case in Goff, J.'s judgment (*supra*), and the reference to Professor O'Connell's article in the judgment of Waller, L.J. (*supra*)).

(b) *any loan (or other transaction) for the provision of finance and any guarantee or indemnity in respect of any financial obligation.*

---

1. [1978] Q.B. 500; 64 I.L.R. 154 (1977).
2. [1980] 1 Lloyds Rep. 23 (C.A.).
3. [1983] 1 A.C. 244; 64 I.L.R. 307 (1981) (H.L.).
4. [1942] Nytt Jurisdisk Arkiv 1.

By virtue of this provision an individual entering into a financial relationship with a central bank which happens to be a department of government and not a separate entity will be able if need arises to gain redress from the courts, and a bank that makes a loan to a State, even for non-commercial purposes, need not fear a plea of immunity.

> (c) *any transaction or activity of a commercial, industrial, financial, professional or other similar character into which a State enters, or in which it engages, otherwise than in the exercise of sovereign authority.*

This is a catch-all provision: if the plaintiff cannot show that the proceedings relate to a "commercial transaction" within the meaning of (a) or (b) above, he may seek to establish that they relate to a transaction which is

(i) of a business character and
(ii) not *actus imperii.*

Thus here the Act places squarely within our law the concept of *acta imperii.* It does not attempt to define the matter further. It will be up to our courts to formulate the criteria for an *actus imperii.* This question is considered below in Chapter 12.

6.2.1 It may be instructive to compare s. 3 with the provisions of the United States Foreign Sovereign Immunities Act of 1976. The main context where immunity will be denied in the United States courts, apart from cases of waiver, is where the action is based upon a commercial activity of the foreign State having a sufficient nexus with the United States.

"Commercial activity" is defined in s. 1603 in the following manner:

> "D. A. 'commercial activity' means either a regular course of commercial conduct or a particular commercial transaction or act. The commercial character of an activity shall be determined by reference to the nature of the course of conduct or particular transaction or act, rather than by reference to its purpose.
> E. A. 'commercial activity carried on in the United States by a foreign State' means commercial activity carried on by such State and having substantial contact with the United States".

One finds in the Congressional Committee Report on this Act of 9 September 1976:

6.2.1 STATE IMMUNITY

"... A commercial activity carried on in the United States by a foreign State would include not only a commercial transaction performed and executed in its entirety in the United States, but also a commercial transaction or act having a "substantial contact" with the United States. This definition includes cases based on commercial transactions performed in whole or in part in the United States, import export transactions involving sales to, or purchases from, concerns in the United States . . . and indebtedness incurred by a foreign State which negotiates or executes a loan agreement in the United States, or which receives financing from a private or public lending institution located in the United States — for example, loans, guarantees or insurance provided by the Export–Import Bank of the United States . . .".

The Judiciary Committee has stated that:

"... Section 1603 defines the term 'commercial activity' as including a broad spectrum of endeavour, from an individual commercial transaction or act to a regular course of commercial conduct. A 'regular course of commercial conduct' includes the carrying on of a commercial enterprise such as a mineral extraction company, an airline or a State trading corporation. Certainly, if an activity is customarily carried on for profit its commercial nature could readily be assumed . . .
As the definition indicates, the fact that goods or services to be procured through a contract are to be used for a public purpose is irrelevant; it is the essentially commercial nature of an activity or transaction that is critical. Thus, a contract by a foreign government to buy provisions or equipment for its armed forces or to construct a government building constitutes a commercial activity. The same will be true of a contract to make repairs on an embassy building. Such contracts should be considered to be commercial contracts, even if their ultimate object is to further a public function".

The Judiciary Committee has also stated that, for example, an indebtedness incurred by a foreign State negotiating or executing a loan agreement in the United States, or receiving financing from a private or public lending institution located in the United States would, in its opinion, be included in the scope of this section.

It has been held that the ownership of an apartment building in Virginia by the German Democratic Republic and the conduct of commercial banking business and the employment of employees in a branch office in Chicago by the State Bank of India are commercial activities carried on in the United States within the meaning of s. 1605(*a*)(2) (see *County Board* v.

German Democratic Republic;[5] *State Bank of India* v. *Chicago Joint Board).*[6]

In *Gemini Shipping Inc.* v. *Foreign Trade Organization for Chemicals and Foodstuffs,*[7] the U.S. Court of Appeals held that a breach by agencies of the Syrian Government of their guarantee in respect of certain demurrage charges arising out of the purchase of grain by the defendants from a U.S. company could not attract immunity, as the enforcement of the guarantee was based on the commercial activity of purchasing the rice.

In *de Sanchez* v. *Banco Central de Nicaragua,*[8] the Eastern Louisiana Federal District Court were prepared to allow immunity in respect of the issuance of cheques by a central bank on behalf of a commercial bank. The court characterized this as a governmental and not a commercial activity (though immunity was in the end result denied on the ground that the case involved rights in property taken in violation of international law . . . another exception written into the Act). (For further reference see Chapter 12, paragraphs 12.15 *et seq.*)

6.3 *Ships*

It should be noted that, by virtue of S. 10(6), this section does not apply in Admiralty proceedings (or proceedings on any claim which could be made the subject of Admiralty proceedings) where the State is party to the Brussels Convention and the claim relates to the carriage of cargo, or to the operation of a ship owned or operated by the State, or the carriage of passengers in such a ship.

6.4 *Treaty*

There is no provision in the Convention similar to s. 3 of the Act. It is in this connection that the Act goes so much further than the Convention, and primarily for this reason that the United Kingdom has been obliged to make a declaration under

5. (1978) 17 I.L.M. 1404.
6. (1977) 16 I.L.M. 853.
7. 647 F. 2d 317 (2nd Cir. 1981); 63 I.L.R. 569 (1981).
8. 515 F. Supp. 900 (E.D. La. 1981).

Article 24 of the Convention (see above Chapter 5, paragraph 5.5). The Convention does not deny immunity to commercial transactions as such; it makes no general rule to that effect. The nearest the Convention gets to that—and it is not close—is Article 7, which denies immunity where the State has in the State of the forum

> "an office, agency, or other establishment through which it engages, in the same manner as a private person, in an industrial, commercial or financial activity, and the proceedings relate to the activity of that office, agency or establishment".

B: Contracts to be performed in the United Kingdom (s. 3(1)(*b*))

6.5 A State is not immune in proceedings which relate to an obligation of the State which by virtue of a contract (whether a commercial transaction or not) falls to be performed wholly or partly in the United Kingdom.

By s. 17(4) "United Kingdom" includes our territorial waters (customarily a distance of three miles from low-water mark). The provision is so framed as to catch all contracts which are to be performed within the United Kingdom, regardless of whether they are of a commercial character or not.

The only exceptions are:

(i) where the parties to the dispute are all States;
(ii) where the parties to the dispute have otherwise agreed in writing;
(iii) contracts of employment between a State and an individual (for which there are separate rules—see Exception C);
(iv) where the contract is (a) not a commercial transaction, (b) was made in the State's territory, and (c) is governed by the State's administrative law.

The reference to a State's "administrative law" is presumably a reference to those jurisdictions which, unlike the common law, have a separate body of law (e.g. droit administratif, public law for matters affecting the relationship between the individual and the State).

Presumably contracts made in a State's ship or aircraft would count as made "in the territory of the State concerned", but not contracts made at the Embassy (see *Radwan* v. *Radwan*[9]).

6.6 It should be noted that by virtue of s. 10(6) these provisions do not apply in Admiralty proceedings (or proceedings on a claim which could be the subject of Admiralty proceedings) where the State is a party to the Brussels Convention and the claim relates to the carriage of cargo, or to the operation of a ship owned or operated by the State, or the carriage of passengers in such a ship.

6.7 *Treaty*

Article 4 is very similar. The words "wholly or partly" do not appear ("an obligation of the State, which, by virtue of a contract, falls to be discharged in the territory of the State of the forum"). The condition set out above at (iv)(a) is not included in the Article, so that a commercial contract made on a State territory and governed by its administrative law may be the subject of immunity before the courts of another State. This is consistent with the Convention's failure to create a general exception for commercial transactions.

C: Contracts of employment

6.8 *The common law*

In *Sengupta* v. *Republic of India*[10] a clerk at the Indian High Commission in London sued the respondents for unfair dismissal. He was first employed in 1975 and dismissed in 1981. The Employment Appeal Tribunal held that the matter fell to be decided at common law as the proceedings were "in respect of matters that occurred" before the Act came into

9. [1973] Fam. 24; 55 I.L.R. 579 (1972).
10. (1983) I.C.R. 221; 64 I.L.R. 352 (1982).

force, within the meaning of s. 23(3) (see Chapter 11). Although a contrary argument, to the effect that the proceedings were "in respect of" the dismissal, not "in respect of" the occurrence of the contract at the time of formation, had great force (particularly as s. 23 specifically removes certain contracts from the scope of the Act were made before it came into force but does not mention contracts of employment), it would not have helped the applicant had the Act applied as he was an Indian national (see the following paragraph).

The court accepted that at common law the restrictive doctrine applied and held that as the performance of this contract and its breach involved participation in the public functions of the foreign State and the hearing of the complaint was likely to involve investigation into that function jurisdiction was excluded and immunity must be accorded (see further Chapter 12 below). The court was assisted by reference to a number of foreign decisions. It said:

"As we understand the cases, decisions in other jurisdictions have consistently granted to a foreign State immunity from claims brought by employees at a diplomatic mission engaged in the work of the mission. In *De Decker* v. *United States of America*,[11] the Belgian Court of Appeal upheld a claim for State immunity from proceedings brought by an official of the United States Foreign Service. In *Luna* v. *Republic of Romania*[12] an Italian court upheld a claim for immunity from proceedings brought by the employee of a commercial agency which the court held to be "simply an office of the Rumanian embassy": the employee was employed at a very low grade. In *Conrades* v. *United Kingdom*,[13] a labour court at Hanover upheld the claim by the United Kingdom Government for immunity from a claim brought by a German national who had been employed for over 30 years as a receptionist and non-confidential clerical worker at the consulate at Hanover. There is no case where immunity has been refused on the grounds that the claimant was not a member of the diplomatic staff.

Those cases are to be contrasted with claims brought by employees at institutions run by foreign States but not as part of their diplomatic mission. Thus immunity has been refused by the Italian court in relation to claims by employees at the Hungarian Academy in Rome, at a hospital run by the Vatican in Rome, and at a lyceé run by the French Government. In each of these cases the fact that the institution at which the claimant was employed was not discharging a sovereign function of the foreign State was a material consideration".

11. 23 I.L.R. 209 (1956).
12. 65 I.L.R. 313 (1974).
13. 65 I.L.R. 205 (1981).

(Further employment cases may be found in Chapter 12 under the various jurisdictions, especially Italy.)

6.9   Statute

Section 4 deals specifically with contracts of employment. The provisions are modelled on those contained in the Convention. The general rule is that there is no immunity in an action upon a contract of employment where

(i) the employee is an individual, and
(ii) EITHER the contract was made in the United Kingdom OR the work is to be performed in the United Kingdom (wholly or partly).

A contract made in London for employment in Abu Dhabi is thus within the scope of this provision. A contract made on the Embassy premises is "made in the United Kingdom". (See *Radwan* v. *Radwan*.[14])

The section is framed to cover proceedings before industrial tribunals; by sub-s. (6) it includes proceedings "in respect of any statutory rights or duties" of employer or employee.

The general rule is displaced (so that immunity will be granted) if (a) the employee is a national of the State when the action began or (b) the employee was neither a United Kingdom national (as defined by sub-s. (5)) nor habitually resident here when the contract was made; or (c) the parties to the contract have otherwise agreed in writing.

Conditions (a) and (b), however, do not operate to displace the "no immunity" rule if (i) the work is for an office, agency or establishment maintained by the State in the United Kingdom for commercial purposes (that means, by s. 17(1) purposes of "commercial transactions" as defined by s. 3(3), for which see paragraph 6.2); AND (ii) the employee was not habitually resident in that State when the contract was made.

6.10 EXAMPLE: would the action of an employee of a State tourist office in London attract immunity, the employee being a national of that State living in London but having a home in that State?

14. *Supra*, fn. 9.

The basic rule of State immunity (see Chapter 3) is displaced by what I have here called the general rule of "no immunity" in actions upon contracts of employment. It appears at first sight that as this employee is a national of the State concerned, condition (a) above operates to take the proceedings out of the scope of the section, so that the basic rule of State immunity applies (sub-s. (2)(a)).

However, his work is for an office or agency maintained by the State in the United Kingdom, so that, provided he can show the office is maintained for commercial purposes AND he is not habitually resident in that State, he keeps his action within the terms of the section (sub-s. (3)).

The purposes of a State tourist office would seem to be the purposes of a "commercial transaction" within the definition of s. 3(3)(c): an activity of a commercial or similar character in which a State engages otherwise than in the exercise of sovereign authority. There is very little authority to elucidate the distinction between *acta imperii* and *acta gestionis*, as it is a concept new to our law (see below Chapter 12). Although tourism has a political and diplomatic aspect, it also has a commercial side in that it attracts foreign currency. Possibly, if the tourist office was only an information service, took no bookings, and charged no fees, it could be argued that its purpose was not commercial but rather the facilitation of communication and understanding between the States, an exercise of sovereign authority.

Whether the employee in this example could show that he was not habitually resident in the State would probably depend on how long he had spent there in recent years, how long his period of sojourn in the United Kingdom was, and what homes he maintained in the two countries. The expression "habitually resident" appears in other statutes, as here, without definition, e.g. Wills Act 1963, s. 1; Recognition of Divorces and Legal Separations Act 1971, s. 3(1)(a). It has been held to mean, in the last statute, regular physical presence enduring for some time (*Cruse* v. *Chittum*[15]).

6.11 Condition (c) above (displacing the "no immunity" rule where the parties have otherwise agreed in writing) does not

15. [1974] 2 All E.R. 940.

apply "where the law of the United Kingdom requires the proceedings to be brought before a court of the United Kingdom" (sub-s. (4)). This provision is difficult to understand. The suggestion of our courts "requiring" proceedings to be brought before them does not strike any responsive chord in the mind of the English lawyer, whether one understands it to indicate a context where the law is ordering proceedings to be brought or, less unlikely, that it is requiring that if proceedings are brought they be brought in the United Kingdom courts. Does our law ever assert that proceedings may not be brought in another jurisdiction? Surely it allows other jurisdictions to entertain such actions as they think fit: to do less would seem an unwarrantable interference with the jurisdiction of other States. Nor does it seem that one can derive much assistance from what appears to be the source of this provision in the Convention: Article 5(2)(c) reads:

> ". . . unless, in accordance with the law of the State of the forum, the courts of that State have exclusive jurisdiction by reason of the subject-matter".

The concept of exclusive jurisdiction may indeed be more relevant to other legal systems. What may be meant by the sub-section is that there is no contracting out of the "no immunity" rule where a special tribunal within the United Kingdom legal system has exclusive jurisdiction. Thus, industrial tribunals are a creature of statute which alone can hear certain actions relating to employment. This would have the effect of preventing the State employer from ousting the jurisdiction of the tribunal by a plea of immunity, based on a prior agreement, just as an ordinary employer is so prevented by s. 140 of the Employment Protection (Consolidation) Act 1978.

6.12 Two exceptions and two definitions should be noted.

By virtue of s. 10(6) the provisions of s. 4 do not apply in Admiralty (or similar) proceedings where the State is a party at the Brussels Convention and the claim relates to the carriage of cargo, or to the operation of a ship owned or operated by the State, or the carriage of passengers in such a ship. This exclusion is designed to avoid conflict with the regime created by the Brussels Convention, but it is not immediately apparent how proceedings relating to a contract of employment could feature in such a context. Secondly, by virtue of s. 16(1)(*a*), the provisions of s. 4 do not apply to the employment of members of a diplomatic mission or a consular post. Thus in a claim by a United Kingdom national in respect of his employment as a consul in London the foreign State may invoke immunity.

Definitions: United Kingdom national is defined by sub-s. (5) to mean

    —a citizen of the United Kingdom and colonies;
    —a person who is a British subject by virtue of ss. 2, 13 or 16 of the British Nationality Act 1948 or by virtue of the British Nationality Act 1965;
    —a British protected person within the meaning of the Act of 1948.

By s. 17(4), references to the United Kingdom include our territorial waters (customarily a distance of three miles, from low-water mark, see *Halsbury's Laws of England* (4th Edn.) Vol. 18 para. 1456 *et seq.*) and any area designated under s. 1(7) of the Continental Shelf Act 1964.

6.13   *Treaty*

Article 5 of the Convention is the source of s. 4 and is very similar to it. The words "wholly or partly" qualifying the performance of the contract of employment are not included.

D: Tort: Personal injuries and damage to property

6.14   *The common law*

At common law there are no exceptions to the rule of absolute immunity in respect of actions in tort. It would have been interesting to see how Lord Denning, M.R., might have decided a claim for immunity in an action for damages for negligence arising out of the careless driving of a State-owned haulage lorry. He might well have extended the *acta gestionis/imperii* distinction from contracts to all matters or acts arising from a State's commercial activity. For it would seem anomalous if the lorry's co-driver, who was in the passenger seat at the time of the accident, could sue his employer, the foreign State, in contract for breach of an implied term to take all reasonable care for his safety, a term vicariously broken by his mate's careless driving, whereas an action in tort by an injured cyclist could be defeated by a claim to immunity.

It may be safely assumed, perhaps, that there are no pending actions of such a nature, which were begun before the Act came into force and so would fall to be decided at common law. It is in fact to be expected that, if a litigant (the cyclist in our example) was considering litigation, his advisers would dissuade him on the ground that a claim to immunity would succeed (of course, the State might in such a case submit to jurisdiction, in which event the point of law would not be canvassed).

6.15   *Statute*

Under the Act (s. 5) there is no immunity in proceedings in respect of

(i) death;
(ii) personal injury;
(ii) damage to, or loss of, tangible property

provided that the cause of the death, personal injury, damage or loss was an act or omission in the United Kingdom.

6.16 By s. 10(6) this section (s. 5) does not apply in Admiralty proceedings, or proceedings on any claim which could be made the subject of Admiralty proceedings, where the State is party to the Brussels Convention and the claim relates to the operation of a ship owned or operated by the State, the carriage of cargo or passengers on board such a ship or the carriage in any ship of cargo owned by the State. This complex provision is designed to avoid conflict between the Act and the provisions of the Brussels Convention.

6.17 It might be difficult to decide in a particular case whether an "omission" has taken place in this country—for example, if a lorry goes out of control because the steering fails, it not having been properly maintained in the State's domestic workshops. If the "injury" is caused by the "omission" to maintain, rather than the "act" of going out of control, the State might have a good claim to immunity. In this respect the text of the Convention (see below) seems clearer.

Though this provision is particularly relevant to traffic accidents it is not so limited. A similar provision in the United States statute has been used to support an action by the wife of the former Chilean ambassador in respect of his alleged murder in Washington by agents of the new Chilean Government. (See 63 I.L.R. 378.)

6.18 It should also be borne in mind that, quite apart from the burden on the plaintiff of showing that his action is such as to fall within the provisions of s. 5, he will also have to obtain leave to serve the writ out of the jurisdiction under R.S.C. Order 11, rule 1 (see Chapter 9, paragraph 9.9).

6.19 *Other torts*

Section 5 is the only provision of the Act that deals with actions in tort to any substantive extent. Section 6(1), which relates to a State's interest in land situate here (see below Exception E), would seem to cover an action for nuisance created upon the premises occupied by a State as well, possibly, as an action for negligence in connection with the State's use of its premises. But such exceptions to the general rule of immunity for actions in tort are not explicit in the section and do not form the burden of it.

It does, however, seem clear that under s. 7 (see below Exception G) an action in tort for, e.g. passing off would not attract immunity.

6.20 It is a matter for conjecture whether under s. 3(1)(*a*), which seems clearly directed at contractual suits, some actions in tort might fall within the exception to the general rule of immunity as being "proceedings relating to a commercial transaction entered into by the State" (e.g. an action for negligence arising in connection with a commercial transaction, which the plaintiff wishes to bring in tort and not in contract, perhaps because he is not in direct contractual relation with the State, or possibly because he is on a stronger footing in tort from the point of view of the relevant period of limitation).

6.21 *Treaty*

Article 11 is similar to s. 5. It provides that there shall be no immunity

> "in proceedings which relate to redress for injury to the person or damage to tangible property, if the facts which occasioned the injury or damage occurred in the territory of the State of the forum, and if the author of the injury or damage was present in that territory at the time when those facts occurred".

The use of the word "facts" in the English text seems better chosen than the "act of omission" of the Act, as it relates unequivocally to the physical fact causing the injury, rather than, as one might construe the Act, the human act that caused it.

However, the final condition, the presence of the tortfeasor within the State, is a little difficult to understand, as it seems to envisage the possibility of damage being caused within a State's boundaries at a time when the tortfeasor has either already left the country (delayed action?) or has never entered it (damage by long-range frequencies?).

E: Ownership, possession and use of property

6.22 *The common law*

It will be remembered that at common law proceedings in respect of land situate in England was one of the few possible exceptions to the general rule of absolute immunity (see above, Chapter 5, paragraph 5.4). It cannot, however, be said to have been conclusively established for, having heard argument on the matter in *Sultan of Johore* v. *Abubakar Tunku Aris Bendahar*,[16] the House of Lords left the point open.

An exception that was established was the trust fund case: the Privy Council said in *The Philippine Admiral*[17] that the court would not be deterred from administering a trust fund here by the claim of a sovereign's interest (see above, Chapter 5, paragraph 5.4). This is not overlooked by the Act (s. 6(3)).

6.23 *Statute*

By s. 6(1) there is no immunity in proceedings relating to

  (i) any interest of a State in land ("immovable property") in the United Kingdom;
 (ii) a State's possession or use of land in the United Kingdom;
(iii) any obligation of a State arising out of such interest, possession or use.

This would seem to include not only actions about possession and sale of land, leases, mortgages, etc., but also actions for nuisances created upon the State's land or negligent use of the land and, conceivably, building disputes (if a contractor sues for the cost of a swimming pool he built in the Embassy, is not this an action relating to a State's use of land? It might, of course, also come within s. 3—see above, paragraph 6.1).

6.24 The provisions of s. 6(1) do not, by virtue of s. 16(1)(*b*), apply to

"proceedings concerning a State's title to or its possession of property used for the purposes of a diplomatic mission".

It would seem that the omission of the words "or use" after "possession" would have the effect of retaining the application of s. 6(1) to an action for nuisance arising from some use to which the occupants might be putting the Embassy. Similarly, the swimming-pool contractor mentioned above would argue

16. [1952] A.C. 318; 19 I.L.R. 182 (1952).
17. [1977] A.C. 373; 64 I.L.R. 90 (1975).

that his action related to the State's "use" of the land and not its
possession of it.

In *Intpro Properties (UK) Ltd.* v. *Sauvel and others*[18] the
plaintiff let premises to the French Government as a private
residence for the Financial Counsellor to the Embassy. When
the diplomat refused the plaintiffs access to effect repairs they
sought an order requiring the defendants to permit entry and
damages against the Government (no injunctive relief can be
obtained against a State, see below paragraph 9.17). Bristow, J.,
held that the proceedings related to the State's possession and
use of the premises and its obligations in connection therewith,
but that the denial of immunity effected by s. 6(1) did not apply
by virtue of s. 16(1)(*b*) because the proceedings "concerned a
State's . . . possession of property used for the purposes of a
diplomatic mission". He did not accept the argument that the
action related only to the State's "use" of the premises, so that
s. 16(1)(*b*) would not apply, though that would seem to have
been the better view.

The Court of Appeal disagreed, saying that the evidence was
insufficient to establish that the premises were "used for the
purposes of a diplomatic mission" within s. 16(1)(*b*) because
the Act contemplated that the premises should be used for the
professional diplomatic purposes of the mission. It was not
enough that they were used as a private residence by a
diplomatic agent, even though incidentally that diplomatic
agent had certain understandable social obligations which he
and his wife carried out on the premises. In addition, the court
said that in any event the proceedings did not concern the
Government's title to or possession of the premises.

6.25 Section 6(2) disallows immunity in proceedings relating
to any interest of a State in *any* property (movable or
immovable) arising by way of succession, gift or *bona
vacantia.*

6.26 It is provided by s. 6(3) that the fact that a State has or
claims an interest in any property is not to preclude a court
from exercising jurisdiction over the property relating to the

18. [1983] Q.B. 1019; 64 I.L.R. 363, 384 (1982/3).

estates of deceased persons or persons of unsound mind, or to insolvency or to the winding up of companies or to the administration of trusts. It is useful, in view of the uncertainty of the common law on these matters, to have the rules framed so clearly.

6.27 Section 6(4) deals with actions to which the State is not a party but which relate to property in which the State is interested. The court is empowered to entertain such proceedings in respect of property in the possession of a State provided that the State would not have been immune had it been itself sued. The court is empowered to entertain such proceedings in respect of property in which a State claims an interest provided that the State would not have been immune had it been itself sued OR its claim is not supported by *prima facie* evidence nor admitted (semble by all interested parties).

6.28 This last provision, the requirement of *prima facie* evidence to support a claim if the action is to be stayed, embodies the effect of the common law rule. It has often been said that an action *in rem* seeks to bring the defendant sovereign before the courts as surely as an action *in personam*, for he has either to come into court or lose his property. Similarly, an action against some other party imperilling property in which the sovereign has an interest in a direct challenge to that interest. Accordingly, the common law has been prepared in the appropriate case to stay the action at his request. He need not own the property, or be in possession of it. It is enough if he is entitled to possession, or if it is held by a bailee, or if he has merely requisitioned it (see *U.S.A.* v. *Dollfuss Mieg et Cie*[19]). However, the courts have been reluctant to accept without question the sovereign's assertion of his interest, for it is a drastic denial of justice for an action between ordinary litigants to be halted at the behest of a third party. In *Juan Ismael & Co. Inc.* v. *Government of the Republic of Indonesia*[20] the defendant State alleged that it had purchased a steamship from the plaintiff company, but the evidence established that the company's agent, as was known

19. [1952] A.C. 582.
20. [1955] A.C. 72; 21 I.L.R. 95 (1954).

to the Government's agent, had no authority to sell. The Privy Council held that a foreign sovereign must show that his claim is not illusory or, as in the instant case, manifestly defective, and that it raises an arguable issue.

See further the decision of Waller, L.J., in *Antoun v. Harrison*.[21]

6.29   *Treaty*

Article 9 of the Convention provides that there shall be no immunity where the proceedings relate to

(a) a State's rights or interests in, or its use or possession of, immovable property situate in the forum State, or
(b) its obligations arising out of such rights, interests, use or possession.

Under Article 10 there is no immunity in proceedings relating to a right in movable or immovable property arising by way of succession, gift or *bona vacantia*.

By Article 14

"Nothing in this Convention shall be interpreted as preventing a court of a Contracting State from administering or supervising or arranging for the administration of property, such as trust property or the estate of a bankrupt, solely on account of the fact that another Contracting State has a right or interest in the property".

F: Membership of bodies

6.30   *Statute*

Under s. 8, where a State is a member of a body, corporate or not (including a partnership), being a body which

(a) has members other than States and
(b) EITHER is incorporated or constituted under United Kingdom law
OR is controlled from the United Kingdom
OR has its principal place of business in the United Kingdom

21. 64 I.L.R. 77 (1965).

there is no immunity in proceedings between the State and the body or its members relating to its membership of the body.

This section does not apply

   (i) if the parties to the dispute have otherwise agreed in writing or

  (ii) if the constitution of the body (or the instrument establishing or regulating it) provides to the contrary.

6.31   *Treaty*

Article 6(1) denies immunity where a State participants with one or more private persons (this condition as to *private* persons does not appear in s. 8 of the Act) in a company, association or other legal entity having its seat, registered office or principal place of business in the forum State AND the proceedings concern the relationship, in matters arising out of that participation, between the State and the entity or any other participant.

Article 6(2), paragraph (1) shall not apply if it is otherwise agreed in writing (this provision is more narrowly, or at any rate more precisely expressed in s. 8(2) of the Act). One does not expect the same nicety of expression from a treaty as in an Act of Parliament.

G: Patents, trademarks, etc.

6.32   *Statute*

Under s. 7 a State is denied immunity in proceedings relating to

  (a) any patent, trademark, design or plant breeders' rights which

    (i) belong to the State, and

   (ii) are already registered or protected in the United Kingdom or for which the State has applied in the United Kingdom;

  (b) an alleged infringement by the State in the United Kingdom of any patent, trademark, design, plant breeders' rights or copyright;

  (c) the right to use a trade or business name in the United Kingdom.

These matters are of a wholly commercial character and clearly need to be excepted from the general rule of immunity if the restrictive doctrine is to be followed. It is doubtful if they would fall within the wording of s. 3, which excepts "commercial transactions".

Although this section might seem primarily designed to cover specialized actions relating to patents and trademarks, it is worth noting two points: first, it also covers, by paragraph (c), an action for passing off; secondly, it could extend to a suit against a State not necessarily commercial in character, e.g. where a State in publishing non-commercial literature in the United Kingdom is alleged to have infringed copyright.

6.33   *Treaty*

Article 8 denies immunity to a State in proceedings relating to

  (a) a patent, industrial design, trademark, service mark or other similar right which, in the State of the forum, has been applied for, registered or deposited or is otherwise protected *and* in respect of which the State is the applicant or owner;
  (b) an alleged infringement by it, in the territory of the State of the forum, of such a right belonging to a third person and protected in that State;
  (c) an alleged infringement by it, in the territory of the State of the forum, of copyright belonging to a third person and protected in that State;
  (d) the right to use a trade name in the State of the forum.

H: Taxes

6.34   *Statute*

By virtue of s. 11 there is no immunity in respect of liability for

  (a) V.A.T., Customs duty, Excise duty, or agricultural levy or
  (b) rates on premises occupied for commercial purposes.

"Commercial purposes" means, by s. 17(1), purposes of any

"commercial transaction" as defined by s. 3(3) (see paragraph 6.2).

By s. 16(5) the Act does not apply to any other proceedings relating to taxation. They would therefore fall, in the absence of any other relevant legislation, within the scope of the general common law rule of immunity.

One may also note here Article 23(1) of the First Schedule of the Diplomatic Privileges Act 1964, which exempts the premises of a mission from all dues and taxes (see below Chapter 14, paragraph 14.20).

6.35 *Treaty*

The Convention contains no similar provisions.

CHAPTER 7

SHIPPING

7.1   (i) The common law

A great part of the law of sovereign immunity has been concerned with actions *in rem* seeking the arrest or detention of ships. Maritime trade has since the earliest days of civilization been a vital link between States. Sea-going nations have built empires, or, more peaceably, spheres of influence, whether by trade, like the Phoenicians and the Greeks, or by warfare like the Spanish and the English. Two-thirds of the surface of the globe is water. The ability to range freely over that watery domain has shaped nations and created our civilization. It is not surprising that a great part of a State's merchant fleet has been and remains State-owned. As the merchant vessel has been responsible for so much of the commercial intercourse between countries, and as the State has had a commanding interest in such trade, it is only to be expected that much of the law governing a State's liability in commercial actions will be concerned with maritime proceedings.

7.2 There is no arcane mystery to Admiralty proceedings. They differ from the more usual proceedings in procedure rather than in substance. An action *in rem* is based on a claim *in personam*. The action is brought against the *res*, usually a ship, but sometimes cargo, freight or an aircraft, in order that the *res* may, in the event of the claim being successful, provide a source for satisfaction of the judgment. At common law the action *in rem* was based on the maritime lien which attached to property the subject of a dispute to the extent of the claim from the moment such claim arose. The right to enforce the lien by an action *in rem* was confined to the property by which the damage was caused or in relation to which the claim arose, and was enforceable against the property in the hands of an innocent purchaser.

7.3 The present law, found in the Administration of Justice Act 1956, preserves this jurisdiction based upon the maritime lien, but extends the action *in rem* to many claims which do not give rise to the lien. Moreover, on the sister ship principle, action may be brought in many cases against any other ship in the same beneficial ownership as the ship in connection with which the claim arose.

The principle in the modern law is this: the foundation of an action *in rem* is the lien resulting from the personal liability of the owner of the *res*. That personal liability may be established by an ordinary action *in personam*, for the Admiralty jurisdiction of the High Court may now in all cases be invoked by an action *in personam* (Act of 1956 s. 3(1)), although the exercise of jurisdiction may be inhibited by the rules as to service out of the jurisdiction, and, further, in collision and similar cases certain conditions must be fulfilled before jurisdiction can be exercised.

7.4 But the origin and nature of an action *in rem*, which may be seen simply as a convenient alternative to establishing the same liability by an action *in personam*, means that there was no sensible justification for what, as we shall see, appeared at one time to be the common law rule, namely that the restrictive doctrine of sovereign immunity applied to action *in rem*, while, anomalously, the absolute doctrine still applied to actions *in personam*. In speaking of this anomaly in *The I Congreso del Partido*[1] Goff, J., said:

> ". . . actions *in rem* and actions *in personam* cannot be conveniently segregated into separate compartments. Invocation of the Admiralty jurisdiction by an action *in rem* presupposes the existence of a claim *in personam* against the person, who, at the time when the action is brought, is the owner of the ship: see section 3(4) of the Act of 1956. If the owner of the ship is a foreign sovereign, he is inevitably impleaded by the action *in rem* because he must either fight the case or surrender his ship. 'To implead an independent sovereign in such a way is to call upon him to sacrifice either his property or his independence': see *The Parlement Belge* (1880) 5 P.D. 197, 219. If he chooses not to surrender his ship, he will effectively be fighting the claim *in personam*, though in addition his property will be at stake. The practical effect of the decision in *The Philippine Admiral* is therefore that in cases concerned with ordinary trading ships foreign

1. [1978] Q.B. 500; 64 I.L.R. 154 (1977).

sovereigns may be forced to contest claims *in personam* in this country, though only where the claim falls within the Admiralty jurisdiction as defined by section 1 of the Act of 1956, and in respect of which an action *in rem* can be commenced in accordance with section 3 of the Act".

7.5 Section 1(1) of the Act of 1956 sets out the claims which (by s. 3) may be made the subject of an action *in rem*. The majority of those claims may be pursued not only against the ship or property in question but also against a sister ship. While the reader is referred to the Act for the full details of these claims, it is noted here that the sovereign is most likely to be concerned with a "claim for loss of or damage to goods carried in a ship" or a claim "arising out of any agreement relating to the carriage of goods in a ship or to the use or hire of a ship"; as well, perhaps, as claims for damage to or by a ship, salvage, towage, pilotage, claims in respect of goods or materials supplied to a ship for her operation or maintenance, claims in respect of the construction, repair or equipment of a ship.

7.6 Although the immunity of the foreign sovereign should not, for the reasons given above, depend on a distinction between actions *in rem* and actions *in personam*, or, even less, between maritime and other actions, it is convenient to view that immunity as falling into two parts. Lord Atkin, in *The Cristina*,[2] distinguished between the direct impleading of a sovereign by an action *in personam* and indirect impleading against property in which he has an interest (see Chapter 3, paragraph 3.1). He said:

"It seems to me clear that, in a simple case of a writ *in rem* issued by our Admiralty court in a claim for collision damage against the owners of a public ship of a sovereign State in which the ship is arrested, both principles are broken. The sovereign is impleaded and his property is seized".

With this in mind let us look at the progress under the common law of the immunity in actions *in rem*.

7.7 Over a hundred years ago the case of a trading vessel was considered by that great international lawyer, Sir Robert

2. [1938] A.C. 485; 9 I.L.R. 250 (1938).

Phillimore, in *The Charkieh*.[3] Admiralty proceedings were instituted *in rem* against the *Charkieh* and her freight for damages arising from a collision in the River Thames. The *Charkieh* was one of a small fleet of trading vessels which had previously belonged to a private trading company but which had been bought by Ismail Pasha, the Khedive of Egypt. She had been sent to England for repairs and, to lessen expenses, she had brought cargo with her. At the time of the collision she was under charter to a British subject and advertised to carry cargo to Alexandria. Sir Robert held that the Khedive was not entitled to the privileges of a sovereign prince, but that even if he had been he would have lost that immunity by assuming the character of a trader.

> "No principle of international law, and no decided case, and no dictum of jurists of which I am aware, has gone so far as to authorize a sovereign prince to assume the character of a trader, when it is for his benefit; and when he incurs an obligation to a private subject to throw off, if I may so speak, his disguise, and appear as a sovereign, claiming for his benefit and to the injury of a private person, for the first time, all the attributes of his character".

By sending the ship to trade here, Sir Robert considered that the Khedive had waived any privilege which might otherwise have attached to the vessel as property of a sovereign. The anomalous distinction between immunity in actions *in rem* and actions *in personam* is foreshadowed in certain passages in Sir Robert's judgment.

The summary given here of that case and following cases is based on the Privy Council's judgment in *The Philippine Admiral*.[4]

7.8 The *Parlement Belge*[5] was a packet owned by the King of the Belgians, officered and manned by persons in his employ and flying the Belgian pennant, which carried both mails and passengers with their luggage between Ostend and Dover. At first instance Sir Robert adhered to the opinion he had given in *The Charkieh* that a vessel engaged in commerce, as in his view the *Parlement Belge* was, was not entitled to immunity even if

3. (1873) L.R. 4 A. & E. 59.
4. [1977] A.C. 373; 64 I.L.R. 90 (1975).
5. (1879) 4 P.D. 129; (1880) 5 P.D. 197 (C.A.).

she was owned by a foreign sovereign and manned by his servants. The Court of Appeal reversed his judgment. Though their decision has, as we shall see, been taken as authority for the proposition that vessels owned by a foreign sovereign are immune from jurisdiction even if used wholly or substantially for trading purposes, the better view (that taken by Mackenna, J., in *Swiss Israel Trade Bank* v. *Government of Salta*[6] and by the Privy Council in *The Philippine Admiral*) is that it lays down two propositions, one, that a foreign sovereign cannot be sued *in personam*, and, two, that an action *in rem* cannot be brought against his ship if she is being used substantially for *public* purposes. The King of the Belgians claimed that the *Parlement Belge* was being used for public purposes, and the Court of Appeal, granting immunity, accepted that.

7.9 Although, then, the question whether a State-owned vessel used wholly or substantially for trading purposes was immune was in fact left open in that case, the Court of Appeal in *The Porto Alexandre*[7] said that they were bound by *The Parlement Belge* to answer that question in the affirmative. The *Porto Alexandre*, which was the property of the Portuguese Government, was being employed by that Government in ordinary trading voyages earning freight. In September 1919, she loaded a cargo of cork shavings for carriage to Liverpool under a bill of lading from which it appeared that the cargo was shipped by and consigned to the Portuguese Import and Export Co. Ltd. She ran aground in the River Mersey. Salvage services were rendered to her by three Liverpool tugs, and a writ *in rem* was issued on behalf of the owners, masters and crews. Hill, J., at first instance, and the Court of Appeal reluctantly held that they were bound by *The Parlement Belge* to grant immunity and set aside the writ against the ship and the freight.

7.10 In 1926 the Supreme Court of the United States reached a similar decision in *The Pesaro*.[8] Proceedings *in rem* had been issued against the vessel on a claim for damages arising out of a

6. [1972] 1 Lloyd's Rep. 497; 55 I.L.R. 411 (1972).
7. [1920] P. 30; 1 I.L.R. 146 (1919).
8. (1926) 271 U.S. 562; 3 I.L.R. 186 (1926).

failure to deliver goods accepted by her at a port in Italy for carriage to New York. On the vessel being arrested the Italian Government asked that the suit be dismissed on the ground that the vessel was owned, possessed and controlled by it and was employed by it in the carriage of merchandise for hire in the service and interest of the whole Italian nation as distinguished from any individual member thereof. Accepting this submission the court said:

> ". . . when, for the purpose of advancing the trade of its people or providing revenue for its treasury, a government acquires, mans and operates ships in the carrying trade, they are public ships in the same sense that warships are. We know of no international usage which regards the maintenance and advancement of the economic welfare of a people in time of peace as any less a public purpose than the maintenance and training of a naval force".

However, the international trend was even then going in the opposite direction, for on 10 April 1926, a total of 20 States signed the Brussels Convention, including the United Kingdom, which, as we shall see (see paragraph 7.23 below), assimilated the position of trading ships owned by a sovereign to ordinary merchant vessels.

7.11 The case of *Compania Naviera Vascongada* v. *S.S. Cristina* (*The Cristina*)[9] has already been considered in Chapter 3, at paragraphs, 3.1, 3.10 where it was described as the high-water mark of the absolute doctrine of immunity. She was a trading ship registered at Bilbao and when that port was occupied by the insurgents in June 1937 the Government of the Spanish Republic issued a decree requisitioning all vessels registered there. The *Cristina* was then on the high seas but when she reached Cardiff the Spanish consul there replaced the master and those of the officers and crew who were thought to be in sympathy with the insurgents with persons well affected to the Government. The owners issued a writ *in rem* claiming to have possession of the vessel as her owners, which the Spanish Government sought to have set aside as infringing its sovereign immunity. What was in issue in the litigation was not whether a trading vessel could be immune, for it was clear that the *Cristina* had been requisitioned by the Government to

9. [1938] A.C. 485; 9 I.L.R. 250 (1938).

assist in putting down the rebellion and was therefore in the fullest sense *publicis usibus destinata*, but whether the Government had a sufficient interest in the ship to attract immunity in respect of it. On that question all five Law Lords agreed that, as the vessel was in the *de facto* possession and control of the Spanish Government when the writ was issued, the writ impleaded a foreign sovereign and must be set aside.

One noteworthy aspect of the case, the far-reaching general propositions found in the judgment of Lord Atkin, has already been considered in Chapter 3, paragraph 3.1. But also significant is the division of opinion among the members of the court on the question whether *The Porto Alexandre*[10] was rightly decided. Lord Atkin thought it had been. Lord Wright said that "as at present advised" he thought *The Porto Alexandre* and *The Pesaro*[11] correctly stated the English law on the point. Lord Maugham, on the other hand, pointed out that the decision in *The Parlement Belge*[12] did not compel the decision in *The Porto Alexandre*. He adverted to the Brussels Convention, the tenor of which ran directly counter to the approach of the courts in *The Porto Alexandre* and *The Pesaro*, and he doubted the correctness of those cases. Lord Thankerton and Lord Macmillan reserved their opinions as to whether *The Porto Alexandre* had been correctly decided.

7.12 In the years following the Second World War the United Kingdom found itself increasingly isolated in its adherence to the absolute theory of sovereign immunity. As noted above (Chapter 3, paragraph 3.12) the United States adopted the restrictive doctrine through the Tate letter of 19 May 1952. Frankfurter, J., had already said, *obiter*, in *Republic of Mexico* v. *Hoffmann*[13] that he agreed with Lord Maugham's view in *The Cristina* that there should be no immunity for ships owned and operated by a foreign State for ordinary trading purposes, and he thought *The Pesaro*[14] had been wrongly decided.

7.13 However, it was not until the mid-1970s that this country

10. *Supra*, fn. 7
11. *Supra*, fn. 8.
12. *Supra*, fn. 5.
13. (1945) 324 U.S. 30.
14. (1926) 271 U.S. 562; 3 I.L.R. 186 (1926).

moved away from the absolute theory. The movement away in actions *in personam* has been described above (Chapter 3, paragraph 3.14 *et seq.*): a contentious decision by the Court of Appeal presided over by Lord Denning, M.R., in the *Trendtex* case,[15] followed by the passing of the State Immunity Act 1978. The movement away in shipping matters was made by the Privy Council in *The Philippine Admiral*[16] and followed by the House of Lords in *The I Congreso del Partido*[17] (see below). The facts in the former case were that a Hong Kong company brought proceedings *in rem* against the *Philippine Admiral* for goods supplied to and disbursements made for the ship. Another plaintiff sued *in rem* for damages for breach of a charter-party. The Government of the Republic of the Philippines applied for the proceedings to be set aside on the ground that the ship was their property. Throughout her life she had been operated as an ordinary merchant vessel earning freight by carrying cargoes. The Privy Council said that *The Porto Alexandre*[18] had been wrongly decided, the court in that case had misunderstood the limited effect of the decision in *The Parlement Belge*,[19] Lord Atkin and Lord Wright had not been correct in *The Cristina*[20] in suggesting that immunity lay in respect of a trading vessel, and accordingly no immunity should be granted to the *Philippine Admiral*.

7.14 In delivering judgment Lord Cross said, at page 402:

"Their Lordships turn now to consider what answer they should give to the main question raised by this appeal—whether or not they should follow the decision of the Court of Appeal in *The Porto Alexandre* ([1920] P. 30). They are clearly weighty reasons for not following it. In the first place the court decided the case as it did because its members thought they were bound so to decide by *The Parlement Belge*, L.R. 4 P.D. 129 whereas—as their Lordships think—the decision in *The Parlement Belge* did not cover the case at all. Secondly, although Lord Atkin and Lord Wright approved the decision in *The Porto Alexandre* the other three Law Lords who took part in *The Cristina* ([1938] A.C. 485) thought that it was at least doubtful whether sovereign immunity

15. *Trendtex Trading Corporation* v. *Central Bank of Nigeria* [1977] Q.B. 529; 64 I.L.R. 111 (1977).
16. [1977] A.C. 373; 64 I.L.R. 90 (1975).
17. [1983] 1 A.C. 244; 64 I.L.R. 307 (1981) (H.L.).
18. [1920] P. 30; 1 I.L.R. 146 (1919).
19. (1879) L.R. 4 P.D. 129; (1880) L.R. 5 P.D. 197 (C.A.).
20. [1938] A.C. 485; 9 I.L.R. 250 (1938).

should extend to State-owned vessels engaged in ordinary commerce. Moreover, this Board in the *Sultan of Johore* case ([1952] A.C. 318) made it clear that it considered that the question was an open one. Thirdly, the trend of opinion in the world outside the Commonwealth since the last war has been increasingly against the application of the doctrine of sovereign immunity to ordinary trading transactions. Lastly, their Lordships themselves think that it is wrong that it should be so applied. In this country—and no doubt in most countries in the western world—the State can be sued in its own courts on commercial contracts into which it has entered and there is no apparent reason why foreign States should not be equally liable to be sued there in respect of such transactions".

7.15 Admirable as this decision was, adherence to the doctrine of precedent meant that, whereas it was possible for the court to argue its way out of *The Porto Alexandre*,[21] the established authority for the doctrine of absolute immunity in actions *in personam* was so great that the Privy Council was unable to do other than endorse it, though admitting the anomalous nature of the situation thus created. The subsequent history of this anomaly is dealt with in Chapter 3, paragraph 3.17, *et seq*.

7.16 In *The I Congreso del Partido*[22] a Cuban State enterprise had contracted to deliver sugar to a Chilean company, but, upon a right-wing coup in Chile in September 1973 Cuba had broken off diplomatic relations and had refused to fulfil the contract. The Chilean company proceeded *in rem* against a sister ship of Cuba. Goff, J., held that, as breaking off diplomatic relations was an *actus imperii*, it was irrelevant that this particular element in the breaking off was a breach of a commercial obligation. The restrictive theory afforded immunity to such an act. On appeal, Waller, L.J., agreed, but Lord Denning, M.R., disagreed so the decision at first instance stood until the House of Lords gave judgment in July 1981. Lord Wilberforce, with whose judgment in this regard all the Law Lords agreed, said that the restrictive doctrine applied at common law to all actions, whether *in rem* or *in personam*, that involved State-owned trading vessels, although there was a fundamental split among the Law Lords as to the effect of

21. *Supra*, fn. 18.
22. [1978] Q.B. 500; [1980] 1 Lloyd's Rep. 23 (C.A.); [1983] 1 A.C. 244; 64 I.L.R. 307 (1981) (H.L.).

applying the doctrine to the facts of the case. (See further Chapter 12, paragraphs 12. 10–13.)

7.17   Conclusion

Therefore no immunity will be accorded at common law in respect of *acta gestionis* in an action involving a ship used wholly or substantially for commercial purposes.

7.18   (ii) Statute

Section 10 of the Act of 1978 contains complicated provisions relevant to

(a) Admiralty proceedings and
(b) proceedings on any claim which could be made the subject of Admiralty proceedings.

By s. 1 of the Administration of Justice Act 1956 the High Court may exercise its Admiralty jurisdiction over specified questions and claims. For the full details the reader is referred to the Act, but it may be noted here that the matters listed include claims to the possession or ownership of a vessel or in respect of a mortgage or charge on a ship, claims for damage done by or to a ship, claims for death or personal injury arising from negligence in connection with the condition or control of a ship, claims for loss of or damage to goods carried in a ship, claims arising out of any agreement relating to the carriage of goods in a ship or to the use or hire of a ship, salvage, towage and pilotage claims, claims in respect of goods or materials supplied to a ship for her operation or maintenance, claims in respect of the construction, repair or equipment of a ship.

Such claims may in all cases be brought by an action *in personam* (s. 3(1) of the Act of 1956), or, if the ship or property in question is to hand, by an action *in rem* against that ship or property. In many cases the action can be brought against a sister ship (s. 3(2), (4)). Section 10 of the Act of 1978 will apply to an ordinary action *in personam* in the Queen's Bench

Division if it could have been brought under the Admiralty jurisdiction.

The provisions of s. 10 are designed to deny immunity in respect of trading ships and commercial cargoes and to harmonize with the Brussels and European Conventions.

7.19 There is no immunity

(i) in an action *in rem* against a ship or any property other than cargo in the ownership, possession or control of a State (or in which it claims an interest) if the ship was being used (or intended for use) for commercial purposes when the cause of action arose.

"Commercial purposes" means, by s. 17(1), the purposes of "commercial transactions" as defined by s. 3(3) (see Chapter 6, paragraph 6.7).

If the action is brought against one ship to enforce a claim in connection with another, both ships must have been in use (or intended for use) for commercial purposes when the cause of action arose.

It seems clear from the wording of s. 10(2) and (3), denying immunity to a State in an action *in rem* against a ship used for commercial purposes, that the approach of Goff, J., and Waller, L.J., and, it would seem, of Lord Wilberforce in *The I Congreso del Partido*[23] (see paragraph 7.16 and Chapter 12, paragraph 12.9) would not be followed if a similar issue fell to be decided under the Act. The wording of the Act offers no scope to the argument that, although a ship was in use as a trading vessel, the acts in respect of which the action is brought were themselves in exercise of sovereign power. Once a claim arises against a trading ship owned by the State immunity cannot be accorded (see further paragraph 7.27).

7.20 There is no immunity

(ii) in an action *in personam* to enforce a claim in connection with a ship or any property other than cargo in the ownership, possession or control of a State (or in which it claims an interest) if the ship was being used (or intended for use) for commercial purposes when the cause of action arose.

23. *Supra*, fn. 22.

It seems, therefore, that here too, no plea of *acta imperii* can be made. If the Act had been in force when the cause of action arose in *The I Congreso del Partido* and Cuba had been sued in an action *in personam*, she would not have been able successfully to claim that, as her act that broke the contract was itself an *actus imperii*, she should be granted immunity.

7.21 Special rules for cargo (sub-s. (4)):
There is no immunity

(iii) in an action *in rem* against a cargo in the ownership, possession or control of a State (or in which it claims an interest) if both the cargo and the ship carrying it were in use (or intended for use) for commercial purposes when the cause of action arose.

(iv) in an action *in personam* to enforce a claim in connection with cargo in the ownership, possession or control of a State (or in which it claims an interest) if the ship carrying it was in use (or intended for use) for commercial purposes. In this last case it appears on the wording of the Act not to be necessary for the cargo also to satisfy the test of commercial purposes.

7.22 By s. 17(1) "ship" includes hovercraft.

7.23   (iii) Treaty

The Brussels Convention assimilates the position of State-owned ships and cargoes used for commerce to that of the private vessel.

Article 1 provides: "Sea-going ships owned or operated by States, cargoes owned by them, and cargoes and passengers carried on State-owned ships, as well as the States which own or operate such ships and own such cargoes shall be subject, as regards claims in respect of the operation of such ships or in respect of the carriage of such cargoes, to the same rules of liability and the same obligations as those applicable in the case of privately-owned ships, cargoes and equipment".

Article 2 provides: "As regards such liabilities and obligations, the rules relating to the jurisdiction of the courts, rights of action and procedure shall be the same as for merchant ships belonging to private owners and for private cargoes and their owners".

7.24 This comprehensive denial of immunity to State-owned ships and cargoes is curtailed by Article 3 which preserves immunity in respect of non-commercial vessels and their cargoes.

Article 3 provides: "The provisions of the two preceding Articles shall not apply to ships of war, State-owned yachts, patrol vessels, hospital ships, fleet auxiliaries, supply ships and other vessels owned or operated by a State and employed exclusively at the time when the cause of action arises *on Government and non-commercial service*, and such ships shall not be subject to seizure, arrest or detention by any legal process, nor to any proceedings *in rem*".

7.25 However, even in respect of such vessels there are exceptions to the rule of immunity, for Article 3 further provides: "Nevertheless, claimants shall have the right to proceed before the appropriate courts of the State which owns or operates the ship in the following cases:

  (i) Claims in respect of collision or other accidents of navigation
  (ii) Claims in respect of salvage or in the nature of salvage and in respect of general average
  (iii) Claims in respect of repairs, supplies or other contracts relating to the ship

and the State shall not be entitled to rely on any immunity as a defence".

7.26 The same rules apply to State-owned cargoes carried on board such ships, (Article 3(2)) but, by Article 3(3): "State-owned cargoes carried on board merchant ships for government and non-commercial purposes shall not be subject to seizure, arrest or detention by any legal process nor to any proceedings *in rem*.

"Nevertheless, claims in respect of collisions and nautical accidents, claims in respect of salvage or in the nature of salvage and in respect of general average, as well as claims in respect of contracts relating to such cargoes, may be brought before the court which has jurisdiction in virtue of Article 2".

7.27 An interesting gloss on the Convention can be found in the judgment of Goff, J., in *The I Congreso del Partido*,[24] where the judge, in dealing with plaintiffs' counsel's submission that the effect of Articles 1–3 was that the immunity of State-owned ships depended solely on the nature of the ship or the use to which it was being put, and that in the case of ships falling outside those specified in Article 3 a sovereign could not invoke sovereign immunity, even where the act complained of either was, or arose by reason of, a governmental act, said:

> "It is, however, to be observed that Article 1, which, subject to Article 3, permits claims in respect of State-owned ships and cargoes, and cargoes and passengers carried on State-owned ships, applies only to 'claims in respect of the operation of such ships or in respect of the carriage of such cargoes' and the Article is therefore open to the interpretation that it excludes claims where the act complained of arises from a governmental act. On the evidence before me relating to the laws of countries which have ratified the Convention, which this country has not, there is certainly no consensus as to the interpretation favoured by [counsel for the plaintiffs]. On the contrary, the Supreme Court of Sweden, a country which has ratified the Convention and enacted it into Swedish law, expressed the opinion in the leading case of *The Charente* ([1942] Nytt Jurisdisk Arkiv 1) that Article 1 of the Convention, as enacted into Swedish law, had no application in the case of an *actus jure imperii*; and the *travaux préparatoires* of the Convention, if regard is to be had to them, provide considerable support for this view. I do not therefore consider that the plaintiffs can derive much support for their argument from the Convention".

It is not easy to understand why the wording of Article 1 is "open to the interpretation that it excludes claims where the act complained of arises from a governmental act". The wording is clear enough. If a claim is in respect of the operation of a ship or the carriage of cargo there is no immunity unless the vessel or the cargo falls within the provisions of Article 3. There is no suggestion that one has to consider the nature of the act giving rise to the claim. As I suggested above (paragraph 7.19) the reasoning of Goff, J., in *The I Congreso del Partido*[25] would appear to be inapplicable under the Act of 1978.

24. [1978] Q.B. 500; 64 I.L.R. 154 (1977).
25. *Ibid.*

CHAPTER 8

SUBMISSIONS TO THE JURISDICTION

8.1 (i) The common law

At common law purported waivers of immunity are strictly construed in favour of the sovereign. There must be an actual submission. Thus no waiver can be inferred from an agreement in writing to submit to the court's jurisdiction (*Kahan* v. *Pakistan Federation*):[1] the promise to submit is not enforceable against the sovereign, and it is not treated as the submission itself. No waiver may be inferred from an agreement to submit to arbitration, nor from an application to set aside an arbitration award (*Duff Development Co. v. Kelantan Government*).[2]

Even where a sovereign has actually submitted to the jurisdiction, execution is not permitted. He submits to the court's adjudication but not to the enforcement of its order. He may remove his assets from the jurisdiction if he so wishes (*Vavasseur* v. *Krupp*).[3] When he does submit to the jurisdiction, he is taken to have submitted also in respect of any appeal in the matter (*Sultan of Johore* v. *Abubakar Tunku Aris Bendahar*).[4]

No submission may be inferred merely from the fact that he has lived in this country incognito and as a private individual entered into a contract under an assumed name (*Mighell* v. *Sultan of Johore*,[5] an action for breach of promise of marriage).

8.2 A submission is made if the sovereign himself institutes proceedings (obviously enough), and, where he does so, he is

1. [1951] 2 K.B. 1003; 18 I.L.R. 210 (1951).
2. [1924] A.C. 797; 2 I.L.R. 124 (1924).
3. (1878) 9 Ch.D. 351.
4. [1952] A.C. 318; 19 I.L.R. 182 (1952).
5. [1894] 1 Q.B. 149.

deemed to have submitted also in respect of any counterclaim arising out of the same transaction but not one independent of and unrelated to the subject-matter of the action. In *High Commissioner for India* v. *Ghosh*[6] the plaintiff was not deemed to have submitted to a counterclaim for slander where his claim had been for money lent or, in the alternative, breach of contract.

A submission is also made where a sovereign takes a step in the action (other than one taken to contest the jurisdiction, e.g. by entering a conditional appearance) with full knowledge of his right to immunity and with proper authorization. Thus, despite the entry of an unconditional appearance, the defendants were granted immunity in *Baccus S.R.L.* v. *Servicio Nacional del Trigo*[7] because their unconditional appearance had been entered in ignorance of the sovereign's privilege and without the authority of the appropriate Minister (but now see R.S.C. Order 12 as amended by S.I. 80/1716 with effect from 3 June 1980).

8.3 (ii) Statute

It is not surprising that, just as the Act makes great inroads into the general principle of immunity at common law, so also it is not prepared to treat the sovereign's position in the matter of submissions with the extreme delicacy of the common law.

8.4 Under s. 2 a submission is inferred in the following circumstances:

(i) if a State institutes proceedings, it is (obviously enough), taken to have submitted;

(ii) a prior agreement in writing may, contrary to the common law rule, amount to a binding submission, but a term of a contract to the effect merely that United Kingdom law is to govern the contract is not to be regarded as a submission (this provision is likely to prove of great significance, for it enables the non-State

6. [1960] 1 Q.B. 134; 28 I.L.R. 150 (1959).
7. [1957] 1 Q.B. 438; 23 I.L.R. 160 (1956).

party to a contract to protect himself before entering into contractual obligations with a State from a later claim to immunity. Some departments of State already have a standard form in which they waive any right they might otherwise have to immunity from jurisdiction. Such a waiver is not in itself an agreement to submit to execution (see Chapter 9, paragraph 9.16 *et seq.*)).

8.4.1 A considerable body of case law has already arisen in United States jurisdictions on the question of Waiver by prior treaty. In one decision of the U.S. Court of Appeals in 1974, before the Foreign Sovereign Immunities Act 1976 was in force, it was held, when an attempt was made to attach Soviet vessels for alleged damage to fishing gear, that the fact that the U.S.S.R. had concluded a treaty with the USA agreeing that Soviet vessels would enter U.S. ports subject to all applicable rules of U.S. law did not amount to a waiver of immunity from attachment (*Southeastern Leasing Corp.* v. *Stern Dragger Belogorsk*[8]).

An example of a fairly comprehensive waiver by treaty may be found in the 1972 U.S.—U.S.S.R. Trade Agreement:

> "Foreign trade organisations of the USSR shall not claim or enjoy in the USA, and private natural and legal persons of the USA shall not claim or enjoy in the USSR, immunities from suit or execution of judgment or other liability with respect to commercial transactions".

8.4.2   *The Act of 1976*

Section 1610(*d*) allows attachment before judgment to be effected upon the property of a foreign State which is used for a commercial activity within the United States, but only provided that the foreign State has explicitly waived its immunity from such pre-judgment attachment and that the purpose of the attachment is to satisfy a judgment which has been or may ultimately be entered against the State and not merely to obtain jurisdiction.

In one case, *New England Merchants National Bank* v. *Iran Power Generation and Transmission Company*,[9] the U.S. District Court for New York (Southern District) decided that

8. 63 I.L.R. 39 (1974).
9. (1980) 19 I.L.M. 1298.

a clause in a treaty between the U.S.A. and Iran of August 1955, which waived immunity for commercial activities by the signatories, had to be strictly interpreted *contra proferentem* and could not be interpreted therefore as a waiver of immunity from pre-judgment attachment, that not being within the clear contemplation of the clause.

In another case the District Court for New Jersey permitted pre-judgment attachment against property of the Imperial Iranian Airforce and Iran Aircraft Industries on the basis not of an explicit waiver, but of a general waiver under the terms of that same treaty. (*Behring International Inc.* v. *Imperial Iranian Airforce*).[10] But another Judge of the District Court for the Southern District of New York did not take that view in *Reading & Bates Corp.* v. *National Iranian Oil Company*[11] and refused to co..firm an ex parte order of pre-judgment attachment, saying

> "It is hard to imagine that a sovereign nation, in entering a treaty supposedly to promote commerce, would at the same time even suggest that it would evade a lawful judgment arising out of its commercial activities".

The California Central District Federal Court has refused to infer a waiver in respect of pre-judgment attachment from the words in the Treaty (a waiver of immunity from "execution of judgment or other liability"). *Security Pacific National Bank* v. *Government of Iran.*[12]

But the U.S. Court of Appeals, Second Circuit, has recently held that an agreement by a state bank to waive "any right or immunity from legal proceedings including suit, judgment and execution" was enough to constitute a waiver of immunity from pre-judgment attachment. The Court said that it was not necessary that the actual phrase "pre-judgment attachment" be used if the words were otherwise clear. (*Libra Bank Ltd.* v. *Banco Nacional de Costa Rica*).[13] And see, further, *S & S Machinery Co.* v. *Masinexportimport.*[14]

8.4.3 The following example of a waiver clause in a loan

10. 475 F. Supp. 383 (D.N.J. 1979); 63 I.L.R. 261 (1979).
11. 478 F. Supp. 724 (S.D.N.Y. 1979); 63 I.L.R. 305 (1979).
12. 513 F. Supp. 864 (C.D. Calif. 1981); 518 F. Supp. 596 (C.D. Calif. 1981).
13. 676 F.2d 47 (2nd Cir. 1982).   14. 706 F.2d 411 (2nd Cir. 1983).

agreement was provided by A.C. Cates & S. Isern-Feliu (see *International Financial Law Review*, July 1984, p. 23).

"The Borrower hereby irrevocably submits to the non-exclusive jurisdiction of the High Court of Justice in England, the Courts of the State of New York and the Courts of the United States of America for the Southern District of New York in relation to any claim, dispute or difference which may arise hereunder or any document entered into pursuant hereto or in connection herewith but without prejudice to the rights of the Agent or the Banks to commence any legal action or proceeding in the courts of any other competent jurisdiction and irrevocably appoints . . . of . . . London, England as its authorised agent for service of process in the High Court of Justice in England and . . . of . . . New York, USA as its authorized agent for service of process in the Courts of the State of New York and the Courts of the United States of America. The Borrower agrees that it will at all times maintain an agent, duly appointed, in England and New York to accept service of process on behalf of the Borrower in respect of the aforesaid courts. The Borrower irrevocably consents to the service of process out of any of the aforesaid courts in any such legal action or proceedings by the mailing of copies thereof by registered or certified airmail (postage prepaid) to the address for the time being for the service of notices on the Borrower under Clause . . . or in any other manner permitted by law. The Borrower hereby irrevocably waives any objection it may have to the laying of venue of any such legal action or proceeding in such courts and any claim that any legal action or proceeding brought in connection with this Agreement in any such court has been brought in an inconvenient forum. The Borrower hereby irrevocably waives any immunity from jurisdiction to which it or its assets might otherwise be entitled (such waiver to have effect under and be construed in accordance with the Foreign Sovereign Immunities Act of 1976 of the United States of America in respect of any legal action or proceeding in the Courts of the State of New York or the Courts of the United States of America) and hereby irrevocably and generally consents in respect of any legal action or proceeding arising out of or in connection with this Agreement to the giving of any relief or the issue of any process in connection with such action or proceeding, including, without limitation, the making, enforcement or execution against any property, assets or revenues whatsoever (irrespective of their use or intended use) of any order or judgement which may be made or given in such action or proceeding".

8.4.3 (iii) Under s. 2 of the U.K. Act a State submits to the jurisdiction if it knowingly (see below at (c))

> EITHER intervenes in the proceedings
> OR takes any step in the proceedings
> BUT that does not include intervening or taking a step

(a) merely to claim immunity (it could hardly be otherwise!)
(b) merely to assert an interest in property where the State would have been immune if it had itself been sued; or
(c) in reasonable ignorance of the facts of entitling it to immunity (i.e. where those facts could not reasonably have been ascertained), provided it puts in its claim to immunity as soon as reasonably practicable (which means, presumably, not merely very soon after those facts are ascertained, but very soon after the moment when they could reasonably be ascertained).

This exclusion (c) may be intended to embody the common law rule, that taking a step in ignorance of the right to immunity is no submission, but the language of the Act in s. 2(5), which follows Article 3(1) of the Convention, is, it is submitted, of much narrower effect than the common law rule, for ignorance of the facts entitling one to claim immunity is not the same as ignorance of one's right to immunity. It is most unlikely that "facts" would be held by a court to include the legal "fact" of the right to immunity. In these circumstances it is not easy to see what situation is envisaged by this sub-section: conceivably an ambassador might instruct solicitors to acknowledge service (formerly enter an appearance) not knowing, for example, that a ship was being used at the relevant time for non-commercial purposes, but it is not easy to see how that fact would be beyond his reasonable ascertainment.

8.5 Section 2(6) follows the common law rule by providing that a submission, once made, extends to

(i) any appeal in the proceedings;
(ii) any counterclaim which arises out of the same legal relationship or facts as the claim.

8.6 A submission may, by sub-s. (7), properly be made by the following persons:

(i) in respect of any proceedings a submission may be made by the ambassador ('the head of a State's diplomatic mission in the United Kingdom") or his deputy;

(ii) in respect of proceedings arising out of a contract made on behalf of and with the authority of a State, the submission may be made by the State's agent who made the contract.

This sub-section should render unnecessary the sort of argument that arose at common law in, e.g. *Baccus S.R.L.* v. *Servicio Nacional del Trigo*.[15]

8.7 By s. 9 an agreement in writing to submit to arbitration extends (contrary to the common law rule) to proceedings in our courts which relate to the arbitration. In such proceedings the State is not immune. This section does not apply

(i) if the parties to the agreement are States

or (ii) if the agreement itself provides otherwise.

It should also be noted that to submit to the jurisdiction is not to submit to execution (see Chapter 9, paragraph 9.16 *et seq.*).

In the United States an agreement to submit disputes to arbitration under Swiss law under International Chamber of Commerce Rules amounted to an implicit waiver (*Ipitrade* v. *Federal Republic of Nigeria*);[16] again in that jurisdiction a mere agreement to arbitrate was held to amount to a waiver in *Birch Shipping Corporation* v. *Embassy of Tanzania*.[17] But choice of Dutch law and an agreement to submit disputes to arbitration in Paris was held not to amount to waiver before United States courts in *Verlinden* v. *Central Bank of Nigeria*[18] (see further *Ohntrup* v. *Firearms Center Inc.*).[19]

15. [1957] 1 Q.B. 438; 23 I.L.R. 160 (1956).
16. 63 I.L.R. 196 (1978) (D.C. Columbia 1978).
17. 63 I.L.R. 524 (1980) (D.C. Columbia 1980).
18. 63 I.L.R. 390 (1980) (S.D.N.Y. 1980).
19. 63 I.L.R. 632 (1981).

8.8 (iii) Treaty

Article 1(1): "A Contracting State which institutes or intervenes in proceedings before a court of another Contracting State submits for the purpose of those proceedings to the jurisdiction of the courts of that State". That would seem obvious enough.

By Article 13, Article 1(1) does not apply where a State intervenes to assert that it has a right or interest in property which is the subject-matter of the proceedings, and the circumstances are such that it would have been entitled to immunity if the proceedings had been brought against it.

8.9 By Article 1(2) there is no immunity on a counterclaim (a) "arising out of legal relationship or the facts on which the principal claim is based", (b) if under the Convention it would not have been entitled to immunity in respect of the counterclaim had separate proceedings been brought against it.

The provision, at first sight, and even upon closer scrutiny, seems to state that immunity shall be denied only where the counterclaim is not independent of the claim AND the subject-matter of the counterclaim is itself an exception under the Convention to the general rule of immunity, instead of making the two conditions alternative. However, the Explanatory Report to the Convention appears to interpret the provision so as to mean that the defendant's counterclaim is not open to a claim of immunity either if it is linked to the State's action or if it is in any event an excepted case. Indeed if this were not the correct interpretation the defendant would derive almost no benefit from what is presumably intended to be a concession to defendants sued by a State. His benefit would merely be that he could claim against the State in the same action, instead of having to bring separate proceedings.

The Act, be it noted, makes no mention of the second condition.

8.10 By Article 1(3) a Contracting State which makes a counterclaim in proceedings before a court of another Contracting State submits to jurisdiction in respect of both claim and counterclaim. (Clearly, for to put in a counterclaim must be to take a step in the proceedings within the meaning of Article 3, below.)

8.11 By Article 3 immunity is waived where a Contracting State "takes any step in the proceedings relating to the merits" (other, of course, than an appearance merely to claim immunity). However, if the State satisfies the court that it could not have acquired knowledge of facts on which a claim to immunity can be based until after it has taken such a step, it can claim immunity based on these facts if it does so at the earliest possible moment.

8.12 By Article 2 a Contracting State may submit to juris- diction

(a) by international agreement;
(b) by a contract in writing;
(c) by consent given after the dispute has arisen (writing is not here stipulated).

8.13 By Article 12 if a Contracting State has agreed in writing to submit to arbitration there is no immunity in proceedings relating to

(a) the validity or interpretation of the arbitration agreement;
(b) the arbitration procedure;
(c) the setting aside of the award
unless the arbitration agreement itself provides otherwise *or* it is an agreement made between States.

CHAPTER 9

PROCEDURAL PRIVILEGES

9.1 (i) The common law

At common law the sovereign, once involved in litigation, enjoyed no privileges save freedom from measures of enforcement. It is generally understood that a submission to the jurisdiction is not a submission to execution, though there are dicta in *Duff Development Co. Ltd.* v. *Kelantan Government*[1] doubting this.

9.2 The sovereign is expected to obey the ordinary rules of court, and, once having submitted, is treated as an ordinary litigant (*King of Spain* v. *Hullett and Widder*).[2] He can be required to provide security for costs (*King of Greece* v. *Wright*),[3] and he must make discovery of documents (*Republic of Costa Rica* v. *Erlanger;*[4] *South African Republic* v. *Compagnie Franco-Belge du Chemin de Fer du Nord;*[5] see further *Halsbury's Laws of England* (4th Edn.) Vol. 18, para. 1559, n. 5).

9.3 If the foreign sovereign fails to comply with an order of the court, the order, whether interlocutory or final, may not be enforced by seizure of his assets, neither to secure obedience to an order nor to satisfy a judgment or an order for costs (*Duff Development Co. Ltd.* v. *Kelantan Government*),[6] for this would amount to a form of execution.

9.4 However, the court may resort to other measures, such as striking out a pleading or debarring a State from defending.

1. [1924] A.C. 797; 2 I.L.R. 124 (1924).
2. (1833) 7 Bli., N.S. 359, 393.
3. (1837) 6 Dow. 12.
4. (1874) L.R. 19 Eq. 33.
5. [1898] 1 Ch. 190.
6. *Supra*, fn. 1.

The State in this way may end up with an adverse judgment but it will not be enforced by the court. Only moral pressures, and those the Foreign and Commonwealth Office might bring to bear, may be used to assist the successful litigant.

9.5 (ii) Statute

A significant procedural privilege is found in s. 1(2) of the Act. Even if the State does not appear, a court must grant immunity if the case does not fall within one of the exceptions set out in the Act. A State does not have to claim immunity to get it.

Where, therefore, it seems to the court that a defendant who does not appear may fall within the meaning of "State" under the Act (see Chapter 4, paragraph 4.8 *et seq.*) the plaintiff will have to satisfy the court (the burden may not be heavy) either that the defendant is not of sovereign status or that the case falls within one of the exceptions set out in the Act to the general rule of immunity. It remains to be seen how quick the court will be to apprehend that a defendant may be of sovereign status.

It is clear from s. 12(4) (see paragraph 9.12) that the Act contemplates judgment being given against a State in default of appearance in appropriate circumstances. For "appearance" we must now read "acknowledgment of service" (S.I.80/1716) in relation to proceedings issued after 3 June 1980.

9.6 The following provisions of the Act follow the rules of the Convention (Article 16):

Service of process

By s. 12(1) service of a writ upon a State (or other document instituting an action) can only be effected by sending it through the Foreign and Commonwealth Office to the State's Ministry of Foreign Affairs, and it is effectively served only with it arrives there. A certificate from the United Kingdom Secretary of State is conclusive evidence as to when the document has been served or received (s. 21(d)).

If a State enters an appearance it waives any irregularity in the prescribed mode of service (sub-s. (3)). If a State agrees to another manner of service the prescribed mode need not be followed (sub-s. (6)). Whereas under Article 16 of the Convention such a writ must be accompanied by a translation where necessary, the Act is silent on the point (future Rules of Court may, however, require this—*cf*. Order 11, rule 6(5), (6)).

Service out of the jurisdiction

9.7 It must be carefully noted that, by s. 12(7), rules of court for service outside the jurisdiction are not affected by the section, so that leave to serve out will have to be obtained under Order 11. It would have been possible to provide for service within the jurisdiction on the Embassy, on the analogy of a foreign company carrying on business within the jurisdiction (it would have had to be made clear that the Embassy was not to be regarded as foreign territory for that purpose). However, it was no doubt considered more diplomatic that the foreign sovereign should not, by reason merely of his mission's presence here for the purpose of diplomatic intercourse between the two countries, be deemed to have a legal presence within the jurisdiction.

9.8 Before starting proceedings a plaintiff will wish, where a submission to the jurisdiction is not expected, to satisfy himself that his action falls within one of the statutory exceptions to the absolute rule of immunity. In addition to satisfying himself of that (and satisfying the court, if a claim to immunity is later made) he will have to show for the purpose of service of the writ that the case falls within the claims specified in Order 11.

9.9 Order 11: It is provided by Order 11, rule 1(1) that service of a writ or notice of a writ out of the jurisdiction is permissible with the leave of the court in specified cases. Section 6(1) of the Act (relating to land in the United Kingdom—see Chapter 6, E) may be considered in connection with Rule 1(1)(*a*) (where the whole subject-matter of the action is land situate within the jurisdiction), (*b*) (where an act, deed, will, contract, obligation or liability affecting land situate within the jurisdiction is sought to be construed, rectified, set aside or enforced) and (*k*) (relating to actions upon a mortgage of property within the jurisdiction).

Section 6(2) (relating to interests by way of succession, gift or *bona vacantia*—see Chapter 6, E) may be considered in connection with Rule 1(1)(*m*) (relating to probate actions). Section 6(3) (relating, *inter alia*, to the estates of deceased persons and trusts) may be considered in connection with Rule 1(1)(*d*) ("if the action begun by the writ is for the administration of the estate of a person who died domiciled within the jurisdiction") and (*e*) (relating to trusts of property within the jurisdiction).

Section 5 (relating to personal injury and damage to property—see Chapter 6, D) may be considered in connection with Rule 1(1)(*h*) ("if the action begun by the writ is founded on a tort committed within the jurisdiction").

9.10 The statutory exceptions which are likely to feature most prominently in actions against a foreign State, actions relating to commercial transactions and contracts to be performed within the United Kingdom, are found in s. 3 (see Chapter 6, A-B). Although s. 3(1)(*a*) denies immunity in respect of a State's commercial transactions, a plaintiff will need to show that his action falls within Rule 1(1)(*f*) or (*g*) if he is to have leave to serve out (as already noted, in the perhaps unlikely event of the State agreeing to service within the jurisdiction, the provisions of s. 12 do not apply).

Rule 1(1)(*f*) permits service out in actions upon a contract ("to enforce, rescind, dissolve, annul or otherwise affect a contract, or to recover damages or obtain other relief in respect of the breach of a contract") which EITHER was made within the jurisdiction OR was made by an agent trading or residing within the jurisdiction on behalf of a principal trading or residing out of the jurisdiction OR is by its terms or by implication governed by English law.

Rule 1(1)(*g*) permits service out in an action for a breach committed within the jurisdiction of a contract made anywhere.

It will therefore be seen that the test under the section for the denial of immunity is not the same as the test under the Rules for service out of the jurisdiction, the main difference being that all proceedings relating to commercial transactions, wherever made, wherever repudiated, and whatever law governs them, are denied immunity under s. 3(1)(*a*).

Appearance

9.11 The time for entering appearance runs from the date of receipt of the writ by the State's Ministry of Foreign Affairs and, by s. 12(2), that time is extended from the usual period of 14 days to two months. However, by sub-s. (6) this extension does not apply if service of the writ has been effected by agreement in some other manner than that laid down by sub-s. (1). (As to "appearance", see now the amendment to Order 12 made by S.I. 80/1716.)

Default judgment

9.12 Before judgment in default of appearance can be obtained a plaintiff must prove that the writ was properly served and that the two-month period for appearance has expired (sub-s. (4)). However, by sub-s. (6) this provision does not apply if service of the writ has been effected by agreement in some other manner than that laid down by sub-s. 1.

Setting judgment aside

9.13 Where judgment is given against a State in default of appearance, the State has, by sub-s. (5), two months to apply to set it aside, reckoned from the date when a copy of the judgment is received through the Foreign and Commonwealth Office by the State's Ministry of Foreign Affairs. A certificate from the Secretary of State is conclusive evidence as to when the document was so received (s. 21(*d*)). Such a copy of the judgment must under the provisions of the Convention (Article 16) be accompanied by a translation if necessary: though the Act is silent on the point one may expect rules of court so to provide (compare Order 11, rule 6(5), (6)).

     By s. 22(2) references to entry of appearance and judgments in default of appearance include references to any corresponding procedure.

Exclusions

9.14 The special rules of procedure contained in s. 12 do not apply to an action *in rem*, which is considered to be already properly covered by rules of court, nor to a counterclaim (for the State has in such a case itself instituted proceedings on the claim in accordance with the ordinary rules of court). They do, however, apply by s. 14(5) to proceedings against a constituent territory of a Federal State.

Disclosure

9.15 Although a State may be ordered, whether in the usual way or by special order, to disclose or produce documents or information in the proceedings, it may not, if it fails to comply with the order, be subjected to any penalty by way of committal or fine (s. 13(1)). One may expect, however, that the court would consider striking out the State's pleading, or debarring it from defending.

Under Article 18 of the Convention, a Contracting State party to proceedings before a court of another Contracting State may not be subjected to any measure of coercion, or any penalty, by reason of its failure or refusal to disclose any documents or other evidence. However, the court may draw any conclusion it thinks fit from such failure or refusal.

Proscribed reliefs and processes

9.16 The question of execution against the property of a State is answered differently in various jurisdictions. In some countries it is prohibited, as it is under the common law, in others it is permitted, or permitted only with government authorization. Thus the highest Swiss court, the Federal Tribunal, has refused to distinguish between immunity from jurisdiction and immunity from jurisdiction and immunity from execution (*Kingdom of Greece* v. *Julius Bar & Co.*,[7] *Republique Arabe Unie* v. *Dame X*),[8] whereas the Paris Court of Appeal has said the two are quite distinct (*Clerget* v.

7. 23 I.L.R. 195 (1956).
8. 65 I.L.R. 385 (1960).

Représentation Commerciale de la Republique Democratique du Vietnam).[9] Even where it is permitted, there is general agreement that it does not extend to property in use for public, i.e. non-commercial, purposes. The distinction between public and non-public purposes is difficult to define, and is not the subject of any general international consensus. It raises the same sort of difficulties as the distinction between *acta imperii* and *acta gestionis* (see Chapter 12).

9.16.1 In 1977 the Bundesverfassungsgericht of West Germany had occasion to consider the question of execution. The Republic of the Philippines had rented a house from a German woman and used it as an office of the Philippine Embassy. When the Embassy determined the contract in 1973 the lessor obtained judgment in the local court for DM.95,000 for breach of contract. She then started execution proceedings which resulted in an order of attachment by the competent court attaching funds on two bank accounts which the Philippine Embassy maintained with a German bank in Bonn. This issue came before the Constitutional Court on a special procedure. In a detailed analysis of the practice of foreign jurisdictions the court found that a significant number of States, in particular Italy, Switzerland, Belgium, the Netherlands, Greece and the United States (the last named under its recent Foreign Sovereign Immunities Act of 1976), no longer granted absolute immunity from execution, but rather distinguished whether the assets against which execution was sought were devoted to the public use of the foreign State or were used for commercial purposes. In the particular case the court ruled that the assets in question were intended for public purposes, being bank accounts from which the salaries of Philippine Embassy employees as well as other Embassy expenses were paid. Accordingly execution was not permitted.

During the course of its judgment the court said:

"It does not follow, simply because general customary international law embodies the minimum obligation in the case of trial proceedings, to grant immunity in respect of sovereign acts, that it also demands only relative immunity in the case of execution . . .

At present, there is no custom which is as yet sufficiently general and is backed by the necessary legal consensus to constitute a general rule of

9. 48 I.L.R. 145 (1967).

customary international law whereby the State of the forum is debarred outright from taking measures of forced execution against a foreign State. . . .

There exists a general rule of international law whereby forced execution of judgment by the State of the forum, under a writ of execution against a foreign State which has been issued in respect of non-sovereign acts of that State, on property of that State which is present or situated in the territory of the State of the forum is inadmissible without the consent of the foreign State if, at the time of the initiation of the measure of execution, such property serves sovereign purposes of the foreign State . . .

Claims arising out of a general current bank account of the embassy of a foreign State which is maintained in the State of the forum for the purpose of covering the embassy's costs and expenses are not subject to measures of execution by the State of the forum . . .

For the executing authorities of the receiving State to require the sending State, without its consent, to provide details concerning the existence or the past, present or future purposes of funds in such an account would constitute interference, contrary to international law, in matters within the exclusive competence of the sending State . . .

No ruling is given on whether, and according to what criteria, claims and other rights arising out of other accounts of a foreign State with banks in the State of the forum, such as special accounts in connection with procurement purchases or the granting of loans, or general-purpose accounts, are to be considered sovereign or non-sovereign property, and what limits, if any, imposed by international law are to be observed when it comes to obtaining evidence in that respect''.

The case is reported at 65 I.L.R. 146.

9.16.2 In April 1983 the same court, in another highly researched decision (65 I.L.R. 215) held against the National Iranian Oil Company, who appealed against attachment orders on accounts it held in certain German banks, on the ground that the funds were held for sovereign purposes, being derived from sales of petroleum and petrol products underaken for the Iranian Government. Under Iranian law such funds had to be transferred to the State Treasury at the Iranian central bank, and the appellant contended it was no more than a trustee for its Government.

The view of the court was that there was no general rule of international law prohibiting the execution of attachment orders against assets such as the ones in dispute, nor any rule requiring a foreign State to be treated as the owner of assets in accounts held at banks in the forum State which were registered in the name of an undertaking of the foreign State possessing legal personality. The rule was that assets belonging to a foreign State which were situate or held in the forum State must not be subject to enforcement or measures providing security without the consent of the foreign State, *in so far as they were serving the sovereign purposes of the foreign State* (my italics). The assets in question, intended for transfer to the central bank to cover the State's budgetary expenditure, could not be defined as assets held for sovereign purposes. Such assets were given as definitive purposes, said the court, only once they had entered into the possession of the central bank. International law did not require the assets before such transfer to be defined as being for sovereign purposes. (The Court of Appeal at The Hague had reached a similar conclusion in a NIOC case in 1974,—see 47 I.L.R. 138.)

9.16.3 Because of the lack of a common international practice in this connection the framers of the Convention proscribed execution and "preventive measures" against the property of a Contracting State except as against the commercial property of a State that has individually, by a specific declaration under Article 24, accepted such an exception to the rule against execution (see below).

The Act, as we shall see, reproduces the Convention's rules vis-à-vis any State party to it, while permitting execution against the commercial property of any other State.

9.17 Under the Act (s. 13(2)) the following reliefs cannot be given against a State:

    (i) an injunction;
   (ii) an order for specific performance;
  (iii) an order for the recovery of land;
  (iv) an order for the recovery of any property

UNLESS (sub-s.(3)) the State gives, or has in a prior agreement already given, its written consent. The head of the State's diplomatic mission or his deputy has authority to give such consent (sub-s. (5)). The consent will be carefully construed to ascertain its precise extent, and it is specifically provided in sub-s. (3) that an agreement merely to submit to the jurisdiction is not to be regarded as such a consent. The consent may be contained in a treaty, convention, or other international agreement (s. 17(2)).

Thus a *Mareva* injunction may not be obtained against a State: it is free to transfer its assets out of the jurisdiction before judgment (*cf.* the common law, Chapter 8, paragraph 8.1).

9.18 No process may be issued against the property of a State

   (i) for the enforcement of a judgment; or
  (ii) for the enforcement of an arbitration award; or
 (iii) for the arrest, detention or sale of the property in an action *in rem* (s. 13(2)(*b*)).

There are two exceptions to the general unavailability of processes of this kind against the property of a State:

  (a) under sub-s. (3), where the State gives, or has already given its written consent (see above);
  (b) most importantly, under sub-s. (4), process may issue against property "in use or intended for use for commercial purposes" (which means by s. 17(1), the purposes of "commercial transactions" as defined by s. 3(3)—see above Chapter 6,A).

If the head of the State's diplomatic mission or his deputy certifies as to any property that is not in use or intended for use for commercial purposes, it is up to the other party to prove the contrary (sub-s. 5)).

9.18.1 In *Alcom Ltd.* v. *Republic of Colombia*[10] the plaintiff obtained judgment for over £40,000 against the defendant for goods sold and delivered. The Master made garnishes orders on the Government's Embassy accounts at the First National Bank of Boston and Barclays Bank. The judge set those orders aside. The question was whether the accounts, which were certified by the ambassador as intended to be used only "to meet the expenditure necessarily incurred in the day-to-day running of the diplomatic mission" were "for the time being in use or intended for use for commercial purposes" within the meaning of s. 13(4). The Court of Appeal allowed the appeal and restored the garnishee orders. The Master of the Rolls,

10. [1984] A.C. 580 (C.A. and H.L.).

with whose judgment the other members of the court agreed, said that the accounts were used for the purposes of "commercial transactions" as so widely defined by s. 3(3) (see above at Chapter 6A):

> "The purpose of money in a bank account can never be 'to run an embassy'. It can only be to pay for goods and services or to enter into other transactions which enable the Embassy to be run".

This decision caused the Foreign and Commonwealth Office considerable anxiety. It had never been envisaged that the Act would enable execution against an Embassy's bank account. So relief was experienced when in April 1984 the House of Lords reversed the lower court and discharged the orders. A united front was presented, no doubt by design. Doubtless the court knew of the views of the Government and their expectations, and the effect on international comity of the decision (though the former would not of course influence the judges). Lord Diplock, with whose judgment the other Law Lords agreed, approved the decision of the Bundesverfassungsgericht in the *Philippine Embassy* case (see above at 9.16.1) and said that, although the existence of a rule at international law precluding execution against Embassy bank accounts was not decisive of the purport of the United Kingdom Act it was "highly unlikely that Parliament intended to require the United Kingdom courts to act contrary to international law unless the clear language of the statute compels such a conclusion". He went on to attach the greatest importance to the fact that in the normal course of events one would expect the Embassy account to be used in part at least for purposes falling outside the statutory definition of commercial purposes, and he said:

> "Unless it can be shown by the judgment creditor who is seeking to attach the credit balance by garnishee proceedings that the bank account was earmarked by the foreign State solely (save for *de minimis* exceptions) for being drawn upon to settle liabilities incurred in commercial transactions, as for example by issuing documentary credits in payment of the price of goods sold to the State, it cannot, in my view, be sensibly brought within the crucial words of the exception for which 13(4) provides".

He said that in the instant case the judgment creditor could not show that, and therefore the ambassador's certificate was conclusive that the bank account in question fell outside s. 13(4).

Although the result is clearly appropriate, it is not satisfactory that the inevitable inability of the creditor to show that the account was used solely for discharging commercial liabilities determines his failure, because the matter then becomes one of evidence rather than law.

But due to the connection made in the Act between commercial purposes and commercial transactions and the semantically precise methods of interpretation traditional to our jurisprudence it would not be open to the court to state baldly what is obvious, namely that it is inappropriate that Embassy accounts be liable to attachment, that that could not have been the intention of the draftsman, and that therefore the logical argument should not be allowed to prevail over the pragmatic one.

9.18.2 We may note by the by that in November 1980 a New York District Court took an opposite view, namely that where a proportion of the assets could be defined as being for "governmental purposes" attachment was permitted under the Foreign Sovereign Immunities Act as being upon property used for a commercial activity" (*Birch Shipping Corporation* v. *Embassy of United Republic of Tanzania*).[11] The court said that the employment of local persons on the staff and the purchase of goods and services involved a commercial activity and the fact that the account was also used for non-commercial payments, that is to say payments of a sovereign nature, which could include the salaries of the Tanzanian staff, did not make the account immune from attachment.

The Ontario High Court held in October 1980 that execution was not permitted upon funds deposited with the Royal Bank of Canada in the name of the Embassy of Cuba (*Re Royal Bank of Canada and Corriveau*).[12]

The Austrian Supreme Court said in 1958, in *Neustein* v. *Republic of Indonesia*[13] that attachment of State funds in an account marked "for the legation" was not necessarily bad: the

11. 63 I.L.R. 524 (1980).
12. 64 I.L.R. 69 (1980).
13. 65 I.L.R. 3 (1958).

question was whether the account existed exclusively for the exercise of sovereign rights of the foreign State or whether it was used for commercial transactions governed by private law.

United States Law

9.18.3 Section 1610(*a*) of the Foreign Sovereign Immunities Act (a) enables property belonging to a foreign State which is in use for a commercial activity within the United States to be subject to attachment in aid of execution or to execution in relation to a judgment of a U.S. court in various circumstances. These include the situation where there has been a waiver of immunity either explicit or implicit by the State; where the property is or was used for the commercial activity *upon which the claim is based* (this nexus with the claim is not necessary under the United Kingdom Act); where the execution relates to a judgment establishing rights in property which has been taken in violation of international law or which has been exchanged for property taken in violation of international law.

The Congressional Report states that the expression "taken in violation of international law" would include

". . . the nationalisation of expropriation of property without payment of the prompt, adequate and effective compensation required by international law. It would also include takings which are arbitrary or discriminatory in nature. Since, however, this section deals solely with issues of immunity, it in no way affects existing law on the extent to which, if at all, the 'act of State' doctrine may be applicable". (See [1976] 15 I.L.M. 1408.)

The property of an agency or instrumentality of a foreign State engaged in commercial activity in the United States is, by s. 1610(*b*), subject to similar attachment where there has been a waiver; or where the judgment relates to a claim in respect of which the agency or instrumentality cannot claim jurisdictional immunity and irrespective of whether the property is or was used for the activity upon which the claim is based.

In addition, execution is permitted against a State's property if it relates to a judgment establishing rights in property acquires by succession or gift, or in immovable property (except diplomatic or consulate property; or if the property consists of proceeds or other payments under a liability or casualty policy covering claims merged into a judgment).

In *Letelier* v. *Republic of Chile*,[14] where the personal representatives of the former Chilean ambassador murdered in Washington by agents of the Chilean Government sought to satisfy judgment in respect of that crime by attaching the assets of LAN, Chile's national airline, a New York District Court somewhat surprisingly held that not only were LAN's activities in the United States "commercial activities" but that there was sufficient nexus between the conspiracy to murder, which was the subject of the claim, and those activities to satisfy the terms of the section. (For the original judgment see 63 I.L.R. 378.)

9.19 There are provisions in s. 13(4) of the United Kingdom Act limiting the right to execute against commercial property belonging to a State party to the European Convention, which apply in all proceedings other than Admiralty proceedings and proceedings on any claim which could be made the subject of Admiralty proceedings.

In such a case process may issue only if

EITHER it is a process for enforcing an arbitration award

OR the process is for enforcing a final judgment (that means by s. 18(1)(*b*), a judgment that is not, or is no longer, subject to appeal, or, if given in default of appearance, liable to be set aside) *and* the State has made a declaration under Article 24 of the Convention (that Article permits a State to declare that its courts will entertain proceedings against Contradicting States to the extent that they entertain proceedings against other States). This provision follows Article 26 (see paragraph 9.22); the thinking seems to be that if a State is going to apply its domestic rules, being more restrictive than the Convention's régime, to other Contracting States, then it is also willing to accept the possibility of forced execution against its commercial assets.

---

14. 567 F. Supp. 1490 (1983); 63 I.L.R. 378 (1980).

Bank funds

9.20 It is specifically provided by s. 14(4) that property of a State's central bank or other monetary authority shall not be regarded as in use or intended for use for commercial purposes. There can thus be no execution or injunction in respect of the funds of such an entity, even if it is a separate entity (and therefore not of sovereign status—see Chapter 4, paragraph 4.11), and even if, also, the proceedings relate to *acta gestionis*.

The injunction available at common law in such a case as *Hispano Americana Mercantil S.A.* v. *Central Bank of Nigeria*[15] is therefore not permitted under the Act.

It is, however, arguable that, as the Act specifically precludes injunctive relief only as against a "State" and as the exemption afforded to the property of a State's central bank relates only to execution, an injunction is permitted against the property of a central bank which is a separate entity. (See Chapter 4, paragraph 4.11.)

There is an interesting distinction between the English and the American statutes in this connection, a distinction noticed in the judgment of Lord Denning, M.R., in the *Hispano Americana Mercantil* case. The United States statute accords immunity in respect of property "of a foreign central bank or monetary authority held for its own account". The last five words constitute a condition which is not part of the English statute, and which is explained by the memorandum attached to the Bill of Congress in these terms: 'funds used or held in connection with central banking activities, as distinguished from funds used solely to finance the commercial transactions of other entities or of foreign States".

A recent decision of a New York District Court brought into relief the different positions obtaining under s. 1611(*b*) of the American statute in respect of pre-judgment attachment against a central bank and the execution of a judgment. In *Banque Compafina* v. *Banco de Guatemala*,[16] a claim against the central bank of Guatemala in respect of guarantees it had given for notes issued by certain Guatemalan entities, the court said that no pre-judgment attachment was possible under

15. [1979] 2 Lloyd's Rep. 277; 64 I.L.R. 221 (1979).
16. 583 F. Supp. 320 (1984).

the section in respect of funds used or held in connection with central banking activities, because in the case of central banks the waiver provisions only applied to attachment after judgment, i.e. execution.

Recognition of judgments

9.21 It is worth noting here that Part II of the Act (ss. 18, 19), implementing Article 20 of the Convention, obliges the courts of the United Kingdom to recognize, subject to certain conditions, any judgment given against the United Kingdom by the courts of any other Contracting State provided that the case falls within the exceptions to the basic rule of immunity contained in the Act. This does not mean, however, that our courts are put under the obligation of enforcing such a judgment (one can hardly imagine the question arising!) but merely that they will regard it as "conclusive between the parties thereto in all proceedings founded on the same cause of action", and in such proceedings it may be relied on also by way of defence and counterclaim (s. 18(2)).

There are in s. 19 complicated exceptions to the duty to recognize such judgments, of which the most important are "if to do so would be manifestly contrary to public policy" or where a party had no adequate opportunity to present his case.

Execution under the Convention

9.22 Article 23: "No measures of execution or preventive measures against the property of a Contracting State may be taken in the territory of another Contracting State except where and to the extent that the State has expressly consented thereto in writing in any particular case".

Article 26 provides that a judgment against a Contracting State in proceedings relating to an industrial or commercial activity in which the State is engaged in the same manner as a private person may be enforced against property used exclusively in connection with such activity provided that both the State of the forum and the State against which judgment has been given have made declarations under Article 24 (and provided that certain other technical conditions are satisfied).

Article 24, as noted above, permits a State to make a formal declaration that its courts will apply to Contracting States the more restrictive regime that its courts apply to other States, provided however, that it does not derogate from the immunity proper to *acta imperii*; nor, by Article 24(2), may it assume jurisdiction by virtue only of certain 'exorbitant" grounds (as the Explanatory Report to the Convention terms them), which are set out in the Annex, unless the defendant State has taken a step in the proceedings without challenging the jurisdiction of the court.

As there was no international consensus on the question whether execution was permissible against the property of States, commercial or otherwise, the framers of the Convention created the basic rule which forbids execution, while at the same time obliging Contracting States to recognize any judgments given against them in the courts of other Contracting States. Execution was, however, to be permitted against commercial property where a State had signified its acceptance of a more restrictive régime than that of the Convention by making, as the United Kingdom has done, a formal declaration under Article 24.

CHAPTER 10

EXCLUSIONS AND INCLUSIONS

Excluded matters (s. 16)

10.1 (i) The Act does not affect the privileges and immunities enjoyed by diplomatic and consular officers under the Diplomatic Privileges Act 1964, and the Consular Relations Act 1968. Similarly, Article 33 of the European Convention provides for the supremacy of the Vienna Conventions (on Diplomatic Relations 1961, Cmnd. 1368 and on Consular Relations 1963, Cmnd. 2113) in the event of a conflict between the European and the Vienna Conventions.

As noted elsewhere (Chapter 13, paragraph 13.5), s. 20 of the Act extends the protection of the Diplomatic Privileges Act 1964 to the sovereign, his family and servants (in place of the protection previously afforded them at common law).

10.2 (ii) The Act does not apply to criminal proceedings. Persons of diplomatic status have immunity from our criminal jurisdiction under the Act of 1964 (see Chapter 14, paragraph 14.7). The sovereign was immune from criminal jurisdiction at common law; he now enjoys that immunity under the Act of 1964. Entities of sovereign status (governments and Departments of State) necessarily enjoy immunity from criminal jurisdiction at common law. It might be thought acceptable that, as the Act of 1978 denies immunity to States in civil proceedings arising out of commercial activities, immunity should be denied also in respect of offences arising out of such activities, such as contraventions of regulations affecting health and safety at work (e.g. in connection with the building or management of a State tourist office). However, such "offences" must be considered part of our criminal jurisdiction, as we have no halfway house between the civil and the criminal jurisdiction, such as administrative or public law might provide. Although commentators have, from time to time, suggested that such matters as selling adulterated milk and unlawfully opening a shop on the Sabbath are not strictly part of the criminal law, there seems no legal ground for arguing that in respect of summonses for such matters a State is not at common law entitled to immunity.

10.3 (iii) The Act does not apply to proceedings relating to anything done by or in relation to the armed forces of a State while present in the United Kingdom. In particular, it has effect subject to the Visiting Forces Act 1952 which resitricts the power of United Kingdom courts to try offenders connected with visiting forces or to entertain proceedings in respect of a person's service as a member of visiting forces.

It is not clear how far this exception will extend. If a car carrying visiting soldiers runs over a pedestrian, is his claim that there can be no immunity by virtue of s. 5 of the Act defeated because the proceedings relate to something "done by the armed forces of a State"? If soldiers of a friendly State put on an exhibition in this country which can properly be said to be a commercial activity, is an action for breach of contract in connection with that activity excepted from the provisions of the Act, in particular s. 3, by the effect of s. 16(4)? And if so, should the plaintiff then argue that the restrictive doctrine must be applied under the common law?

10.4 (iv) The Act does not apply to proceedings under s. 17(6) of the Nuclear Installations Act 1965 whereby a foreign State that is the operator of a nuclear installation is deemed to have submitted to jurisdiction (but not to execution) in respect of claims for nuclear accidents, that is, occurrences causing personal injury or damage to property arising from the radioactive, toxic, explosive or other hazardous properties of nuclear matter. In such an action the procedural privileges afforded by the Act of 1978 (see Chapter 9) will therefore not be relevant.

10.5 (v) The Act does not apply to any proceedings relating to taxation other than those set out in s. 11 (see Chapter 6, paragraph 6.34).

Power is given by s. 15 to restrict or extend by Order in Council the immunities and privileges afforded to a State under Act on the principle of reciprocity.

Included matters

10.6 **(i)** By s. 17(3), for the purposes of ss. 3-8 the "territory" of the United Kingdom includes any dependent territory in respect of which the United Kingdom is a party to the European Convention. By s. 22(4) "dependent territory" means

- (a) any of the Channel Islands;
- (b) the Isle of Man;
- (c) any colony other than one for whose external relations a country other than the United Kingdom is responsible;
- (d) any country or territory outside Her Majesty's dominions in which Her Majesty has jurisdiction in right of the Government of the United Kingdom.

(ii) By s. 17(4), in ss. 3(1), 4(1), 5 and 16(2) (see Chapter 6, A-B, 6, C, 6, D; Chapter 10, paragraph 10.3 respectively) references to the United Kingdom include references to its territorial waters (customarily extending to a distance of three miles from low-water mark) and any area designated under s. 1(7) of the Continental Shelf Act 1964.

(iii) In the Act references to a "ship" include hovercraft (s. 17(1)).

CHAPTER 11

RETROSPECTIVE?

11.1 The Act is not retrospective. By s. 23(3) the statutory rules contained in Part I of the Act "do not apply to proceedings in respect of matters that occurred before the date of the coming into force of this Act", i.e. 22 November 1978.

The courts' recognition of this is illustrated by the cases of *Uganda Co. (Holdings) Ltd.* v. *Government of Uganda*[1] at first instance, and, in the Court of Appeal, *Hispano Americana Mercantil S.A.* v. *Central Bank of Nigeria*.[2] In the latter case the court refused to be influenced, when asked to lift an injunction freezing assets of the defendant bank, by the statutory rule (ss. 13(4), 14(4)) that assets of a central bank are immune from process.

11.2 To the generality of non-retrospection the Act gives particular illustrations for the following contexts:

(a) For a prior agreement to fall within s. 2(2), whereby a State may submit in advance to the jurisdiction (see Chapter 8, paragraph 8.4), or within s. 13(3), whereby a State may give written consent to certain proscribed reliefs and processes (see Chapter 9, paragraph 9.17), it must be made after 22 November 1978. As noted above (Chapter 8, paragraph 8.1) such agreements will be ineffective at common law.

(b) The denial to a State under s. 3 of immunity in respect of commercial transactions and contracts which fall to be performed within the United Kingdom (see Chapter 6, A–B) only applies to transactions and contracts entered into after 22 November 1978. Earlier transactions and contracts will be governed by the common law. Reference may be made to *Planmount Ltd.* v. *Republic*

---

1. [1979] 1 Lloyd's Rep. 481; 64 I.L.R. 209 (1978).
2. [1979] 2 Lloyd's Rep. 277; 64 I.L.R. 221 (1979).

120

of Zaire,[3] where the contract sued upon was made some ten months before the Act came into force.

(c) The denial of immunity to a state under s. 4 in relation to certain contracts of employment (Chapter 6, C) applies only to contracts made after 22 November 1978.

In *Sengupta* v. *Republic of India*[4] the Employment Appeal Tribunal took the view that a claim for unfair dismissal was "in respect of" the original contract as at the date of its formation, i.e. before the Act came into force, rather than the dismissal that occurred after it came into force (they went on to apply the restrictive doctrine at common law and granted immunity—see above, paragraph 6.8). This view seems strained, as the cause of action was the dismissal, but may be explained by the fact that the applicant would have been shut out *in limine* had the Act applied, being an Indian national, and the court wanted to give him the benefit of a full hearing at common law.

(d) The provisions of s. 9, whereby a written consent to submit to arbitration necessarily involves a submission to court proceedings arising therefrom, applies only to consents given after 22 November 1978. (The rule at common law is that a submission to arbitration entails nothing more.)

11.3   Treaty

By Article 35 the Convention applies only to proceedings introduced after it entered into force with respect to the relevant State.

---

3. [1981] 1 All E.R. 1110; 64 I.L.R. 268 (1980).
4. (1983) I.C.R. 221; 64 I.L.R. 352 (1982).

CHAPTER 12

ACTA IMPERII, ACTA GESTIONIS

12.1 The distinction between acts of a foreign sovereign in exercise of his sovereign authority (*acta imperii*) and his non-sovereign acts is new to English law. It influenced the judgment of Sir Robert Phillimore in *The Charkieh*[1] and was effectively the ratio of his decision in *The Parlement Belge*[2] (see above, Chapter 7, paragraphs 7-8) but after this brief appearance it disappeared from the English stage until Lord Denning, M.R., formulated it, first as a lone voice in the House of Lords in 1958 in the *Rahimtoola* case[3] and then as the majority view in 1977 in the *Trendtex* case.[4] The distinction had in the meantime been accepted in 1975 for actions *in rem* by the Privy Council in *The Philippine Admiral*.[5] The history of this matter is set out above in Chapter 3.

12.2 The distinction remains fundamental for such cases as still fall to be decided at common law (see Chapters 10 and 11). It is clearly fundamental to actions concerning State-owned trading vessels and, if the Court of Appeal's majority view in the *Trendtex* case[6] is good law, as it very likely is, it is applicable generally (see Chapter 3, paragraph 3.18). Under the Act, which applies the distinction to English law, *acta gestionis* (commercial activities) are to a large extent defined by s. 3 (see Chapter 6, A). But the dichotomy may arise for analysis in the following contexts: the catch-all provision, s. 3(3)(c) speaks of transactions or activities of a State "otherwise than in the exercise of sovereign authority". If a transaction does not fall

1. (1873) L.R. 4 A. & E. 59.
2. (1879) L.R. 4 P.D. 129.
3. *Rahimtoola* v. *Nizam of Hyderabad* [1958] A.C. 379; 24 I.L.R. 175 (1957).
4. *Trendtex Trading Corporation* v. *Central Bank of Nigeria* [1977] Q.B. 529; 64 I.L.R. 111 (1977).
5. [1977] A.C. 373; 64 I.L.R. 90 (1975).
6. *Supra*, fn. 4.

within the specific definitions of sub-s. (3)(*a*) or (*b*) the court will have to consider this catch-all provision and decide (assuming the transaction is shown to be of a commercial character within the meaning of s. 3(3)(*c*)) whether the State engaged in it "in the exercise of sovereign authority".

The dichotomy is also relevant under s. 14(2)(*a*) which speaks of a separate entity's immunity for acts "in the exercise of sovereign authority" (see Chapter 4, paragraph 4.11); under s. 10, which speaks of ships and cargo used "for commercial purposes", i.e. the purposes of commercial transactions as defined by s. 3(3) (see Chapter 7, paragraphs 7.19-21); and under s. 13(4) which speaks of process against property used for "commercial purposes" (see Chapter 9, paragraph 9.18).

12.3 The distinction between *acta imperii* and *acta gestionis* has been drawn for many years in some European jurisdictions. Belgian and Italian courts have based decisions on this dichotomy since the late 19th century (it is of interest that Sir Robert's judgments were given at about the same time). However, there was no unanimity on how the test for *acta imperii* should be formulated or, even assuming a similar formulation in different jurisdictions, how it should be applied. Thus a contract to supply cigarettes to the Vietnamese army has been declared by the Cour de Cassation in France to be a sovereign act (*Guggenheim* v. *State of Vietnam*);[7] a contract for the purchase of army boots has been declared by a United States court to be a sovereign act (*Kingdom of Romania* v. *Guaranty Trust Co. of New York*);[8] while a similar contract, for the purchase of army boots, has been declared by an Italian court not to be an act of the sovereign authority (*Governo Rumeno* v. *Trutta*).[9] (Romania seems to have had some difficulty at that time with its contracts for army boots!)

12.4 A common formulation of the distinction refers to "acts which a private person can do", but that test may be applied so as to yield different results: if an architect gives his service to a foreign government for the building at Canada's "Expo 67"

7. 22 I.L.R. 224 (1955).
8. 250 Fed. 341 (1918).
9. Guir. It. 1926 pt. 1(1) 774.

exhibition of a national pavilion, is one to argue that a private person cannot commission a national pavilion at "Expo 67", or is the answer that a private person can certainly commission a building. When one asks whether certain acts are sovereign or commercial acts how far does one specify them? A private person can contract for a yacht, but only a State for a battleship. Is the type of boat important when one asks whether a contract for a State's purchase of a battleship is *acta imperii*? In one sense every act of a government is a public act. The purchase of cement for a hospital project is, in that sense, as much a public act as the purchase of cement to build an army base.

In the face of these difficulties some commentators have maintained that the distinction is unworkable. Nevertheless, as can be seen from an examination of the cases abstracted below, if one concentrates on the nature of the transaction, and the legal relationship created by it, ignoring its purpose or motive, a fairly workable test emerges.

12.5 Our courts will have to make up their own minds in due course on how the dichotomy is to be interpreted and applied. In view of the natural paucity of English authorities on this novel point it may be helpful to study the approach of other jurisdictions. One will, of course, bear in mind the sturdy independence, not to say insularity, of the English judge. One may also bear in mind the words of Lord Wilberforce in *James Buchanan & Co.* v. *Babco Forwarding & Shipping Co.*[10] when, considering the suggestion that our courts should now adopt the Continental approach to statutory construction, he said that there was "no universal wisdom available across the Channel on which our insular minds could draw", and that "the assumed and oft repeated generalization that English methods were narrow, technical and literal, whereas Continental methods were broad, generous and sensible, seemed . . . insecure". In *The I Congreso del Partido*[11] Lord Denning, when considering the many affidavits produced about foreign law on the subject, said:

10. [1978] A.C. 141.
11. [1980] 1 Lloyd's Rep. 23 (C.A.).

"On this point we were referred to masses of cases and textbooks in many languages of many countries and to masses of affidavits by professors of international law all over the world. I stand amazed at the time and money which the parties have expended on this case".

But Lord Wilberforce later said that he had "derived much assistance from the reasoning and learning contained in these affidavits and for the explanation which their deponents give of decisions of their courts, direct resort to which may be hazardous".[12]

Nevertheless, it may be thought that as the issue concerns a difficult concept, new to our law but the subject of many decisions in other jurisdictions, it may well be illuminating to consider in some measure the approach of those other jurisdictions.

12.6   A: England

First, however, it may be helpful to abstract what has been said on this issue in those few English cases in which it has so far featured.

In *Trendtex Trading Corporation* v. *Central Bank of Nigeria*,[13] the facts of which are set out above in Chapter 3, at paragraph 3.18, Lord Denning, M.R., said, at page 558:

"So I turn to see whether the transaction here was such as to attract sovereign immunity, or not. It was suggested that the original contracts for cement were made by the Ministry of Defence for Nigeria: and that the cement was for the building of barracks for the army. On this account it was said that the contracts of purchase were acts of a governmental nature, *jure imperii*, and not of a commercial nature, *jure gestionis*. They were like a contract of purchase of boots for the army. But I do not think this should affect the question of immunity. If a government department goes into the market places of the world and buys boots or cement—as a commercial transaction—that government department should be subject to all the rules of the market place. The seller is not concerned with the purpose to which the purchaser intends to put the goods . . .

It is interesting to find that the German courts have had to deal with a precisely similar point. In February, 1975, the Ministry of Defence in Nigeria agreed to purchase 240,000 tons of cement from a firm in

12. [1983] 1 A.C. 244; 64 I.L.R. 307 (1981) (H.L.).
13. [1977] Q.B. 529; 64 I.L.R. 111 (1977).

Liechtenstein. The Central Bank of Nigeria issued letters of credit through its correspondent the Deutsche Bank in Frankfurt. The goods were shipped. The price paid. The vessel arrived at Lagos but, owing to the congestion, had to wait. The holders of the letters of credit claimed demurrage. They levied distress on the assets of the Central Bank of Nigeria then in Germany. The Central Bank claimed the release of these assets on the ground of sovereign immunity. On December 2, 1975, the Commercial Court of Frankfurt in *Y.M.N. Establishment* v. *Central Bank of Nigeria* rejected the plea. Their reasons were as follows:

> 'According to the decision of the Federal Constitutional Court of 1962 and 1963 . . . a foreign State may be granted immunity from jurisdiction only in respect of its sovereign activity (*acta jure imperii*) but not in respect of its non-sovereign activity (*acta jure gestionis*), because no general rule of public international law exists under which the domestic jurisdiction for actions against a foreign State in relation to its non-sovereign activities is precluded' ''.

12.7 Stephenson, L.J., said, at page 566:

"The movement or trend of opinion towards restricting sovereign immunity is based on the distinction between ordinary trading transactions and governmental acts. The new doctrine would restrict immunity to the latter, labelled in Latin as *acta jure imperii*, and deny it to the former under the description of *acta jure gestionis*. The distinction between the two categories has been found as difficult to draw as the distinction between a State's agents who are not immune and a State's agencies which are. But I entertain no doubt that the issue of this letter of credit in payment for this cement fell on the private and commercial side of the line and was an ordinary trading transaction. It was a separate transaction from the sale to the English company in whose favour the first letter of credit was issued by the bank . . .

If it were necessary, or permissible, to look at that underlying contract of sale, or below it at the purpose for which the cement was required, namely, to build barracks for the Nigerian Ministry of Defence, I would still regard the whole transaction as commercial . . . There are those who regard the purpose of the transaction as determining the question whether it is public and governmental or private and commercial; I prefer the view incorporated in the Bill introduced into the United States House of Representatives in 1975:

> 'the commercial character of an activity shall be determined by reference to the nature of the course of conduct or particular transaction or act, rather than by reference to its purpose': see section 1603(*d*) of the Foreign Sovereign Immunity Act 1976.

This accords with the judgment of the German Federal Constitutional Court in the *Claim against the Empire of Iran* case, 45 International Law Reports 57,80''.

12.8 Shaw, L.J., said, at page 579:

"In my judgment, therefore, even if the Central Bank of Nigeria is part of the government of that country, it is not immune from suit in respect of the subject matter of the present action. In coming to this conclusion I should make it clear that I regard the intrinsic nature of a transaction rather than its object as the material consideration in determining whether entering into that transaction is a commercial activity or an exercise of sovereign authority".

12.9 In *The Philippine Admiral*[14] Lord Cross, giving the judgment of the Privy Council, said:

"In this country—and no doubt in most countries in the western world—the State can be sued in its own courts on commercial contracts into which it has entered and there is no apparent reason why foreign States should not be equally liable to be sued there in respect of such transactions. There is, of course, no clear-cut dividing line between acts done *jure imperii* and acts done *jure gestionis* and difficult borderline cases may arise. *Republic of Congo* v. *Venne* (22 D.L.R. (3d) 669) is an example of such a case and others are given in the textbooks on international law . . .".

12.10 Next one may consider the case of *The I Congreso del Partido*, the most important case on State immunity since *The Cristina*.[15] It is reported at first instance at [1978] Q.B. 500 and was heard by a two-judge Court of Appeal in October 1979.[16] The House of Lords gave judgment in July 1981.[17] The salient facts of that case were these:

A Cuban State enterprise had contracted to deliver quantities of sugar to a Chilean company. Before the two Cuban cargo ships had unloaded at Valparaiso, Chile suffered, on 11 September 1973, a right-wing coup, displacing President Allende's Marxist Government, and displeasing the Cuban Government. The latter severed diplomatic relations with Chile and ordered the ships to leave with their cargo unloaded.

One ship, the *Playa Larga*, was owned at all relevant times by the Cuban Government; the other, the *Marble Islands*, was owned by a trading enterprise that was not in any event entitled

14. *Supra*, fn.5.
15. *Compania Naviera Vascongada* v. *S.S. Cristina* [1938] A.C. 485; 9 I.L.R. 250 (1938).
16. [1980] 1 Lloyd's Rep. 23 (C.A.).
17. [1983] 1 A.C. 244; 64 I.L.R. 307 (1981).

to immunity; later, after this ship had left Chile, when it was on the high seas, the Cuban Government took it over and ordered it to unload its cargo at Haiphong. Thus, as regards that vessel, there was no pre-existing commercial relationship between the Cuban State and the Chilean company but an action would lie *in tort* against Cuba for interference with goods. The *I Congreso del Partido* was merely another ship owned by Cuba, recently completed in the Sunderland yards, against which the Chilean company sought to enforce their claims in respect of the two cargoes.

One of the questions that arose for consideration in the case was whether, granted that the original contract was *acta gestionis*, the act constituting the breach should be examined to see if it too was *actus gestionis*, and, if it was not, whether that affected the issue of immunity. As pointed out above (Chapter 7, paragraph 7.20) under the statute consideration of the act constituting the breach appears to be irrelevant, but this case fell to be decided at common law, as the contract in question was made long before the Act came into operation. If there was immunity for an act in breach of a commercial obligation done in exercise of the sovereign authority (a rider which has been argued in the similar context of the Brussels Convention by certain commentators (see Chapter 6, paragraph 6.2)), then one had to ask whether the refusal to deliver the sugar became *actus imperii* because it was done in implementation of the decision to sever diplomatic relations (a policy decision to establish or sever diplomatic relations is clearly an *actus imperii*).

12.11 It is worth observing what was said in the lower courts on this question as it was not in principle refuted by the House of Lords, and all guidance is welcome on this difficult topic. Goff, J., said, at page 529:

"It is clear that in most jurisdictions no distinction is drawn between actions *in rem* and actions *in personam* as is drawn in this country; but it is also clear that in most jurisdictions a restrictive doctrine of sovereign immunity is applied in all actions, the doctrine being applicable in the case of an *actus jure imperii* but not in the case of an *actus jure gestionis*. Indeed, the evidence before me reveals only too clearly the isolated position which was until very recently occupied by this country in adhering to the absolute doctrine of sovereign immunity in the case of actions *in personam*. However, there appears to be no consensus as to where the dividing line should be drawn between the two categories of *actus jure imperii* and *actus jure gestionis*. Differences of opinion were revealed in relation to contracts for public purposes. In a case of that kind, courts generally look to the nature of the contract rather than to its purpose in deciding whether or not the contract is to be characterised as *jure gestionis* or *jure imperii*; and Mr Alexander relied on these cases in support of his submission that, once the sovereign has entered the market place, he cannot invoke sovereign immunity in respect of a breach of contract even where such breach arises from a governmental act.

But, in my judgment, the cases only demonstrate that in the case of a contractual claim the nature of the contract will be *relevant*, not that it will necessarily be *decisive* of the question whether or not the case is concerned with an *actus jure imperii*. If the nature of the contract is such that it is itself an *actus jure imperii*, then any claim under it may be the subject of sovereign immunity. If it is itself an *actus jure gestionis*, then an ordinary breach of the contract cannot be the subject of a claim to immunity, but the character of the contract cannot necessarily preclude a breach from being held to result from an *actus jure imperii*, in which event sovereign immunity may be claimed in respect of such breach.

Although I have found no direct guidance on this question in the foreign authorities cited to me, there are statements of principle to be found in those authorities which are consistent with the view that regard must be had, not only to the nature of the transaction, if any, between the parties, but also to the nature of the act complained of. For example, in the *Claim against the Empire of Iran* case (1963) 45 International Law Reports 57 the Federal Constitutional Court of the Federal Republic of Germany stated, at page 80:

'As a means for determining the distinction between acts *jure imperii* and *jure gestionis* one should rather refer to the nature of the State transaction or the resulting legal relationships, and not to the motive or purpose of the State activity. It thus depends on whether the foreign State has acted in exercise of its sovereign authority, that is in public law, or like a private person, that is in private law'.

Similarly, in the Italian case of *Consorzio Agrario di Tripolitania* v. *Federazione Italiana Consorzi Agrari*, December 5, 1966, n. 2830 the question was said by the Italian Corte di Cazzazione to depend on whether 'the act in respect of which the controversy has arisen has been enacted in the exercise of sovereign powers'. In the present case the act complained of, namely, the diversion of the two cargoes from Valparaiso to Cuba and Vietnam and their disposal there, was essentially an act of foreign policy. Such an act must surely be characterised as an *actus jure imperii*: see, for example, *Victory Transport Inc.* v. *Comisaria General de Abastecimientos y Transportes* (1964) 336 F. 2d 354, 360 where 'acts concerning diplomatic activity' are listed among those acts in respect of which sovereign immunity may be invoked".

12.12 In the Court of Appeal, Waller, L.J., agreeing with

Goff, J., referred to the *Empire of Iran*[18] case (see above) and said:

"There are observations cited from decisions of courts in different countries which are helpful in showing the approach made in those countries when distinguishing between *acta jure imperii* and *acta jure gestionis*. In Belgium the Court of Appeal of Ghent in 1879 said:
  'When however the State having regard to the needs of the community does not limit itself to its political role but acquires and owns property, concludes contracts, becomes a creditor or debtor or even engages in trade, it is not acting in the sphere of public authority but as a civil or private person'.
And the Austrian Supreme Court asserted jurisdiction over Turkey in respect of a claim for payment for certain building works carried out at the Turkish Embassy in Vienna and said:
  'In private law actions which in no way touched on the sovereignty of the State claimed against the foreign State also had to be subject to courts of the State where the business was situated'.
And in another Austrian case also cited the court, following the decision just quoted, examined
  'Whether the plaintiff is claiming against the sued State on the strength of a private law relationship or one in its sovereign domain. In order to decide whether a private or sovereign act was involved the act (which was carried out by organs of the State) is to be judged not by its aim or its purpose; whether an act of one or the other sort is involved is to be determined from the nature of the legal proceeding, i.e. from the inherent internal character of the transaction or from the legal relations created'.
And a quotation in relation to the Greek courts was
  'State immunity is limited to activities which a State engages in as a sovereign political power and does not extend to matters which arise from activities—such as the administration of property—which in no way concern sovereignty'.
And later in the judgment the court said this
  'As a means for determining the distinction between acts *jure imperii* and *jure gestionis* one should rather refer to the nature of the State transaction or the resulting legal relationships and not to the motive or purpose of the State activity. It thus depends on whether the foreign State has acted in exercise of its sovereign authority, that is in public law, or like a private person, that is in private law'.
And lastly
  'National law can only be implied to distinguish between a sovereign and non-sovereign activity of a foreign State in so far as it cannot exclude from the sovereign sphere and thus from immunity such State dealings as belong to the field of State authority in the narrow and proper sense according to the predominantly held view of States'.

18. *Claim against the Empire of Iran Case*, 45 I.L.R. 57 (1963).

These quotations do lend support to the argument that the act which causes the claim has to be examined and that the claim for sovereign immunity is defeated when the whole activity is commercial and the act is in no way concerned with sovereignty . . .

It appears that from the many authorities cited not every country draws the line between *acta jure imperii* and *acta jure gestionis* in the same place but I draw the inference from the passages which are quoted in the *Empire of Iran* that one way of posing the question is to ask whether the State has acted in exercise of its sovereign authority or as a private person. And if there is borne in mind the passage quoted above from *Victory Transport* the Republic of Cuba clearly has an interest in being free to perform political acts without undergoing the embarrassment or hindrance of defending the propriety of such acts before foreign courts. I do not read the affidavits of foreign lawyers as doing anything to dispel this approach, on the contrary some, at any rate, give such a view clear support.

In my opinion in this case it was the act of the government of the Republic of Cuba which prevented these cargoes from being delivered. I do not think it is possible to say that the act was clearly commercial in nature. It was not like the *Empire of Iran* a mere refusal to pay the bill for the work done. It was not like the case of *Trendex Trading Corporation* v. *Central Bank of Nigeria* [1977] 1 Q.B. 529, where there was a cancellation of contracts because too much had been ordered. No suggestion has been made that it was in the commercial interests of the Republic of Cuba to cease trading with Chile. On the contrary, it was a political decision, a foreign policy decision which bore no relation to commercial interests. The dispute would bring into question 'Legislative or international transactions of a foreign government, or the policy of its executive' (see per Lord Denning, M.R., in *Rahimtoola* [1958] A.C. 422). I am of opinion therefore that subject to certain subsidiary points with which I must deal the Republic of Cuba is entitled to claim sovereign immunity in these two cases''.

12.13 However, Lord Denning, M.R., disagreed. He said:

". . . I think it is plain that the absolute doctrine is no longer part of international law. The restrictive theory holds the field in international law: and by reason of the doctrine of incorporation it should be applied by the English courts, not only in actions *in rem* but also in actions *in personam*. The difficulty lies, however, in applying it to the various situations which arise . . .

So, in regard to State trading vessels, I take it that when a sovereign chooses to go into the markets of the world so as to let out his vessel for hire or to carry goods for freight—just like an ordinary private shipowner for commercial purposes—then he clothes himself in the dress of an ordinary ship's captain. He is liable to be sued on his contract or for his wrongs in the courts of any country which has jurisdiction in the cause. He cannot renounce the jurisdiction by a plea of sovereign immunity. He can, of course, plead frustration, or *force majeure*, if and in so far as they afford a defence. But he must face the music. He seeks like an actor to run behind the arras and come out saying: 'Look, I am no longer a ship's captain. I wear the crown of a king. You cannot sue me'. That he should not be allowed to do . . .

It was submitted, however, by Mr Bingham, Q.C., that, in these cases and in all others, the sovereign can claim immunity when the acts that caused the loss or damage were done by him in the exercise of his sovereign authority—or as it is put in Latin *jure imperii*—as distinct from *jure gestionis*. This is a very elusive test. As to what acts fall within it is anyone's guess. As Terence says: '*Quot homines, tot sententiae: suo quoque mos*' (so many men, so many opinions: his own a law to each).

But, however elusive the test, Mr Bingham submits that action in the foreign relations or diplomatic field falls squarely within the category of 'sovereign governmental acts'. In the present case, he said, the acts done by the Government of Cuba were taken in the foreign relations field following a violent military coup against the government of a close ally: and were therefore sovereign governmental acts—*jure imperii*. . . .

One thing seems to be reasonably clear. Immunity depends on the nature of the act and not on its purpose . . .

Sovereign immunity depends on the nature of that action: not on the purpose or intent or motive—use whichever word you like— with which it is done. To prove this I would take the old chestnut. All the pundits say that when a Government Department places an order for boots for the army, it is acting *jure gestionis*, no *jure imperii*: but when it places an order for guns it is *jure imperii*. I cannot accept that distinction. Suppose the Navy Department of a foreign government orders a helicopter for military purposes: and its Agriculture Department orders a like helicopter for surveying the fields. In neither case is the foreign government entitled to sovereign immunity. The seller is not concerned with the purpose for which the helicopter is required. Likewise with a gun. The seller is not concerned whether the foreign government wants it to kill an enemy or to fire a salute or to train recruits. Whenever a foreign government orders goods or services of a trader, it ought to pay for them, no matter for what purpose it intends to use them. Especially in these days when foreign governments order many goods and engage many services in the name of their State trading enterprises. If it refuses to take delivery, it ought to pay damages—unless it has some defence such as frustration or *force majeure*.

This view is supported by the case of the *Empire of Iran* (1963) 45 I.L.R. 57 . . . in the Foreign Sovereign Immunities Act 1976 of the United States in Section 603 it says:

'The commercial character of an activity shall be determined by reference to the nature of the course of conduct or particular transaction or act, rather than by reference to its purpose'.

. . . In the case of *The Playa Larga* the origin of all that happened was a simple commercial transaction by which the Government of Cuba agreed to carry sugar to Chile and deliver it to the Chilean importers. When the *Playa Larga* got to Valparaiso and failed or refused to deliver the cargo of sugar there—and afterwards refused at Callao—that was a plain repudiation and breach of that contract. Such an act—a plain repudiation of a contract—cannot be regarded as an act of such a nature as to give rise to sovereign immunity. It matters not what was the purpose of the repudiation. If it had been done for economic reasons—as, for instance, because the market price of sugar had risen sharply—it could not possibly have given rise to sovereign immunity. If it had been done for humanitarian reasons—as, for instance, because the Cuban Government were short of sugar for their own people—or wanted to give it to the people of North Vietnam—equally it could not possibly have given rise to sovereign immunity. It was in fact done out of anger at the coup d'état in Chile—and out of hostility to the new régime. That motive cannot alter the nature of the act. Nor can it give sovereign immunity where otherwise there would be none. It is the nature of the act that matters, not the motive behind it. This is supported by the decision itself in *Trendtex* v. *Bank of Nigeria* [1977] Q.B. 529 and the parallel decisions in Germany and the United States. No one suggested that the policy of the new Nigerian Government afforded any answer. It is also supported by the reasoning of four wise judges of the United States Supreme Court in *Alfred Dunhill* v. *Republic of Cuba* (1976) 48 L.Ed. 2nd at D, page 312, who held that

'the concept of an Act of State should not be extended to include the repudiation of a purely commercial obligation owed by a foreign sovereign or by one of its commercial instrumentalities'.

That case concerned the U.S. doctrine of Act of State: which is similar to our doctrine of sovereign immunity.

In the case of *The Marble Islands* the origin of all that happened was a simple commercial transaction by which one of the State organisations of Cuba agreed to carry sugar to Chile and deliver it to the Chilean importers. The Cuban Government induced its State organisation to repudiate that contract and ordered it to carry the sugar to North Vietnam. The Cuban Government then bought the vessel and, by its conduct, adopted the repudiation as its owner. It continued the repudiative act and went on to carry the sugar to North Vietnam and handed it to the people there. The nature of the transaction was again the repudiation of a purely commercial obligation. Its purpose was two-fold—to show its hostility to Chile and to help the people of Vietnam. But the purpose does not matter. The act by its very nature was an act of repudiating a binding commercial obligation. Such an act does not give rise to sovereign immunity".

12.14 The House of Lords was, as explained elsewhere (see Chapter 3), unanimously of the view that the restrictive doctrine applied to the case. But they were fundamentally at variance as to the effect of its application upon the instant facts, eloquent testimony to the great difficulty of manifesting the theory in practice.

Lord Wilberforce said:

". . . merely to state that the restrictive doctrine applies is to say little more than that a State has no absolute immunity as regards commercial or trading transactions, but where immunity begins and ends has yet to be determined. . . .

When . . . a claim is brought against a State . . . and State immunity is claimed, it is necessary to consider what is the relevant act which forms the basis of the claim: is this, under the old terminology, an act *jure gestionis* or is it an act *jure imperii*: is it . . . a 'private act' or is it a 'sovereign or public act', a private act meaning in this context an act of a private law character such as a private citizen have entered into . . .".

Referring to the plea that the contract was wholly commercial and therefore immunity should not be accorded, he said:

"In my opinion this argument, though in itself generally acceptable, burkes, or begs, the essential question, which is 'what is the relevant act?' It assumes that this is the initial entry into a commercial transaction and that this entry irrevocably confers upon later acts a commercial, or private law, character. Essentially it amounts to an assertion 'once a trader always a trader'. But this may be an over-simplification.

If a trader is always a trader, a state remains a state and is capable at any time of acts of sovereignty. The question arises, therefore, what is the position where the act upon which the claim is founded is quite outside the commercial, or private law, activity in which the State has engaged, and has the character of an act done *jure imperii*. The 'restrictive' theory does not and could not deny capability of a State to resort to sovereign, or governmental action: it merely asserts that acts done within the trading or commercial activity are not immune. The inquiry still has to be made whether they were within or outside that activity".

And later:

". . . it may not be easy to decide whether the act complained of is within the area of non-immune activity or is an act of sovereignty wholly outside it. The activities of States cannot always be compartmentalized into trading or governmental activities; and what is one to make of a case where a State has, and in the relevant circumstances, clearly displayed, both a commercial interest and a sovereign or governmental interest? To which is the critical action to be attributed? Such questions are the more difficult since they arise at an initial stage in the proceedings and, in all probability, upon affidavit evidence. This difficulty is inherent in the nature of the 'restrictive' doctrine, introducing as it does an exception, based upon a certain state of facts, to a plain rule. But as was said in the *Empire of Iran* case, 45 I.L.R. 57, 79–80:

'The fact that it is difficult to draw the line between sovereign and non-sovereign State activities is no reason for abandoning the distinction. International law knows of other similar difficulties . . . The distinction between sovereign and non-sovereign State activities cannot be drawn according to the purpose of the State transaction and whether it stands in a recognizable relation to the sovereign duties of the State. For, ultimately, activities of State, if not wholly then to the widest degree, serve sovereign purposes and duties, and stand in a still recognizable relationship to them. Neither should the distinction depend on whether the State has acted commercially. Commercial activities of States are not different in their nature from other non-sovereign State activities.'

. . . The conclusion which emerges is that in considering, under the 'restrictive' theory whether State immunity should be granted or not, the court must consider the whole context in which the claim against the State is made, with a view to deciding whether the relevant act(s) upon which the claim is based, should, in that context, be considered as fairly within an area of activity, trading or commercial, or otherwise of a private law character, in which the State has chosen to engage, or whether the relevant act(s) should be considered as having been done outside that area, and within the sphere of governmental or sovereign activity''.

The learned Law Lord held in relation to *The Playa Larga* that Cuba had not acted in the exercise of sovereign authority. He said:

"Everything done by the Republic of Cuba . . . could have been done, and, so far as evidence goes, was done, as owners of the ship: it had not exercised, and had no need to exercise sovereign powers. It acted, as any owner of the ship would act, through Mambisa, the managing operators. It invoked no governmental authority. . . . The action taken by that vessel was caused by instructions issued by the Cuban Government as owner to Mambisa as operator of the vessel.

It may well be that those instructions would not have been issued, as they were, if the owner of *Playa Larga* had been anyone but a State: it is almost certainly the case that there was no commercial reason for the decision. But these consequences follow inevitably from the entry of States into the trading field. If immunity were to be granted the moment that any decision taken by the trading state were shown to be not commercially but politically, inspired, the 'restrictive' theory would almost cease to have any content and trading relations as to State-owned ships would become impossible. It is precisely to protect private traders against politically inspired breaches, or wrongs, that the restrictive theory allows States to be brought before a municipal court. It may be too stark to say of a State 'once a trader always a trader': but, in order to withdraw its action from the sphere of acts done *jure gestionis*, a State must be able to point to some act clearly done *jure imperii*. Though, with much hesitation, I feel obliged to differ on this issue from the conclusion of the learned judge, I respectfully' think that he well put this ultimate test [1978] Q.B. 500, 528:
'. . . it is not just that the purpose or motive of the act is to serve the purposes of the State, but that the act is of its own character a governmental act, as opposed to an act which any private citizen can perform' ''.

12.14.1 Their Lordships were unanimous in holding that no immunity should be accorded in respect of *The Playa Larga*. But in relation to *The Marble Islands* opinion was divided.

Lord Diplock said that the evidence showed that everything that was done, principally the unloading of the cargo at Haiphong, was done on the express directions of the Cuban Government, and it was deliberately treated by the Government as being effected under private and not in the exercise of any sovereign powers. The elaborated legal machinery adopted to discharge and dispose of the cargo at Haiphong was done in purported reliance on the private law rights of those in possession and not upon any *ius imperii* of the Cuban State itself. Therefore no immunity could be granted on the claim over the *Marble Islands* cargo either.

Lord Keith, agreeing, said that the Cuban Government did not profess at the time to be exercising any sovereign powers; the transactions which it instructed were presented as being authorized by the terms of the bills of lading and the Cuban Commercial Code.

Lord Bridge was the third judge to refuse immunity. He said that there was no suggestion that the acquisition of the *Marble Islands* was itself a sovereign act, and he could not suppose that any civilized system of law would not recognize that an international carrier of goods acquiring a laden vessel in mid-voyage from another incurs private law obligations to the cargo owners. Thereafter what was done by Cuba, effected in purported exercise of private law rights, was a breach of the private law obligation previously assumed.

However, Lords Wilberforce and Edmund-Davies were strongly of the opposite view. The former said that the private law transactions, on which the majority of the court heavily relied, were carried out by the demise charterer, Mambisa, a Cuban body separate, for the purposes of immunity, from the Cuban State.

"The Republic of Cuba never entered into these operations . . . Its actions were confined to direction transfer of the sugar to North Vietnam, and to the enactment of Law No 1256".

He argued that Cuba never assumed any commercial obligation, and never entered the trading area, and its acts were and remained in their nature purely governmental, any civil wrong being committed by Mambisa.

Lord Edmund-Davies said there was no scope for the trader theory in relation to the *Marble Islands* claim, for there was never at any time any commercial relationship between the Chilean purchasers and the State of Cuba falling within the ambit of the restrictive doctrine of immunity. He added that if in those circumstances it were held that Cuba could not rely on State immunity, he found it impossible to imagine circumstances where the doctrine could operate.

12.14.2 Although the court was unanimous in accepting the restrictive theory of immunity, and in looking to the nature of the act and not its purpose or motive, two judges saw it clearly as an act of sovereign power when Cuba took over the *Marble Islands* and directed the cargo to be unloaded at Haiphong, while three judges found it to be a private law transaction. The analytical distinction between the two views seem to depend on whether the State of Cuba or Mambisa was the seller of the cargo to North Vietnam.

But behind that lies a more fundamental distinction. The legal machinery adopted by the Cuban Government for disposing of the cargo, which was intended as a gift to North Vietnam, was that the demise charterers, Mambisa, sold the sugar to another Cuban State enterprise, called Alimport, by ordinary private law sale, and in purported reliance on a term in the bill of lading permitting the sale in certain circumstances of perishable cargo. Alimport then donated the sugar to Vietnam, while the proceeds were frozen under the Cuban legislation, Law No 1256.

The majority of the court, therefore, saw in that dealing an assertion by Cuba that it was entitled under private law to dispose of the cargo, which excluded the possibility that it was acting in exercise of sovereign authority. However this would seem to involve an unjustified reliance on the form in which the disposition of the cargo was effected. Surely the reality of the matter is that the Cuban Government took over the ship and denied the cargo to the owners as an act of State policy, which could not in the case of this vessel be overruled by a pre-existing commercial context, for there was none.

It is submitted that the minority view is preferable, and that there is, moreover, no need to split hairs about whether the Government was merely directing Mambisa and Alimport to carry out the transaction or whether it was in fact disposing of the cargo itself.

Nevertheless it may well be that broad justice was done, in the sense that the distinction drawn between the Government as owners from the first of the *Playa Larga* while uninterested in the *Marble Islands* until after the *coup d'etat*—between the Government being accountable for the former's cargo at the outset and Mambisa for the latter's—although legally correct, was an unreal one.

The formalistic training of the common lawyer would not permit a decision to be based on that ground. The Government was in reality, however, directing all the actions which Mambisa took and it might well be thought an unsatisfactory result if the outcome of the litigation depended on whether the Government appeared on the documents to be the owner of the vessel from the start or not, a fortuitous circumstance which was irrelevant to the commercial reality of a single bulk sale of sugar.

12.14.3 We may also note that in *Planmount Ltd* v. *Republic of Zaire*,[19] a claim for the cost of building works carried out at the official London residence of the ambassador, Lloyd, J., after considering the *Claim against the Empire of Iran* case (45 I.L.R. 57) said:

> "To my mind, it is hard to imagine a clearer case of an act or transaction of a private or commercial nature than the repairs to the ambassador's residence".

12.15   B: United States of America

As noted above in Chapter 3, paragraph 3.12, the American courts only themselves decide the issue of immunity where the State Department is non-committal (though the U.S. statute of 1976 shifts the responsibility to the courts). Such a case was *Victory Transport* v. *Comisaría General*.[20] This was a decision by the United States Court of Appeals in 1964 in proceedings

19. [1981] 1 All E.R. 1110; 64 I.L.R. 268 (1980).
20. 336 F. 2d 354, 360; 35 I.L.R. 110 (1963/4).

against a branch of the Spanish Ministry of Commerce to compel arbitration of a dispute under a charter-party. The court took the occasion (at page 359) to consider the nature of the restrictive doctrine and the scope of *acta imperii*:

"Through the 'Tate letter' the State Department has made it clear that its policy is to decline immunity to friendly foreign sovereigns in suits arising from private or commercial activity. But the 'Tate letter' offers no guide-lines or criteria for differentiating between a sovereign's private and public acts. Nor have the courts or commentators suggested any satisfactory test. Some have looked to the nature of the transaction, categorizing as sovereign acts only activity which could not be performed by individuals. While this criterion is relatively easy to apply, it ofttimes produces rather astonishing results, such as the holdings of some European courts that purchases of bullets or shoes for the army, the erection of fortifications for defense, or the rental of a house for an embassy, are private acts . . . Furthermore, this test merely postpones the difficulty, for particular contracts in some instances may be made only by States. Others have looked to the purpose of the transaction, categorizing as *jure imperii* all activities in which the object of performance is public in character. But this test is even more unsatisfactory, for conceptually the modern sovereign always acts for a public purpose . . . Functionally the criterion is purely arbitrary and necessarily involves the court in projecting personal notions about the proper realm of State functioning . . .

. . . The conceptual difficulties involved in formulating a satisfactory method of differentiating between acts *jure imperii* and acts *jure gestionis* have led many commentators to declare that the distinction is unworkable. However, the Supreme Court has made it plain that when the State Department has been silent on the question of immunity in a particular case, it is the court's duty to determine for itself whether the foreign sovereign is entitled to immunity 'in conformity to the principles accepted by the department of the government charged with the conduct of foreign relations'. *Republic of Mexico v. Hoffman, supra*, 324 U.S. at 35, 65 S. Ct. at 532. And since the State Department has publicly pronounced its adherence to the distinction, we must apply it to the facts of this case.

. . . The purpose of the restrictive theory of sovereign immunity is to try to accommodate the interest of individuals doing business with foreign governments in having their legal rights determined by the courts, with the interest of foreign governments in being free to perform certain political acts without undergoing the embarrassment or hindrance of defending the propriety of such acts before foreign courts. Sovereign immunity is a derogation from the normal exercise of jurisdiction by the courts and should be accorded only in clear cases. Since the State Department's failure or refusal to suggest immunity is significant, we are disposed to deny a claim of sovereign immunity that has not been 'recognized and allowed' by the State Department unless it is plain that the activity in question falls within one of the categories of strictly political or public acts about which sovereigns have traditionally been quite sensitive. Such acts are generally limited to the following categories:

(1) internal administrative acts, such as expulsion of an alien.
(2) legislative acts, such as nationalization.
(3) acts concerning the armed forces.
(4) acts concerning diplomatic activity.
(5) public loans.

We do not think that the restrictive theory adopted by the State Department requires sacrificing the interests of private litigants to international comity in other than these limited categories. Should diplomacy require enlargement of these categories, the State Department can file a suggestion of immunity with the court. Should diplomacy require contraction of these categories, the State Department can issue a new or clarifying policy pronouncement.

. . . The Comisaría General's chartering of the appellee's ship to transport a purchase of wheat is not a strictly public or political act. Indeed, it partakes far more of the character of a private commercial act than a public or political act.

The charter-party has all the earmarks of a typical commercial transaction. It was executed for the Comisaría General by 'El Jefe del Servicio Commercial', the head of its commercial division. The wheat was consigned to and shipped by a private commercial concern. And one of the most significant indicators of the private commercial nature of this charter is the inclusion of the arbitration clause. The French Court of Appeal, in dismissing a claim of sovereign immunity where the governmental charterer had agreed to arbitration, pointed out:

'A contract relating to maritime transport is a private contract where the owner merely puts his ship and the ship's crew at the disposal of the State and does not take a direct part in the performance of the public service undertaken by the State in the latter's capacity as a charterer. The charter-party does not contain any clause peculiar to public law or unusual in private law. It provides for a time charter of the vessel which is put at the disposal of the State chartering it. The insertion of the arbitration clause underlines the intention of the parties to make their agreement subject to private law'. *Myrtoon Steamship Company* v. *Agent Judicaire Du Tresor*, 24 Int.L.Rep. 205, 206 (1957).

Maritime transport has been included among the commercial or business activities specifically mentioned in recent United States treaties restricting sovereign immunity. And the 1926 Brussels Convention, the first major international attempt to restrict sovereign immunity, which Spain signed but never ratified, denied immunity to all maritime governmental activities except vessels operated exclusively on non-commercial service, such as warships, patrol vessels, or hospital ships.

Even if we take a broader view of the transaction to encompass the purchase of wheat pursuant to the Surplus Agricultural Commodities Agreement to help feed the people of Spain, the activity of the Comisaría General remains more in the commercial than political realm. Appellant does not claim that the wheat will be used for the public services of Spain;

presumptively the wheat will be resold to Spanish nationals. Whether the Comisaría General loses money or makes a profit on the sale, this purchasing activity has been conducted through private channels of trade. Except for United States financing, permitting payment in pesetas, the Comisaría General acted much like any private purchaser of wheat.

Our conclusion that the Comisaría General's activity is more properly labelled an act *jure gestionis* than *jure imperii* is supported by the practice of those countries which have adopted the restrictive theory of sovereign immunity. Thus the Commercial Tribunal of Alexandria declined to grant immunity to this same Spanish instrumentality in a more difficult case—a suit arising from the Comisaría's purchase of rice to help the people of neutral Spain during wartime.

'It is not contended in the present case that the rice in question was bought by the Comisaría General for the needs of the Spanish public services. On the contrary, it seems clearly established that the rice was bought for the feeding of the Spanish population during a difficult period. In negotiating this purchase herself, instead of leaving the matter to private enterprise, Spain proceeded in much the same manner as any other Spanish trader would have done who wanted to buy rice in Egypt; that is to say, she got it out of Egypt with the necessary permits and carried it to Spain in a Spanish ship in order to re-sell it on the usual commercial lines. This being so, the Comisaría General cannot claim immunity from jurisdiction, and the judgment entered against it must be confirmed'.

Though there are a few inconsistencies, the courts in those countries which have adopted the restrictive theory have generally considered purchasing activity by a State instrumentality, particularly for resale to nationals, as commercial or private activity.

Finally, our conclusion that the Comisaría General's claim of sovereign immunity should be denied finds support in the State Department's communication to the court in *New York and Cuba Mail S.S. Co.* v. *Republic of Korea*, 132 F.Supp. 684, 685 (S.D.N.Y. 1955). There the Republic of Korea was allegedly responsible for damaging a ship while assisting in the unloading of a cargo of rice for distribution without charge to its civilian and military personnel during the Korean War. Though suggesting that Korea's property was immune from attachment, the State Department refused to suggest immunity 'inasmuch as the particular acts out of which the cause of action arose are not shown to be of a purely governmental character'. If the wartime transportation of rice to civilian and military personnel is not an act *jure imperii*, *a fortiori* the peacetime transportation of wheat for presumptive resale is not an act *jure imperii*".

12.16 The case of *Alfred Dunhill of London (Inc.)* v. *Republic of Cuba*[21] arose out of an alleged act of State by Cuba in

---

21. 96 Sup. Ct. Rep. 1854 (1976); 66 I.L.R. 212 (1976).

expropriating Cuban sugar companies. White, J., giving a judgment in which the majority concurred, said, at page 1846:

> "Nothing in our national policy calls on us to recognise as an act of State of repudiation by Cuba or an obligation adjudicated in our courts and arising out of the operation of a commercial business by one of its instrumentalities. For all the reasons which led the Executive Branch to adopt the restrictive theory of sovereign immunity, we hold that the mere assertion of sovereignty as a defence to a claim arising out of purely commercial acts by a foreign sovereign is no more effective given the label 'act of State' than if it is given the label 'sovereign immunity' . . .
> We decline to extend the acts of State doctrine to acts committed by foreign sovereigns in the course of their purely commercial operations. Because the act relied on by the respondents in this case was an act arising out of the conduct by Cuba's agents in the operation of cigar businesses for profit the act was not an act of State".

12.17 The purchase by the Republic of Haiti of military equipment for use by Haitian armed forces was declared a public or political act and immunity was granted by a New York District Court in 1974 (*Aerotrade Inc.* v. *Republic of Haiti*[22]).

The sale of wheat flour to Bolivia was held to be purely commercial by a District Court for Columbia in 1975 (*ADM Milling Co.* v. *Republic of Bolivia*[23]). Similarly, the purchase by a Syrian Government agency of foodstuffs under a United States Government programme was held in 1981 by a United States Court of Appeals to be a commercial transaction and therefore not attracting immunity (*Gemini Shipping* v. *Foreign Trade Organization for Chemicals & Foodstuffs*[24]).

In *NAC* v. *Federal Republic of Nigeria*[25] a New York District Court held that the sale of cement to the defendants was commercial in character, both in nature and purpose, and could not attract immunity whether under the Act of 1976, which speaks of "commercial activity" (see above, para. 6.2.1), or under the earlier pre-existing law; and a similar view was taken by Courts of Appeal in similar suits in 1981.[26]

A New York District Court held in 1978 that the sending by

22. 63 I.L.R. 41 (1974).
23. 63 I.L.R. 56 (1975).
24. 63 I.L.R. 569 (1981).
25. 63 I.L.R. 137 (1978).
26. See 63 I.L.R. 557.

the USSR Ministry of Culture of Soviet artists to perform in the United States under a United States impresario was a commercial activity (*United Euram Co.* v. *USSR*[27]).

A Texas District Court held in 1980 that a military training agreement whereby a Saudi soldier was in the United States was not of a commercial character (*Castro* v. *Saudi Arabia*[28]).

The New York Supreme Court has held that Argentine Airlines are involved in commercial activities (*Argentine Airlines* v. *Ross*[29]); and a Court of Appeals took a similar view in 1980 of Aeromexico.[30]

As indicated in the text above, later cases are decided under the United States Foreign Sovereign Immunities Act of 1976, but the criteria of "commercial activity" remains the same.

A federal court in Alabama has recently (27 February 1984) set aside a default judgment it had entered against the People's Republic of China in respect of an action by holders of bonds issued in 1911 by the Imperial Qing Government to finance the construction of the well-known Huguang railway. This bizarre action was begun in 1979 when the United States recognized the People's Republic. The court, possibly swayed by the diplomatic repercussions threatened by China (who hold fast to the absolute theory of immunity) if the action was admitted, said that the characterization of the bond issue as a "commercial activity" needed further consideration.

A United States Court of Appeals has said that the issuance in Mexico City of certificates of deposit by a State-owned Mexican bank was a commercial activity within s. 1605(*a*)(2) of the Act of 1976 (though the claim against the bank was rejected for other reasons *Allied Bank International* v. *Banco Credito Agricola de Cartago*.[31]

The issuance of Polish Treasury notes in the early 1930s to finance the purchase of railway carriages was recently held by a New York District Court to be a commercial activity (*Schmidt* v. *Polish People's Republic*).[32]

27. 63 I.L.R. 228 (1978).
28. 63 I.L.R. 419 (1980).
29. 63 I.L.R. 195 (1978).
30. See 63 I.L.R. 446.
31. N.Y. Ct. of App. (2nd Cir.) 23 April 1984.
32. 579 F. Supp. 23 (1984).

12.18 Across the border in the neighbouring jurisdiction of Canada the Supreme Court took a different, view of the question in *Government of Democratic Republic of the Congo v. Venne*.[33] By a majority of five to two the court held that where an architect was commissioned to draw plans for the construction of a State's national pavilion at the "Expo 67" exhibition, the transaction involved a public sovereign act on behalf of the State and the employment of the architect was a step taken in performance of that sovereign act. The court, strangely, found it of particular significance that the request for the architect's services had been made by the accredited representatives of the Congo. However, governments will normally act through accredited representatives. This case illustrates an interpretation of the restrictive doctrine (which was assumed for the purpose of this argument to be applicable in Canadian law) that is so narrow as effectively to deny it any real scope. Ritchie, J., with whose judgment the majority concurred, said:

> "This makes it plain to me that, in preparing for the construction of its national pavilion, a Department of the Government of a foreign State, together with its duly accredited diplomatic representatives, were engaged in the performance of a public sovereign act of State on behalf of their country and that the employment of the respondent was a step taken in the performance of that sovereign act . . .
>
> In an area of the law which has been so widely canvassed by legal commentators and which has been the subject of varying judicial opinions in different countries I think it would be undesirable to add further *obiter dicta* to those which have already been pronounced and I am accordingly content to rest my opinion on the ground that the appellant's employment of the respondent was in the performance of a sovereign act of State".

Two judges dissented, saying that the test should be one of function and not of status and that immunity should be denied to the State. On the other hand, the Quebec Court of Appeal held in 1977 that a contract appointing the plaintiff sole agent and distributor of the defendant's films in Canada was a purely commercial transaction (*Zodiak International Products* v. *Polish People's Republic*[34]). Canada now has its own State Immunity Act of 1982.

33. (1972) 22 D.L.R. (3d) 669; 64 I.L.R. 24 (1971).
34. 64 I.L.R. 51 (1977).

C: Continental jurisdictions

When studying these decisions one has to bear in mind the fundamental distinction in civil law jurisdictions between public and private law.

12.19   *Belgium*

The Belgian courts deny immunity where the acts are not limited to the political role (*actes de la vie politique*) but involve acting as a civil or private person.

In March 1879 the Court of Appeal in Ghent denied immunity to the Peruvian Government in respect of the sale of guano on the ground that it was *actus gestionis* (see 45 I.L.R. 64).

The Court of Cassation in 1903 asserted jurisdiction over a claim by a railway company against the Netherlands (*S.A. des Chemins de Fer Liégois-Luxembourgeois* v. *Etat Néerlandois*,[35] declaring itself competent to determine claims for reimbursement arising out of works executed for the enlargement of a Dutch railway station. The court said that where a State acquires and possesses goods, enters into contracts, becomes a creditor or debtor and generally engages in commercial activities, it is not exercising its sovereign authority, but is doing what any private individual can do and is accordingly acting as a private person. In this and later cases stress was laid on the nature of the act as determining whether immunity should be accorded. Acts relating to contracts of sale (even if involving war booty), contracts for the purchase of arms, the lease of immovable property, the management of railway lines, the engagement of merchant seamen have all been treated as acts *jure gestionis*. On the other hand, acts relating to the lease of immovable property for the installation of a foreign embassy, military requisitions, the annulment of securities and bills held by enemy aliens and the regulation of foreign trade have been treated as acts *jure imperii*.

In 1971 the Civil Tribunal of Brussels said that the attachment of films made for the Liberian Ministry of

---

35. Clunet 31 (1904) 417.

Information was not lawful as the films were in use for a purpose which concerned *ius imperii* (*NV Filmpartners* case[36]).

12.20 *Italy*

In 1876 the Court of Cassation in Florence, in a decision upheld by the Court of Cassation in Rome, distinguished between the State as the bearer of sovereign authority (*ente politico*) and the State as the subject of private law (*ente civile*) (see 45 I.L.R. 63).

In 1886 the Court of Cassation assumed jurisdiction in respect of proceedings instituted in the Italian courts concerning services rendered for the Bey of Tunis, and, in the same year, denied a plea of immunity entered by the Greek Government in a suit for the payment, in accordance with a contract made by the Greek consul, of the expenses of maintenance of a Greek subject in a lunatic asylum. While the Italian courts have consistently assumed jurisdiction over foreign States in matters of a private law nature, they have declined to do so with respect to acts *jure imperii*. Thus in the case of *Little* v. *Riccio* in 1934 the Court of Cassation declined jurisdiction in an action for dismissal brought against a committee responsible for the maintenance of the British cemetery at Naples, holding that the cemetery was maintained by Great Britain in exercise of a public law function and therefore *jure imperii*.

A contract for the construction of drains on premises used for American forces stationed in Italy was held by the same court to be a matter of private law in *United States Government* v. *Irsa*,[37] and so were loans to a Libyan State consortium to enable it to lend money to Italian farmers in Italy (*Consorzio Agrario di Tripolitania* case[38]).

An ordinary lease of premises for use as a consular residence was held to be a private law transaction (*United States Government* v. *Bracale Bicchierai*,[39] Court of Appeal of

36. 65 I.L.R. 26 (1971).
37. 65 I.L.R. 262 (1963).
38. *Consorzio Agrario di Tripolitania* v. *Federazione Italiana Consorzi Agrari*, 65 I.L.R. 265 (1966).
39. 65 I.L.R. 273 (1968).

Naples 1968), as was a lease of property for use as an Embassy (the *Moroccan Embassy* case,[40] Court of Appeal of Rome 1979). In the latter case the court said: "If the Italian courts were to attach primary importance to the aims pursued by a foreign State they would have to deny any practical effect to the distinction between acts performed in the exercise of sovereign powers and acts carried out under private law, inasmuch as any activity performed by foreign States and their agencies is in some way connected with the institutional ends of such States" (a neat summation of the argument accepted now by most jurisdictions that one looks to the nature and not the purpose of the act or activity to decide whether it is "commercial" or "sovereign"). In 1974 the Court of Cassation, in the case of *Luna* v. *Republica Socialista di Romania*[41] declined jurisdiction in proceedings for unfair dismissal brought by an Italian national in respect of his employment with the economic section of the Romanian Embassy in Rome, holding that "the employment relationship in question falls within the framework of activities of a public nature of a foreign State, which are by their very nature correlated to the institutional ends of the State itself". By way of contrast the Court of Cassation, in the case of *Malloval* v. *Ministère des Affaires Etrangères Français*, also decided in 1974,[42] denied immunity in proceedings for unfair dismissal brought by an Italian national in respect of her employment with a French lycée in Rome, the court holding that the lycée, although depending on the French Ministry of Foreign Affairs and not having an autonomous legal personality, was not exercising in Italy a public function which was an expression of the sovereignty of France.

Other cases. The claim of an employee of the defendants who was not given an official position and performed ancillary duties not related to the Bureau's institutional functions was held to fall within the sphere of private law (*Paravicini* v. *Commercial Bureau of the People's Republic of Bulgaria*,[43] Tribunal of Milan 1969); but an assistant librarian who took

40. 65 I.L.R. 331 (1979).
41. 65 I.L.R. 313 (1974).
42. 65 I.L.R. 303 (1974).
43. 65 I.L.R. 282 (1969).

part in the public activity of the United States Government in the field of overseas propaganda and information was outside private law as that function was an expression of State sovereignty (*De Ritis* v. *United States*,[44] Court of Cassation 1971). In holding that a fireman employed at a United States military base could claim under private law the Court of Cassation in 1977 said that the categorization of a particular employment relationship was to be made according to the kind of organization involved and the basic treatment officially secured for the employee rather than the extent to which the employment was related to the institutional aims of the sending State (*Bruno* v. *United States*[45]). The same court in *Velloso* v. *Borla*[46] held that permanent employment within the administration of an Embassy, involving the running of Embassy offices in furtherance of institutional aims of a public nature, fell outside the field of private law. And the Praetor at Venice recently accorded immunity to the United Kingdom when sued by an employee of the British Consulate as the duties were said to be correlated with the institutional aims of the Foreign Office and involved participation in the public activity of the State employer (*Bulli* v. *United Kingdom*[47]).

12.21   *Switzerland*

In March 1918 in the *Dreyfuss* case,[48] the Swiss Federal Court asserted jurisdiction over foreign sovereigns for relationships of a private law nature.

In 1928 the Swiss Federal Government told a League of Nations committee that restrictions on State immunity were desirable, that the main difficulty was to differentiate between *acta imperii* and *acta gestionis*, and that immunity should be recognised only for acts which were genuine manifestations of sovereignty, and that the distinction should be based not on the purpose of the transaction but on its true nature (*nature*

44. 65 I.L.R. 283 (1971).
45. 65 I.L.R. 316 (1977).
46. 65 I.L.R. 328 (1979).
47. 65 I.L.R. 343 (1981).
48. BGE 44 I 49.

intrinsèque), so that only an act which could be carried out by a private individual should enjoy full immunity.

Where the United Arab Republic sought to set aside orders for execution made against their funds in a bank account, the orders having been made in respect of claims arising out of a contract made in Vienna with the diplomatic representation of the Kingdom of Egypt (the U.A.R.'s predecessor) for the renting of a house in Vienna, the court said the nature and not the purpose of the transaction should be examined, to see whether it depended on public authority (*puissance publique*) or could have been performed by any private individual (65 I.L.R. 385).

The same court, the Federal Tribunal, held in 1979 that an agreement for the leasing of a film from a Liechtenstein company to the Egyptian State Television Authority was a matter for private law (*Arab Republic of Egypt* v. *Cinetelevision*[49]).

12.22   *The Netherlands*

In *NV Exploitatie-Maatschappij Bengalis* v. *Bank of Indonesia*[50] the Court of Appeal of Amsterdam said that the refusal of the defendant bank to pay compensation in respect of gold stolen by revolutionaries was to be equated with an act of government in exercise of sovereign function namely the maintenance of the monentary position of the State.

In *NV Cabiolent* v. *National Iranian Oil Co.*[51] the Court of Appeal at The Hague held that the defendants, when concluding with the plaintiffs' predecessors in title a concession agreement for the exploration and possible production of petroleum, were not acting *jure imperii*. The court said that their investigation of the character of the defendants and the principal provisions of the agreement led to

"no other conclusion than that the Agreement contains mainly provisions of a private law nature and that it was concluded between two parties who in entering into that Agreement were equal, or at least of equivalent status. Accordingly when NIOC concluded the Agreement it did not perform an

49. 65 I.L.R. 425 (1965).
50. 65 I.L.R. 348 (1963).
51. 47 I.L.R. 138 (1968).

act which *ex jure* must be regarded as a pure act of State on the part of the State of Iran".

A contract to construct a railway was held to be a matter of private law, and it was irrelevant that the railway might have a military or strategic purpose (*Société Européenne d'Etudes* v. *Socialist Federal Republic of Yugoslavia*,[52] Court of Appeal of The Hague). A normal contract of carriage by sea was held to be a matter of private law in *ICC Handel Maatschappij* v. *USSR*,[53] (District Court of Amsterdam 1976). So was a contract for the purchase of onions (*Parsons* v. *Republic of Malta*,[54] District Court of Alkmaar 1977), and a contract engaging a teacher at the Portuguese Ministry of Education's school in Amsterdam (*de Sousa* v. *Republic of Portugal*,[55] Amsterdam Local Court 1979).

On the other hand, the function of typing and filing for a Consulate-General was held to be within the field of sovereign activity in *Gootjes* v. *Kingdom of Belgium*,[56] Rotterdam Local Court 1978. So also, consistent with the German case cited below, were the actions of the German CID in communicating information about the plaintiffs in the *Church of Scientology* case,[57] District Court of Amsterdam 1980.

12.23   *Greece*

The Court of Appeal in Athens has asserted jurisdiction in respect of the Romanian envoy's premises in Athens, stating that immunity is limited to activities in which the State engages as a sovereign political power and does not extend to matters which arise from activities such as the administration of property which in no way concerns its sovereignty (Annual Digest 16 (1949) 291).

The Athens Tribunal of First Instance held in 1967 that the purchaser of a house intended exclusively for use as a residence for the families of members of the staff of an Embassy and not

52. 65 I.L.R. 356 (1973).
53. 65 I.L.R. 368 (1976).
54. 65 I.L.R. 371 (1977).
55. 65 I.L.R. 378 (1979).
56. 65 I.L.R. 372 (1978).
57. 65 I.L.R. 380 (1980).

for use as premises for the mission or even as the private residence of the ambassador, was not a sovereign act (*Purchase of Embassy Staff Residence* case.[58]

12.24   *France*

The French courts were among the slowest to adopt the restrictive view. In December, 1961, a decision of the Court of Cassation gave immunity to Vietnam upon a contract for the supply of cigarettes to the Vietnamese army, as being an exercise of *fonctions étatiques de gestion publique*. On the same day the court denied immunity to Turkey on a bank guarantee given by Turkey in respect of a loan to Constantinople (see 45 I.L.R. 74).

In 1964 the Court of Cassation granted immunity to the United States on building contracts they had entered into to provide accommodation for American officials, as containing "provisions alien to private law pertaining to the prerogatives of public power of the United States" (*Enterprise Perignon v. United States*[59]).

In March, 1966, the same court held that a contract for the survey and construction of water distribution and drainage works was a contract for "public works" and hence a "public act". The contract contained "clauses which are outside private law and pertain to the prerogatives of the public power of the State of Pakistan" (*Société Transhipping* v. *Federation of Pakistan*[60]).

In *Administration des Chemins de Fer Iraniens* v. *Société Levant Express Transport* (1969) the Cour de Cassation said that immunity might only be accorded to the extent that the act giving rise to the dispute constituted an act of sovereign authority (acte de puissance publique) *or* had been carried out in the public service. These words were echoed in 1976 in the case of *Blagojevic* v. *Banque du Japan*, although in the interim the court had in *Société Hotel George V* v. *État Espagnol* refused to grant immunity to Spain in respect of a lease of premises to the Spanish Tourist Office in Paris, on the ground

58. 65 I.L.R. 255 (1967).
59. 65 I.L.R. 39 (1964).
60. 47 I.L.R. 150 (1966).

merely that the entering into the lease was not an act of sovereign authority.

12.25   *Austria*

In *Dralle* v. *Republic of Czechoslovakia*,[61] a claim against a Czech nationalized firm to restrain the use in Austria of certain trademarks, the Austrian Supreme Court said that immunity should be granted only in respect of acts which the State had undertaken in exercise of its sovereign authority.

In February, 1961, in the *Collision with Foreign Government-Owned Motorcar (Austria)* case,[62] the court examined the question "whether the plaintiff is claiming against the sued State on the strength of a private law relationship or one in its sovereign domain". The act was to be judged not by its aim or purpose, but "from the inherent internal character of the transaction or from the legal relationship created". Thus the purchase of land was still a private law act even if the land was to be used for setting up a military post; a building contract would be a matter of private law even if it was for the construction of an Embassy; and damage caused by the driving of an Embassy car was of a private law nature.

In *Neustein* v. *Republic of Indonesia*[63] the Supreme Court held that the appointment of an Austrian University professor to an Indonesian University was a private law relationship and therefore justiciable. In 1963 the same court said that the treaty obligation assumed in 1940 by the German Reich to pay to persons transferred from Romania compensation for property left behind was not a matter of private law and therefore not justiciable by the Austrian courts (*X* v. *Federal Republic of Germany*[64]). Reference may also be made to *Steinmitz* v. *Hungarian People's Republic*.[65]

---

61. 17 I.L.R. 155 (1950).
62. 40 I.L.R. 73 (1961).
63. 65 I.L.R. 3 (1958).
64. 65 I.L.R. 10 (1963).
65. 65 I.L.R. 15 (1970).

12.26   West Germany

The *Claim against the Empire of Iran* case[66] was a claim for 292 Deutschemarks for repairs carried out at the Iranian Embassy at the Ambassador's request. The matter was referred to the Federal Constitutional Court by the Regional Court of Cologne. The Federal Minister of Justice submitted on behalf of the Federal Government that immunity should be granted as the contract "stands in recognizable relationship to the sovereign activities of the foreign State irrespective of the fact that such a contract would otherwise be characterized as a private law agreement by German law".

The court, in not acceding to that plea, said (page 61):

> "There is no general rule of international law according to which municipal jurisdiction is excluded in the case of claims against a foreign State in connection with its non-sovereign activities".

And (at page 79):

> "The fact that it is difficult to draw the line between sovereign and non-sovereign State activities is no reason for abandoning the distinction ... The distinction between sovereign and non-sovereign State activities cannot be drawn according to the purpose of the State transaction, whether it stands in a recognisable relationship to the sovereign duties of the State. For, ultimately, activities of a State, if not wholly then to the widest degree, serve sovereign purposes and duties, and stand in a still recognisable relationship to them. Neither should the distinction depend on whether the State has acted commercially. Commercial activities of States are not different in their nature from other non-sovereign State activities.
>
> As a means of determining the distinction between acts *jure imperii* and *jure gestionis* one should rather refer to the nature of the State transaction, and not to the motive or purpose of the State activity. It thus depends on whether the foreign State has acted in exercise of its sovereign authority, that is in public law, or like a private person, that is in private law".

In 1969 the Federal Supreme Court said that the purchase of real property and the assumption of mortgage obligations were private law activities (the *Hungarian Embassy* case).[67] In 1972 the Coblenz Oberlandesgericht said that whereas an agreement for the sale of arms might have a public law character the plaintiff's claim for commission in connection

66. 45 I.L.R. 57 (1963).
67. 65 I.L.R. 110 (1969).

therewith was based on an agreement which had an independent nature partaking of private law (*Arms Sale Commission Agreement* case).[68]

In 1974 the Oberlandesgericht of Munich asserted jurisdiction over an estate agent's action for commission due from a foreign government on the purchase of land for a consulate, on the ground that such a contract with the estate agent was not a sovereign act (*Land Purchase Broker's Commission* case).[69]

In the *Central Bank of Nigeria* case[70] in 1975, which arose out of the over-ordering of cement by the Nigerian administration, like our *Trendtex* case[71] (see above at 12.6) the Frankfurt Landgericht held that the opening of a letter of credit at the bank was a private law activity. The use of music in which copyright subsisted by the Spanish State Tourist Office has been held to be a matter for private law (65 I.L.R. 140, Frankfurt Oberlandesgericht, 1977).

The action of New Scotland Yard in giving the German police information on the plaintiffs in pursuance of treaty obligations was a matter of public and not private law (the *Church of Scientology* case),[72] and so was the performance of consular duties, even ordinary secretarial duties (*Conrades v. United Kingdom*,[73] Hanover Labour Court 1981).

A dispute over the financial performance of a contract for the building of oil and gas pipelines was held to be on a purely private commercial basis in the *NIOC Pipeline Contracts* case,[74] (Frankfurt Oberlandesgericht 1982). In the *FTI Bank Account* case[75] (Hamburg Landgericht 1981) the purposes of the Foreign Trade Institute, which functioned chiefly in the sphere of public relations and advertising, were held to be commercial.

---

68. 65 I.L.R. 119 (1972).
69. 65 I.L.R. 125 (1974).
70. 65 I.L.R. 131 (1975).
71. [1977] Q.B. 529; 64 I.L.R. 111 (1977).
72. 65 I.L.R. 193 (1978).
73. 65 I.L.R. 205 (1981).
74. 65 I.L.R. 212 (1982).
75. 65 I.L.R. 209 (1981).

12.27   D: South Africa

This jurisdiction was slow to come to terms with the restrictive doctrine. Although it can be said that South Africa has, in common with that most intransigent of the absolutists, the Soviet Union, a government that does not take kindly to judicial supervision, nevertheless the South African judiciary have always shown an independence of the executive branch consistent with the common law traditions of their legal structure. But although the jurisprudence of South African law is based on the Roman-Dutch system their case law suffers similarly with ours from the icy clutch of precedent. In *Lendlease Finance Co. v. Corporation de Mercadeo Agricola*[76] it was argued that the modern rule in international law was that of restricted immunity but the Cape Provincial Divisional Court stated that it felt bound to adhere to the traditional view of absolute immunity, and although on appeal this particular question did not fall to be decided the Appellate Division made it clear that it regarded the issue as a difficult one. Then in *Prentice Shaw and Schiess Inc. v. Government of Bolivia*[77] the Transvaal Divisional Court left the question open, but only by the judge's taking a very narrow view of the restrictive doctrine so that he was able to say that even if it was applied in that case immunity will still fall to be accorded (he followed the reasoning of the Canadian case of *Government of Democratic Republic of the Congo v. Venne*[78] (see paragraph 12.18). For a criticism of the failure at that point of the South African courts to move with the times on this issue see Cartoon: "The Doctrine of Sovereign Immunity: Another Chance Lost" (*South African Law Journal*, March 1979, p. 26).

But then in 1979 the Supreme Court of Transvaal declared that it accepted the restrictive doctrine (see *InterScience Research v. Republica Popular de Mocambique*;[79] and in 1980 the Supreme Court for the Eastern Cape held that a contract

---

76. (1976) (4) S.A. 464 (A); 64 I.L.R. 675 (1975).
77. (1978) (3) S.A. 938 (T); 64 I.L.R. 685 (1978).
78. (1972) 22 D.L.R. (3d) 669; 64 I.L.R. 24 (1971).
79. 64 I.L.R. 689 (1979).

for the carriage of fertilizer was commercial in character and denied immunity (*Kaffraria Property Co. v. Government of the Republic of Zambia*).[80]

80. 64 I.L.R. 708 (1980).

BOOK 2

DIPLOMATIC IMMUNITY

CHAPTER 13

INTRODUCTION TO BOOK 2

13.1 At common law diplomatic immunity first arose as an extension of sovereign immunity. The inviolability, in theory, of the herald and the flag of truce had been recognized as a practical necessity from earliest times, but, as a matter of law, it was the consideration that the sovereign's dignity and independence must be preserved that gave protection to his diplomatic agents. In his own person the issue was unlikely to be put to the test; his dealings with other countries were, before the days of State commerce, conducted through his accredited representatives. They would be likely, pursuant to their presence in the foreign State, to involve themselves at some time, within or without the course of their official duties, in matters susceptible to litigation civil or criminal. It was therefore considered that the diplomatic agent, while occupying that position, must be accorded the same immunity as the sovereign. The topic is discussed above in Chapters 1 and 2.

We shall here merely cite as illustration the words of Lord Talbot in *Barbuit's* case:[1]

> ". . . the privilege of a public minister is to have his person sacred and free from arrests, not on his own account, but on account of those he represents . . . The foundation of this privilege is for the sake of the prince by whom an ambassador is sent".

13.2 The sovereign's personal immunity at common law, whereby he may not be directly impleaded, is total, though he may waive it by an actual submission (a prior agreement will not bind him; he must institute proceedings or take a step in them as to the merits). It is as an extension of this immunity that immunity may be accorded to entities of sovereign status, whether the State (which may itself be a party to proceedings),

1. (1737) 25 E.R. 777.

the Government, or a department of or under the supervision or control of the State.

13.3 As we have seen (Chapter 3, paragraph 3.18) the immunity of States may be subject even at common law to exceptions for transactions of a commercial character, but, even accepting the restrictive doctrine applied in the *Trendtex* case.[2] it should not be taken for granted that in actions against the head of State himself the former rule of absolute immunity would be similarly modified. It is one thing to assume jurisdiction over an entity, another (at least, in diplomatic terms) to assume jurisdiction over the head of State himself.

13.4 The sovereign's personal immunity extended to immunity from being indirectly impleaded, by an action which put property of his in peril. This might be done by an action *in rem* which has been described as a writ "directed primarily against the ship and accordingly, through the ship, against all persons claiming any right or interest in the ship" (*The Jupiter*[3]): such a writ issued against a sovereign's property is a way of obliging the sovereign to come into court or forfeit his property.

His property might also be put in peril in an action *in personam* to which he is not a party: he may be accorded immunity if he makes out a *prima facie* claim to the property (see Chapter 6, paragraph 6.28). It was, then, from this immunity of the sovereign that the immunity of his diplomatic agents arose. His immunity included his wife, and children if still under his parental control (*In re C* (*an infant*[4])), and his diplomatic "family", i.e. his counsellors, secretaries, clerks and domestic servants (*Engelke* v. *Musmann*[5]). Similarly, the "family" of the diplomatic agent share his immunities.

13.5 The sovereign's personal immunity was found in the common law until the State Immunity Act 1978 came into force on 22 November 1978, providing by s. 20(1) that the

2. *Trendtex Trading Corporation* v. *Central Bank of Nigeria* [1977] Q.B. 529; 64 I.L.R. 111 (1977).
3. [1924] P. 236, 238; 3 I.L.R. 136, 139 (1924/5, 1927).
4. [1959] Ch. 363.
5. [1928] A.C. 433, 450; 4 I.L.R. 362 (1928).

privileges and immunities afforded to the head of a mission, his family and servants by the Diplomatic Privileges Act 1964 should be extended to a sovereign or other head of State, the members of his family forming part of his household, and his private servants.

It may be noted that it is expressly provided by s. 20(5) of the Act of 1978 that the section does not affect the sovereign's position with regard to immunity for acts performed in his public capacity, which is governed by Part 1 of the Act. Under s. 14(1) references to a State include references to a sovereign in his public capacity (Chapter 4, paragraph 4.9 above) so that, whereas a sovereign enjoyed complete immunity at common law (subject to the acceptability of the *Trendtex* decision and its applicability to the sovereign in person), his immunity for acts in his public capacity now falls within the restrictive doctrine set out in the Act of 1978, while his immunity for acts not in his public capacity is governed by the liberal régime of the Act of 1964. (See further Chapter 4, paragraph 4.9.)

The Vienna Convention on Diplomatic Relations 1961 (Cmnd. 1368)

13.6 Some of the Articles of the Convention are incorporated into United Kingdom law by the Diplomatic Privileges Act 1964, and these are considered in detail in the next chapter. At this point it will be helpful if the terms of the treaty as a whole are briefly noted. Its scope and success are impressive. It is almost universally regarded as embodying binding international legal rules on diplomatic intercourse between States.

There had been earlier attempts to create a régime in this field, for example the Vienna Regulation of 1815, the Havana Convention of 1928, the Resolution of the Institute of International Law of 1929, and the Harvard Draft Convention of 1932, but none had been anything like as comprehensive as the Convention of 1961, which has itself provided a starting point for other treaties, for example the Vienna Convention on Consular Relations and the New York Convention on Special Missions.

Its gestation (1956-59), a comparatively short period for so extensive an undertaking, was attended by considerable goodwill and co-operation and a great deal of hard work. This almost unique impetus towards international accord is best explained by the fact that the rules had for the most part long been stabilized, at least since their description by Vattel in 1758 in *le Droit des Gens*, and also by the fact that the rights and obligations proposed by the Convention were reciprocal. Every State would get as good as it gave.

13.7 In the preamble the parties

> Recall that peoples of all nations from ancient times have recognized the status of diplomatic agents,
>
> Have in mind the purposes and principles of the Charter of the United Nations concerning the sovereign equality of States, the maintenance of international peace and security, and the promotion of friendly relations among nations,
>
> Believe that an international convention on diplomatic intercourse, privileges and immunities would contribute to the development of friendly relations among nations, irrespective of their differing constitutional and social systems,
>
> Realize that the purpose of such privileges and immunities is not to benefit individuals but to ensure the efficient performance of the functions of diplomatic missions as representing States,
>
> Affirm that the rules of customary international law should continue to govern questions not expressly regulated by the provisions of the Convention.

13.8 Article 1 is the interpretation paragraph, defining "head of the mission", "members of the mission", "members of the staff of the mission", "members of the diplomatic staff", "members of the administrative and technical staff", "members of the service staff", "diplomatic agent", "private servant", and "premises of the mission".

Article 2 states that the establishment of diplomatic relations between States and of permanent diplomatic missions, takes place by mutual consent. So diplomatic relations may exist in the absence of a permanent diplomatic mission, or even of a special mission, for example where no mission has yet been created, or as when the United States, in November 1973, closed their Embassy in Kampala and withdrew all diplomatic and consular representatives from Uganda, making it clear nevertheless that they were not actually severing diplomatic relations.

Article 3 sets out the functions of a diplomatic mission as consisting *inter alia* in

(*a*) representing the sending State in the receiving State;

(*b*) protecting in the receiving State the interests of the sending State and of its nationals, within the limits permitted by international law;

(*c*) negotiating with the Government of the receiving State;

(*d*) ascertaining by all lawful means conditions and developments in the receiving State, and reporting thereon to the Government of the sending State;

(*e*) promoting friendly relations between the sending State and the receiving State, and developing their economic, cultural and scientific relations.

So included therein are, as one would expect, the three traditional functions of diplomatic missions—listed in all the diplomatic handbooks—protection, negotiation and observation.

13.9 Article 4 provides that the sending State must obtain the agrément (approval or consent) of the receiving State to its nomination for the head of the mission, and that reasons for refusal of agrément do not have to be given. The sending State does not have to obtain approval for any other members of the mission (Article 7), save that the receiving State may require that its approval be sought for the appointment of military, naval and air attaches (such appointments may raise security issues for the receiving State).

In its report of January 1985 (House of Commons Paper 127), arising out of the shooting of the woman police constable outside the Libyan People's Bureau the previous April, the Foreign Affairs Committee of the House of Commons regretted the fact that the sending State could freely appoint to the mission, and urged the Foreign Office to find out as much as it could about prospective staff in advance of their arrival and to limit the size of the mission where appropriate (there is power to do this under Article 11). See Appendix 4, part B.

The United Kingdom had observed the practice of agrément since Tsar Nicholas had refused in 1832 to receive

163

the ambassador on the ground that his appointment had been made by Palmerston without prior notice to the Tsar; and, though there were different schools of thought on this, thereafter for a long time the United Kingdom Government expected reasons for any refusal to be specified.

Articles 5 and 6 deal with multiple accreditation. Article 8 provides that members of the diplomatic staff should in principle be of the nationality of the sending State, and appointments of the receiving State's nationals require the consent of that State. Nationals of the receiving State enjoy little in the way of immunity (see the next chapter and Articles 37 and 38).

13.10 Article 9 is important. It gives a State the right to expel or refuse to admit a person on the ground that he or she is *persona non grata* without any obligation to give reasons. The Foreign Affairs Committee were disturbed by the failure of the Government to act under this Article in certain cases and urged them to make it clear to every diplomat that, should he break the criminal law, apart from minor matters, he was likely to be required to leave the country. See Appendix 4, part B.

The term *persona non grata* is applicable to heads of mission or members of the diplomatic staff, "not acceptable" to any other member of the staff.

Article 10 deals with notification of staff appointments and movements. It provides *inter alia* that the Ministry for Foreign Affairs of the receiving State shall be notified of the appointment of members of the mission, their arrival and their final departure or the termination of their functions with the mission. This provision has been considered by the English courts: in *Fenton Textile Association* v. *Krassin*,[6] decided before the days of the Convention, it was made clear that no immunity could be accorded under the Act of 1708 or at common law until the agent had been accepted or received by this country. In *R.* v. *Governor of Pentonville Prison, ex parte Teja*[7] Lord Parker, C.J., said: ". . . certainly in the case of an ambassador it is implicit that he cannot come to this country claiming immunity until his presence has been indicated as

6. (1921) 38 T.L.R. 259; 1 I.L.R. 295 (1921).
7. [1971] 2 Q.B. 274.

persona grata in this country, and the same is true it seems to me of any diplomatic agent of whatever status". And in the recent case of *R. v. Lambeth Justices, ex parte Yusufu, R. v. Governor of Brixton Prison, ex parte Yusufu*[8] the applicant, a Nigerian national, was being held in custody after being committed by examining justices for trial on charges in connection with the kidnapping of the former Nigerian Minister Mr Umaru Dikko. It was argued that the applicant was entitled to diplomatic immunity. He had been issued by the Nigerian Government with a diplomatic passport and had entry clearance to be in the United Kingdom on official business for one month, but the Foreign Office had not been notified of his entry into the United Kingdom as a diplomat, nor had his credentials ever been presented to the Queen. The Divisional Court said that, although Article 10 had not been incorporated into municipal law by the Act of 1964 and so was of evidential value only, it clearly was incumbent on the sending State under international law to comply with it, and if it did not then no question of diplomatic immunity could arise.

Article 11, as we have seen, empowers the receiving State to limit the size of a mission to what the receiving State considers reasonable and normal. This was new law. Problems had been experienced as early as the 17th century, when the prestige of a State was proportional to the magnificence of its mission, but no rules about size had previously been made. It is to be noted that the issue of what is reasonable and normal is determined by the receiving State.

Article 12 prohibits the establishing without consent of offices in locations away from the mission itself. Articles 13–19 are concerned for the most part with protocol.

Article 20 gives the mission and its head the right to use their flag and emblem on the premises of the mission, including the residence of the head of the mission, and on his means of transport. Eileen Denza notes in her excellent volume on the Convention, *Diplomatic Law* (1976), presumably with her tongue in her cheek: "It was stressed by the representative of Yugoslavia that the term 'means of transport', while wide enough to include private boats and planes as well as motor

---

8. (1985) *The Times*, 20 February 1985.

vehicles, did not extend to public transport used by the head of the mission".

Article 21 imposes an obligation on the receiving State to help the mission and its staff acquire suitable accommodation.

Article 22, on the inviolability of the mission premises, is considered in the next chapter as it is incorporated into the Act of 1964.

Articles 22 to 40 are considered in the next chapter as they are incorporated into municipal law by the Act of 1964, with the exception of Article 28, which grants the traditional exemption from taxes to the official fees and charges levied by a mission, and Article 25 which provides that the receiving State shall accord full facilities for the performance of the functions of the mission. This is no more than a statement of general principle and adds nothing to the more specific obligations created by the rest of the Convention. It is too general to support a ground for complaint in the case of a particular alleged breach.

13.11 With a glance at Article 43, which deals with the coming to an end of the function of a diplomatic agent, we come to the important provision that imposes obligations on the diplomatic personnel to respect the laws of the receiving State, not to interfere with its internal affairs, and not to use the premises of the mission in any way incompatible with the proper functions of the mission or rules of general international law. It should be understood that the diplomat is subject to the laws of the receiving State save in so far as those laws specifically exempt him, for example as to taxes or military service. His immunity from most legal process (considered in the next chapter) is not an exemption from liability, merely a procedural bar. For that reason, guarantors and insurers of a diplomat's obligations and liabilities cannot shelter behind his immunity from process.

Finally, Article 42 forbids the diplomatic agent (but not his family) to practise for personal profit in the receiving State any professional or commercial activity. In *Taylor* v. *Best*[9] Jervis, C.J., said: "If an ambassador or public minister, during his residence in this country, violates the character in which he is

9. (1854) 14 C.B. 487, 519.

accorded to our court by engaging in commercial transactions, that may raise a question between the government of this country and that of the country by which he is sent . . .".

The intent of this Article was to ensure that the diplomat would limit his activities to his official duties and avoid the impression that he was using his position to further his private interests. However, some commercial activity of a minor and incidental character, as opposed to the carrying on of a business, is unlikely to be in breach of the provision, and in such a case the diplomat would be subject to civil process under the exception embodied in Article 31(1)(c) (see the next chapter).

13.12 Consular privileges and immunities are found in the Vienna Convention on Consular Relations 1963 (see Chapter 15). For similar immunities reference may also be made to the Convention on Special Missions 1969; the Vienna Convention on the Representation of States in their Relations with International Organizations of a Universal Character 1975; the United Nations Charter 1945; the Convention on the Privileges and Immunities of the Specialized Agencies of the United Nations 1947; the Convention on the Privileges and Immunities of the United Nations 1946; and various bilateral agreements made with international bodies having their headquarters in London, such as the International Maritime Organization (Headquarters Agreement of 1968, Cmnd 3964); the International Sugar Organization (Headquarters Agreement 1969, Cmnd 4127 and 6287); the International Whaling Commission (Headquarters Agreement 1975, Cmnd 6278), and so forth.

The United Kingdom is thus party to many international agreements which provide for the legal status, privileges and immunities of international organizations and their officials. The Charter of the United Nations stipulates that the UN is to have in the territory of each member State such privileges and immunities as are necessary for the fulfilment of its purpose. This functional approach to immunities is reflected also in the stipulation that officials of the United Nations are to enjoy such immunities as are necessary for the independent exercise of their functions (Article 105). These provisions are supplemented by the Conventions above referred to. There also exist agreements covering the status, privileges and immunities of other bodies such as NATO, the EEC and the Council of Europe. (For the receipt of such provisions into municipal law, see for example the International Organizations Act 1968.)

CHAPTER 14

THE DIPLOMATIC PRIVILEGES ACT 1964

14.1 The immunities the subject of this statute were formerly found in the Diplomatic Privileges Act 1708, which, however, was itself merely declaratory of the common law. The common law rules arose, as we have seen, out of the need both to encourage communication between countries and to preserve the dignity and independence of the foreign sovereign.

14.2 On 1 October 1964 the Diplomatic Privileges Act 1964 came into force, giving the force of law to the relevant provisions of the 1961 Vienna Convention on Diplomatic Relations (Cmnd. 1368). The Convention came into force on 24 April 1964. The Act provides a complete code in respect of the privileges and immunities accorded to members of a State's mission, including staff and private servants. It is a subject which, more than most, calls for international agreement. The Act of 1964 may be contrasted with the State Immunity Act 1978 in two respects: first, it incorporates the actual Articles of the Vienna Convention in a Schedule, whereas the Act of 1978 transforms the Articles of the European Convention into sections, altering them substantially in places. Secondly, the Act of 1964 abrogates the common law rules, providing by s. 1 that

"The following provisions of this Act shall, with respect to the matters dealt with therein, have effect in substitution for any previous enactment or rule of law";

whereas the Act of 1978, even in the limited area of its operation, the immunity of the State in most civil proceedings, makes no such statement. In those contexts in which the Act of 1978 does not apply (see Chapter 10) the common law must still be consulted.

Although the High Commissioners of independent

Commonwealth countries and members of their staff fall
under this Act, it does not cover the privileges and immunities
of persons from foreign sovereign States and Commonwealth
countries and the Republic of Ireland attending conferences,
nor those of international organizations and persons
connected therewith, which are governed by the Diplomatic
Immunities (Conferences with Commonwealth Countries and
the Republic of Ireland) Act 1961, and the International
Organizations Act 1968 respectively.

14.3 Two points should be noted here: the status of a person,
i.e. what rank he is, whether he is on and what part of the staff,
is determined by a certificate from the United Kingdom
Secretary of State. Section 4 provides that on any question
whether or not any person is entitled to any privilege or
immunity under the Act such a certificate

> "stating any fact relating to that question shall be conclusive evidence of
> that fact".

Therefore a certificate stating that a person was or was not a
member of the family of a diplomatic agent and formed part of
his household would render inadmissible any contrary
evidence on the point. (See *Kerr* v. *John Mottram Ltd.*[1] *cf, A-G*
v. *Bournemouth Corporation.*[2])

This reproduces the common law rule. In *Engelke* v.
Musmann[3] the House of Lords, reversing the decision of the
Court of Appeal, held that a statement made to the court by the
Attorney-General on the instructions of the Foreign Office as
to the status of a person claiming diplomatic immunity,
whether as ambassador or as a member of his staff, was
conclusive. *Cf.* the position under the State Immunity
Act—see Appendix 4, part A.

Secondly, power is given by s. 3 to limit by Order in Council
the diplomatic immunities accorded to a State's personnel on a
"tit-for-tat" basis, the principle of reciprocity: where a State
accords to United Kingdom diplomatic personnel privileges
less extensive than those the Act accords to the State's agents

1. [1940] Ch. 657.
2. [1902] 2 Ch. 714.
3. [1928] A.C. 433; 4 I.L.R. 362 (1928).

then that State's entitlement under the Act may be limited in such a manner as the Crown thinks proper.

14.4   The Diplomatic Agent

A "diplomatic agent" is, by Article 1, the head of a State's Mission or a member of the staff of a Mission having diplomatic rank. The immunities he enjoys are also accorded to such members of his family as form part of his household provided they are not United Kingdom nationals (Article 37), which means, by s. 2(2), citizens of the United Kingdom and Colonies.

"Members of the family of a diplomatic agent forming part of his household": this is an attempt to define the scope of the immunity sufficiently precisely to avoid dispute. The practice of the United Kingdom Government, upon which the Minister's conclusive certificate for court purposes will be based, is to interpret the words as including the spouse and minor children, i.e. those under 18, and certain other persons in exceptional circumstances, in practice (a) a person who fulfils the social duties of hostess to the diplomatic agent, such as the sister of an unmarried diplomat or the adult daughter of a widowed diplomat; (b) the parent of a diplomat living with him and not engaged in paid employment on a permanent basis; and (c) the child of a diplomat living with him who has attained majority but is not engaged in paid employment on a permanent basis. Students are included here provided they reside with the diplomat at least during vacations.

It should also be borne in mind that, as noted above, by virtue of s. 20(1) of the Act of 1978, the foreign sovereign and members of his household enjoy the same privileges, and moreover, unlike the family of the diplomatic agent, members of the sovereign's household are not disqualified by United Kingdom nationality (s. 20(2)).

14.5 The diplomatic agent enjoys the following immunities (subject to certain exceptions if he is a United Kingdom national or permanently resident here—see paragraph 14.15).

171

Inviolability of person

(i) The person of a diplomatic agent is inviolable. He is not liable to any form of arrest or detention.

Less specifically, it is also provided that the United Kingdom must treat him with due respect and must take all appropriate steps to prevent any attack on his person, freedom or dignity (Article 29).

This inviolability of the diplomat is the oldest established and the most fundamental rule of diplomatic law. Even if conspiring against the monarch he could not be tried and punished, merely expelled. Although writers have long maintained that there is a right of self-defence against immediate threat of violence from a diplomat (which might have been invoked had the assassin in the Libyan People's Bureau in St James's Square in April 1984 constituted a continuing threat) there does not appear to have been any instance where a State has relied on such a right.

The duty to protect the diplomat is particularly relevant in a time where he is so often threatened and affected by terrorist acts. Feeling ran so high at one time that the Assembly of the United Nations in 1973 approved a Convention on the Prevention and Punishment of Crimes against Internationally Protected Persons, under which the signatories are obliged to make the murder, kidnapping or other attack on a diplomat "punishable by appropriate penalties which take into account their grave nature".

What are "appropriate steps" in any case is best decided by co-operation between the affected States. It may be appropriate to yield to demands, to stall for time, to bargain, to reject demands, or to take offensive action, depending on the situation.

14.6

Inviolability of property

(ii) His private residence, and his papers and correspondence, are inviolable. So, subject to (vi) below, is his property. United Kingdom agents (which by s. 2(2) include any constable and anyone exercising a power of entry to premises under any enactment) may not enter his residence and consent and all appropriate steps must be taken to protect it against intrusion or damage and to prevent disturbance to its peace or impairment of its dignity. (Articles 30, 22.)

The definition provision, Article 1, provides that the premises of the Mission include the residence of the head of the Mission, so that Article 30(1), which gives the private residence of the diplomatic agent the same inviolability and protection as the Mission premises is unnecessary in his case. But as diplomatic agent includes any member of the diplomatic staff of the Mission, under Article 1, this protection is extended by Article 30 to a diplomat who is not in fact the head of the Mission.

It was said in *Agbor v. Metropolitan Police Commissioner*[4] that Article 30 only enables the police to defend the premises against intruders, not to evict without prior application to the court someone in occupation under a claim of right.

The inviolability accorded to the diplomat's papers and correspondence goes beyond the archives and documents of the Mission, which are protected by Article 24 (see below), and applies to all his personal and other correspondence. Presumably it is not a breach of this provision if his post is electronically scrutinized for letter-bombs, thought it were best to seek his consent in advance. However, it does mean that in an action in respect of commercial activities for which he has no immunity (see below) the court could not order disclosure against him.

On the question what interest a diplomat must have in property before it can be regarded as his for the purposes of the Article, reference may be made to *The Amazone*,[5] an action for the possession of the yacht of a diplomatic agent. The court said that the immunity accorded to a diplomat's property was not confined to undisputed property, but extended to property of which the diplomat was clearly in possession.

The United Kingdom Government takes the view that in respect of a diplomat's car that is causing an obstruction complete inviolability is not to be accorded. The official cars of

4. [1969] 1 W.L.R. 703; 52 I.L.R. 382 (1969).
5. [1940] P. 40 (C.A.); 9 I.L.R. 417 (1939).

the Mission are only accorded immunity from "search, requisition, attachment or execution" (Article 22(3)), and it would be strange if the private car of the diplomat enjoyed greater protection. Therefore such a vehicle will be towed away, although no charge may be made for recovery. "Clamping" is regarded as penal, and so contrary to Article 31.1, and has been discontinued since December 1983.

14.7

Jurisdiction of the courts

(iii) He is immune from our criminal jurisdiction (Article 31).

The immunity of an ambassador from the criminal jurisdiction of the receiving State was, after inviolability, the earliest of the basic rules of diplomatic law to be established. The view of the public, until recently, tended to be that our parking laws were blatantly flouted by most Missions and that occasionally there were more serious infringements of the criminal law. It is true that in 1983, for example, over 100,000 fixed penalty notices were cancelled on the ground of diplomatic immunity whereas offences of violence in respect of which immunity has precluded prosecution average about four a year, offences under the Theft Act, including shoplifting, about 20, and with regard to drug offences there have been only two instances in the last five years. However, what should be borne in mind is that the overwhelming majority of the diplomatic community are law-abiding. A very small number of Missions are responsible for most of the parking offences, and even they have the excuse that parking may be difficult in the vicinity of the Mission and the Convention can be interpreted so as to lay on the receiving State the duty, by way of facilitating the performance of the Mission's functions under Article 25, of providing parking. A number of Embassies investgate parking tickets and pay them if they were not unavoidably incurred on official business.

The murder of WPC Fletcher in April 1984 by a shot fired from within the Libyan People's Bureau in St James's Square, and the discovery of Dr Dikko at Stansted airport, drugged and crated for export, have focused the attention of the public on the more serious consequences of this immunity. But the clamour to bring the perpetrators to justice, though eminently understandable, does not take into account the political exigencies. The safety of United Kingdom nationals in less civilized lands, where we are obliged to maintain a presence for political or commercial reasons, is likely to be imperilled if we sought to curtail the full extent of the traditional immunity accorded under the Convention. Nor is it advisable to seek to amend the Convention so as to restrict immunity, because as the United Kingdom Government indicated in their evidence to the House of Commons Foreign Affairs Committee (1985 Commons Paper 127), any attempt to alter the fabric of agreement would be likely to create chaos. See Appendix 4, part B.

14.8

(iv) He is immune from our civil and administrative jurisdiction except in

  (a) a 'real' action relating to private premises in the United Kingdom, unless he holds them on behalf of his State for the purposes of the Mission;
  (b) succession, in which he is involved as executor, administrator, heir or legatee, as a private person and not on behalf of his State;
  (c) any professional or commercial activity he follows in the United Kingdom outside his official functions.
  (Article 31(1).)

The immunity from civil process was established later than that from criminal jurisdiction. Lord Hewart, C.J., said in *Dickinson* v. *Del Solar*:[6] "Diplomatic privilege does not import immunity from legal liability but only exemption from local jurisdiction". The court there held that an insurer cannot take advantage of the privileged position of a diplomatic client to refuse to pay either on the ground that a waiver of immunity amounted to a breach of a condition in the insurance contract or on the ground that there was no legal liability giving rise to

6. [1930] 1 K.B. 376; 5 I.L.R. 299 (1929).

an obligation to indemnify. Nevertheless, the Foreign Office obtains from all authorized motor insurers an assurance that they will not attempt to rely on a client's immunity nor require him to plead it.

Where proceedings are contemplated the FCO is prepared to let parties know informally whether the defendant has diplomatic status, and then his Government can be asked if they are willing to waive his immunity. If proceedings are already begun, the defendant may ignore them or enter a conditional appearance (acknowledgment of service under protest). The court may then request a formal certificate under s. 4 (see above 14.3). The certificate will be confined to matters peculiarly within the Minister's knowledge, such as the notification by sending States of appointments made; questions of law, such as whether a diplomat is disqualified from immunity under Article 38 through permanent residence in the United Kingdom will be decided by the court.

As to exception (a): it had long been accepted that the home State retained in principle jurisdiction over immovable property situated within its boundaries (*cf.* the attitude of the common law in the context of State immunity, see Chapter 6E), but it was not clear, nor is it now clear under the Convention, (but see below for a United Kingdom court's view) to what extent this principle applied to the principle private residence of a diplomat who is not the head of the Mission. A Polish court said in 1925: "Municipal courts have jurisdiction in regard to the private immovable property of a public minister, except in regard to such immovable property as is devoted to the official use of the Embassy or legation".[7] In 1932 a German court said: "The immunity of an extraterritorial person from the jurisdiction of the receiving State was without effect in an action *in rem* concerning real property owned by such person and situated in the territory of the receiving State".[8] In 1950 a New York court said: "There appears to be no doubt that real property held by diplomatic officers in a foreign State, and not pertaining to their diplomatic status, is subject to local laws".[9] This principle was echoed by the Supreme Restitution Court

7. *Annual Digest of Public International Law Cases* 1925–26, 324–325.
8. *Ibid.*, 1931–32 179.
9. *Agostini* v. *de Antveno*, 17 I.L.R. 295, 298 (1950).

for Berlin in 1959,[10] which recognized immunity in respect of "the Embassy buildings and Embassy precincts", those words embracing "the Embassy buildings used by foreign States to house their diplomatic representatives" and buildings "used by the ambassador or his staff for recuperative or recreational or similar purposes".

In *Intpro Properties* v. *Sauvel and the French Government*[11] the plaintiffs had let premises to the French Government for occupation by the Embassy's Financial Counsellor. The diplomat would not let the landlord in to effect repairs, and the latter sought an order requiring the diplomat to permit entry and damages against the Government. The involvement of the State is considered above in Chapter 6E. As far as the diplomat was concerned, the trial judge accorded immunity on the ground that this was not a "real" action. A "real" action has in fact been unknown to English law since the Middle Ages, but it appears from the commentators that "action réelle" in the original text of the Convention is an action where the ownership or possession of land is in question, and therefore it would be straining the meaning to say that a claim to effect repairs, as opposed to one to take over possession of the premises, was a real action. Denza states at page 160: "the essence of the term 'real action' is that the relief sought is either a declaration of title to the property, an order for sale by authority of the court, or an order for possession. The term is used in the sense of an action *in rem*, and the action *in rem* is given the sense which it has in many civil law jurisdictions which, unlike the English law, allow proceedings *in rem* in respect of immovable property".

By the time of the Court of Appeal hearing the diplomat had vacated and the Government had handed over the keys, so the claim for damages was all that was left. But the court did say, in the context of diplomatic immunity, that, had the diplomat himself been the tenant rather than the State, he could not have been said to have been holding the property for the purposes of the Mission. This conclusion would appear not to be consistent with the approach of the Berlin court. The court also pointed out that no order could have been made against the diplomat

10. *Tietz* v. *People's Republic of Bulgaria*, 28 I.L.R. 369 *et seq.* (1959).
11. [1983] Q.B. 1019; 64 I.L.R. 363, 384 (1982/3).

requiring him to permit the landlord to enter in view of the inviolability of his residence under Article 30.

As to exception (c): this may be compared with the denial of immunity to States in respect of commercial transactions under s. 3 of the State Immunity Act and in respect of commercial activities under the United States Foreign Sovereign Immunities Act (see Chapter 6A). This exception was not recognized in English law before the Diplomatic Privileges Act despite the fact that many other jurisdictions had recognized such a rule at international level and some had even legislated for it. But in *Taylor* v. *Best*[12] Jervis, C.J., said that the immunity was not forfeited when an ambassador or public minister engaged in trade, though it would be for an ambassador's servant. And in *Magdalena Steam Navigation Co.* v. *Martin*[13] Lord Campbell, C.J., said: "It certainly has not hitherto been expressly decided that a public minister duly accorded to the Queen by a foreign State is privileged from all liability to be sued here in civil actions; but we think that this follows from well established principles, and we give judgment for the defendant".

"It is clear that the ideas of remuneration and of a *continuous* activity are central to the purpose of Article 31(1)(*c*). Although the provision is drafted in unnecessarily wide terms it is not intended to cover commercial contracts incidental to the ordinary conduct of life in the receiving State" (Denza, at page 166). In this regard it is substantially different from the exception to state immunity, which applies to any contract that involves a commercial transaction.

14.9

(v) He is not a compellable witness in any proceedings (Article 31(2)).

It was clear at a very early stage that the diplomat's inviolability meant that he could not be obliged to give evidence. When the Dutch Government refused in 1856 to permit their Minister to give evidence of a homicide he had

12. (1854) 14 C.B. 487.
13. (1859) 2 El. & El. 94.

witnessed in Washington, the United States Government was so put out that it required that the diplomat he recalled to the Netherlands. In 1864, when it was intended to subpoena the French ambassador in England, the law officers advised that compulsion was out of the question.

The sending State may waive the immunity and permit their diplomat to testify, but he is not obliged to even in those cases, listed above, where he is not in fact immune from civil suit. There are no facilities in United Kingdom law whereby the evidence of a diplomat can be given in any different form from that available to the ordinary compellable witness; but they exist in some jurisdictions, and the United Kingdom Government sometimes takes advantage of them, particularly where the evidence may relate to official functions (in other cases the diplomat is generally permitted by the Government to give evidence in the ordinary way).

14.10

(vi) No measures of execution may be taken in respect of a diplomatic agent except in the cases stated above at (iv) (a), (b) and (c): in such cases his property is not inviolable, but any measures taken must not infringe the inviolability of his person or his residence (Article 30(3)).

This may be compared with the provisions of the State Immunity Act whereby execution is only permitted against property of a State used for commercial purposes and that in limited circumstances (see Chapter 9, paragraph 9.16).

Article 31 also provides, in accordance with customary international law, that the diplomat is not immune from the jurisdiction of his own State. But it is unlikely that it will profit the plaintiff to mount an action in the foreign courts against a defendant upon whom it may well in any event be difficult to effect service. The more realistic course where the claim attracts immunity is to ask the Foreign Office to intercede. As explained in their Report on Diplomatic Immunity presented to Parliament in 1952 the United Kingdom Government does not see the immunity as doing any more than protecting the sending State in respect of its official business. Therefore in other cases they will ask for a waiver or suggest a private arbitration, and if those are refused they may require the diplomat to be recalled. In practice they seek to produce a settlement at an early stage, having satisfied themselves that the claim is *prima facie* properly brought, and it is in this way that most cases brought to their attention are resolved. This is in accord with the Resolution on the consideration of civil claims adopted by the Vienna Conference recommending "that the sending State should waive the immunity of members of its diplomatic Mission in respect of civil claims of persons in the receiving State when this can be done without impeding the performance of the functions of the Mission, and that, when immunity is not waived, the sending State should use its best endeavours to bring about a just settlement of the claims".

14.11

Taxes, etc.

(vii) The diplomatic agent is exempt from all United Kingdom dues or taxes, personal or real, national, regional or municipal, except:

- (a) indirect taxes normally incorporated in the price of goods or services (e.g. he must pay V.A.T. to the builder);
- (b) taxes on private premises, unless held for his State and for the purposes of the Mission;
- (c) estate, succession or inheritance duties (but, by Article 39(4) such duties may not be levied on movable property on the death of a member of the Mission or his family where such property is in the United Kingdom solely due to the deceased's presence here);
- (d) taxes on private income arising here and capital taxes on commercial investments here;
- (e) charges levied for specific services rendered;
- (f) various fees, including stamp duty, on land (but by Article 23 the head of the Mission is exempt from all taxes on the Mission premises except such as represent payment for specific services rendered) (Article 34).

There is considerable scope for debate on the precise ambit of these provisions in the context of the different tax structures created by States, but as interest in the matter is virtually confined to the revenue authorities it is not proposed to do more here than refer the reader to some relevant English authorities (a full treatment of the argument can be found in Denza at page 194 *et seq.*).

In regard to the liability to pay rates reference may be made to *Parkinson* v. *Potter*[14] and *Macartney* v. *Garbutt*[15] where it was assumed that if it were shown that the diplomat was entitled to immunity under the Act of 1708 he was therefore a person "not liable to pay such rate".

It was said in *Novello* v. *Toogood*:[16] "whatever is necessary to the convenience of an ambassador, as connected with his rank, his duties or his religion, ought to be granted". But it did not follow that a servant of the ambassador who carried on business as a lodging-house keeper was entitled to be exempt from rates in respect of the lodging-house.

14.12

(viii) The diplomatic agent is exempt from social security provisions with respect to services rendered for his State.

He must conform to social security provisions in respect of those he employs, but private servants in his sole employ are excepted if they are not United Kingdom nationals or permanently resident here and are covered by another State's social security provisions (Article 33).

By s. 2(4) these exemptions do not apply in respect of insurable employment or where contributions are required under certain enactments relating to National Insurance.

14.13

Public services

(ix) The diplomatic agent is exempt from all personal services,

14. (1885–6) 16 Q.B.D. 152.
15. (1890) 24 Q.B.D. 368.
16. (1823) 1 B. & C. 554.

from all public service of any kind, and from military obligations such as those connected with requisitioning, military contributions and billeting (Article 35).

He will not find himself called up! Nor will he be required to serve on a jury.

14.14

Baggage

(x) (a) Articles for his personal use, or his family's, or for the official use of the Mission, must be allowed into the United Kingdom free of all charges (except for storage, cartage and similar services).

(b) His baggage may not be inspected, unless there are serious grounds for presuming it contains articles not of the above-mentioned sort or illegal articles or ones subject to quarantine. He or his representative has a right to be present at any inspection (Article 36).

The reservation of the right to inspect suspected parcels must be seen as an exception to the inviolability accorded to the diplomat's property under Article 30 (see above), and the distinction between this context, that of the diplomat's personal baggage, and that of the diplomatic bag should be noted. As explained below, it has been for a long time a moot point whether the diplomatic bag may be electronically scanned when suspected, or requested to be opened and in the event of refusal rejected.

14.15

An important exception

A diplomatic agent who is a United Kingdom national or permanently resident here enjoys under the Act only immunity from jurisdiction, and inviolability, in respect of official acts performed in the exercise function (Article 38(1)).

This exception does not apply to the foreign sovereign or other head of State or members of his household (State Immunity Act, s. 20(2)), who therefore do not lose any immunities by being United Kingdom nationals or permanently resident here.

Whether a national of the receiving State was thereby disqualified from immunity was a moot point among the older writers. In *Macartney* v. *Garbutt*[17] it was held that he was not, unless at the time of his reception it had been made a condition of his acceptance that he should not be entitled to privileges or immunities. However, United Kingdom nationals in diplomatic Missions were deprived of immunities by the Diplomatic Immunities (Commonwealth Countries and the Republic of Ireland) Act 1952 and the Diplomatic Immunities Restriction Act 1955.

It can be seen that the immunity afforded under the Convention is a narrow one. It is only in respect of the official acts themselves that it is accorded. So if, for example, a diplomat is involved in a motor accident when travelling on official business, immunity would not be attracted.

One class of United Kingdom national does not lose comprehensive immunity: members of Commonwealth Missions in London who are also United Kingdom nationals are treated as if they had only the nationality of the sending State (Diplomatic Privileges (Citizens of the United Kingdom and Colonies) Order 1964).

Much more problematic is the question whether a diplomat is permanently resident here. This has created difficulty, particularly in the case of women members of a Mission married to Englishmen and remaining in the United Kingdom for longer than the normal five-year tour. The Foreign Office explained the view it took in a circular sent to missions in 1969. The test is normally whether or not the diplomat would be in the United Kingdom but for the requirements of the sending State. In applying that test considerations are: (a) the intention of the individual—whether he intends to move on when his appointment ends, what are his links with the sending State, e.g. payment of taxes, participation in social security schemes,

17. *Supra*, fn. 15.

ownership of immovable property, payment of return passage by the sending State; (b) if his appointment has continued or is likely to continue for more than five years he will be regarded as permanently resident here, unless the Head of the Mission states that the extended stay is due to state and not personal reasons; (c) a person who is locally engaged is normally presumed to be permanently resident here; a woman member of a mission married to a permanent resident of the United Kingdom is normally presumed, in the absence of contrary indications from the Head of the Mission, to be staying in the United Kingdom permanently.

14.16   Staff of the Mission

(i) The administrative and the technical staff of the Mission (that means by Article 1, staff employed in the administrative or technical service of the Mission), and such members of their family as form part of their household, enjoy, unless they are United Kingdom nationals or permanently resident here, all the immunities listed above for the diplomatic agent under numerals (ii) to (ix), with the exception that the immunity from our civil administration (numeral (iv) above) does not extend to acts performed outside the course of their duties. They also enjoy a limited privilege in respect of the importation of baggage, in that they have the privilege set out at (x) (a) above in respect of articles imported at the time of first installation (Article 37(2)).

The practice of States about according privileges to the staff of the mission had been extremely varied and it was not easy to get agreement on this issue at the Convention. Some States, mostly those who argued for limiting the immunity of administrative and technical staff, made reservations about this Article on ratifying the Convention, but those reservations were treated by others, including the United Kingdom and the United States, as invalid. In practice problems have not arisen since. 'Outside the course of their duties" is clearly wider than the phrase in Article 38, "official acts performed in the exercise of his functions" (see above). It would in this context not be right to deny immunity in respect of a traffic accident arising when the vehicle was on the way to an official engagement.

In *Empson* v. *Smith*[18] the Court of Appeal said that the issue was whether acts done in relation to the tenancy of a private residence were done outside the course of official duties and the case was sent back to the County Court for that issue to be decided.

14.17

(ii) Members of the service staff of the Mission (that means, by Article 1, staff in the domestic service of the Mission) enjoy, if they are not United Kingdom nationals or permanently resident here,

(a) immunity in respect of acts performed in the course of their duties;
(b) exemption from dues and taxes on their wages ("the emolument they receive by reason of their employment");
(c) the social security exemption of Article 33 (see numeral (viii) above) (Article 37(3)).

14.18

(iii) Private servants of members of the Mission (that means, by Article 1, persons who are in the domestic service of the head of the Mission or any member of the staff and who are not employees of the sending State) are, if not United Kingdom nationals or permanently resident here, exempt from dues and taxes on their wages. No other immunity need be accorded them. However, the United Kingdom must exercise jurisdiction over them in such a manner as not to interfere unduly with the performance of the functions of the Mission (Article 37(4)).

Private servants in the sole employ of a diplomatic agent are exempt from United Kingdom social security provisions

18. [1966] 1 Q.B. 426; 41 I.L.R. 407 (1965).

provided they are not United Kingdom nationals or permanently resident here and are covered by the social security provisions of another State (Article 33(2)). By s. 2(4) this exemption does not apply in respect of insurable employment or where contributions are required under certain enactments relating to National Insurance.

14.19   *Exception*

Members of the administrative, technical and service staff, and private servants of members of the Mission, who are United Kingdom nationals or permanently resident here are not entitled to any immunity. However, jurisdiction must be exercised over them in such a manner as not to interfere unduly with the performance of the functions of the Mission (Article 38(2)).

The private servants of a foreign sovereign or other head of State do not, however, lose their privileges (listed immediately above at numeral (iii)) by being United Kingdom nationals or permanently resident here (State Immunity Act 1978, s. 20(2)).

14.20   The Mission

(i) The premises of the Mission are inviolable. The premises of the Mission are, by Article 1, the buildings or parts of buildings and the land ancillary thereto, irrespective of ownership, used for the purposes of the Mission including the residence of the head of the Mission.

The agents of the United Kingdom (which, by s. 2(2), includes any constable and anyone exercising a power of entry under any enactment) may not enter the premises of the Mission without the consent of the head of the Mission. The United Kingdom is under a special duty to take all appropriate steps to protect the premises of the Mission against any intrusion or damage and to prevent any disturbance of the peace of the Mission or impairment of its dignity (Article 22(1), (2)).

The premises of the Mission, and their furnishings, and other property thereon, and the means of transport of the

Mission, are immune from search, requisition, attachment or execution (Article 22(3)).

Article 22 embodies two aspects of inviolability, the restraints placed upon the receiving State as to jurisdiction over the Mission premises and the obligation imposed upon it to preserve the integrity of the premises from encroachment. Although no official act by the receiving State may be done in the premises without the consent of the Mission they are not to be thought of as extra-territorial. Crimes committed there remain crimes committed within the jurisdiction (see, among many examples, of the inapplicability of the supposed doctrine of extraterritoriality, *Radwan* v. *Radwan*[19] and *Tietz* v. *People's Republic of Bulgaria*[20]).

14.20.1 English law was slow to give effect to the inviolability rule. In 1896 in the case of Sun Yat Sen[21] some change was evident when the court refused a writ of *habeas corpus* in respect of a Chinese political refugee who was being imprisoned in the Chinese legation. In *Dass* v. *Rennie*,[22] it was held that the offence of obstructing a police officer in the execution of his duty could be committed on the premises of a diplomatic Mission even though the police had not been called for by the Mission or any request made for the removal of the offender. In *Kamara* v. *DPP*[23] the House of Lords dismissed the appeal of defendants who had been convicted of conspiracy to effect a public mischief when they occupied the High Commission of Sierra Leone on political grounds. Under s. 9 of the Criminal Law Act 1977 it is an offence punishable with imprisonment to trespass on the premises of a diplomatic Mission (or on consular premises) or premises which are the private residence of a diplomatic agent. A certificate from the Home Secretary is conclusive as to whether premises are diplomatic premises, etc., but proceedings may not be instituted without the consent of the Attorney-General.

---

19. [1973] Fam. 24; 55 I.L.R. 579 (1972).
20. 28 I.L.R. 369 (1959).
21. (1896) *Revue Generale du Droit International Publique* 693.
22. *The Times*, 9 February 1961.
23. [1974] A.C. 104.

14.20.2 As it was clear that there existed substantial differences of opinion on the question of how far, if at all, diplomatic premises should or could be used to give political asylum the matter was dropped from the agenda at the Vienna Conference and remains unresolved. It was similarly impossible, particularly in view of opposition from Communist States, to write in any exception from inviolability for the case of emergencies. When in 1973 the Pakistan Government insisted, despite protests, on searching the Iraqi Embassy they were able to justify their conduct and take strong diplomatic action when a large quantity of arms was found in crates on the premises.

14.20.3 Again, no agreement was reached on the question whether Mission premises could properly be expropriated on the ground of public interest. When the Fleet Line underground railway was being constructed the usual compulsory purchase procedures were not followed in respect of the land beneath Mission premises, but consent was sought at a diplomatic level.

14.20.4 Two questions that exercised the minds of the Foreign Affairs Committee of the House of Commons who, during 1984, prepared a report on the abuse of diplomatic privilege (arising out of the shooting of the woman police officer from within the Libyan People's Bureau in St James's Square) were: when did inviolability begin and when should it be deemed to end, and how far did the duty to protect the premises from, e.g. demonstrations, extend? The Committee concluded that the duty to protect the Mission could not be given so wide an interpretation as to require the Mission to be insulated from expressions of public opinion within the receiving State. Provided always that work at the Mission could continue normally, that there was untrammelled access and egress, and that those in the Mission were never in fear that the Mission might be damaged or its staff injured, that was enough.

14.20.5 In the case of *R. v. Roques*, heard in the Bow Street Magistrates' Court on 15 June 1984, the court took the view, in respect of an anti-apartheid demonstration outside South

Africa House, that impairment of the dignity of a Mission required abusive or insulting behaviour and that political demonstrations did not in themselves amount to such.

14.20.6 The Committee suggested that the Government could have been slower to grant or permit to continue diplomatic status in respect of the premises in St James's Square in the months before the incident, particularly as the Libyan Government had failed to nominate a head of Mission. But once the status had been given, the Committee said, the use of the premises for unlawful purposes did not justify the termination of inviolability, nor was there any principle of self-defence which would have permitted the police to enter after the shooting. (But it is submitted that, had more shooting been imminent, entry could properly have been effected.)

14.20.7 The practice of the United Kingdom Government is to regard premises as having diplomatic status from the time when they are placed at the disposal of the Mission, as long as all necessary planning consents have been obtained and there is the intention to use the premises for the purposes of the Mission once any building works undertaken have been completed. That a remote or antique intention to use the premises for the purposes of a Mission will not suffice is illustrated by the Berlin cases reported in 28 I.L.R. 369 *et seq.* (in one the Government of Bulgaria conceded that "the mere purchase of real property for ambassadorial purposes did not suffice to found its extraterritoriality, but that it was founded only when the property was in fact used for diplomatic purposes").

14.20.8 Paragraph 3 does not preclude the towing away of diplomatic vehicles where that is necessary (it does not say "immune from any other form of interference", for example, as does the United Nations Convention on Immunities). But, as Denza explains at page 90, this is only done where the driver proves unfindable, serious obstruction is being caused and there is no nearby location to which the car may be taken. In any event no charges are made for its reclamation.

14.20.9 The Convention does not tell us whether legal action in respect of the Mission premises not involving search, requisition, attachment or execution is permitted. The German Federal Constitutional Court said, in the *Jurisdiction over Yugoslav Military Mission (Germany)* case[24] that there was no general rule of international law precluding jurisdiction in all cases concerning Mission premises, and that jurisdiction could be exercised where that would not interfere with the performance of diplomatic functions. In that case, an action for rectification of the land register, no interference with such functions would arise. But as the diplomatic agent is immune from civil suit in an action relating to Mission premises (see above) it seems unlikely that the English court would hold that in respect of premises in the name of the sending State itself the immunity was less comprehensive.

14.20.10 (ii) The sending State (and the head of the Mission) are exempt from all national, regional or municipal dues and taxes in respect of the premises of the Mission, whether owned or leased, other than such as represent payment for specific services rendered (Article 23).

14.20.11 (iii) The archives and documents of the Mission are inviolable at any time and wherever they may be (Article 24).

Though the immunity of the diplomatic bag was an old tradition it was only by the Vienna Convention that it was finally established that archives which were not on the Mission premises, not manifestly of a diplomatic character and not in diplomatic custody were nevertheless entitled to immunity. In *Rose* v. *The King*[25] papers that had been stolen from the Soviet Embassy were admitted as evidence by a Canadian court in the trial of a Canadian national for spying (the Soviet Government did not intervene).

The immunity, on the wording of the provision, is not affected by the termination of the Mission ("at any time"), nor, as already indicated, by where they may be found ("wherever they may be").

"Archives" is a term not here defined, but reference may

24. 38 I.L.R. 162 (1962).
25. [1947] 3 D.L.R. 618.

sensibly be made to the definition of consular archives (see below at 15.8). If the advent of the new technology creates articles of record that seem not on the face of it to be covered by the wording "archives and documents", such as software, laserdiscs, holographic material or whatever the future holds for us, one can expect that a court would reach a decision that reflected the spirit of the Article rather than its letter.

14.20.12 (iv) The fees and charges levied by the Mission in the course of its official duties are exempt from all dues and taxes (Article 28).

14.21 Communications

The United Kingdom must permit and protect the free communication of the Mission for all official purposes. The Mission may use secret codes, couriers, and all appropriate means for its official communications, but needs the United Kingdom's consent to the use of a wireless transmitter (Article 27(1)).

All correspondence relating to the Mission and its functions is inviolable (Article 27(2)).

The diplomatic bag must be clearly marked as such and must not contain anything except diplomatic documents and articles intended for official use (Article 27(4)).

It may not be opened or detained (Article 27(3)).

What does Article 27(2) add to the protection given to the archives and documents of a Mission by Article 24. *Pace* Denza (page 124) it is submitted that this provision must cover all correspondence addressed to the Mission (as well of course as that coming from it). It must be presumed that letters sent to the Mission relate in one way or another to the Mission or its functions. So although the original proposal to the Conference was such as to cover only outward bound material it is clear that inward mail is protected from interference, including use without consent as evidence in court.

14.21.1 Abuse of the diplomatic bag is today a serious problem. The customary practice was that a bag about which suspicions had arisen had to be withdrawn by the sender if unwilling to comply with a request from the receiving State to open it in the presence of a member of the Mission. But this Article makes no such concession. It has been generally recognized that upon accession to the treaty a State had then the right to make a reservation to itself of the customary rule. Kuwait did so in 1969 and Libya in 1977, but it has never yet been taken advantage of. The issue became of prime importance in this country after the appearance of arms in the hands of Libyan personnel and the discovery of the boxed Nigerian, Dr Dikko, at Stansted. There is a division of opinion as to whether it is a breach of the provision to subject the bag to electronic screening. The United Kingdom Government, with our tradition of literal interpretation behind them, take the view that that is not proscribed by a rule which forbids opening, but other observers, such as the Bulgarian Special Rapporteur at the International Law Commission, opine that any technique for finding out what is in the bag is in breach of the spirit of the Article. In any event, even if such screening was able to disclose the possibility of the misuse there would be a problem what then to do, as the United Kingdom made no such reservation as is mentioned above when it signed the treaty. So the position remains unclear and for that reason unsatisfactory.

The bag must be marked as such. The Nigerian crate containing Dr Dikko was not, and therefore could properly be opened, fortunately for the occupant. But about the dimensions of the bag nothing is specified; it would however, *pace* the USSR, seem somewhat over the top to present a State with a container lorry.

14.21.2 The diplomatic courier must be protected by the United Kingdom in the performance of his functions: he enjoys personal inviolability and is not liable to any form of arrest or detention (Article 27(5)).

Diplomatic couriers may be appointed *ad hoc*, in which case their immunity ceases when they have delivered the bag to the consignee. The airline pilot to whom a diplomatic bag is entrusted is not a diplomatic courier of any description, and an airline is entitled to refuse to carry a package, whether accompanied by a courier or not, if it is refused to be offered for screening (see Article 27(6) and (7)).

14.22   Waiver

Under Article 32 immunity may be waived by the sending State in respect of its personnel. The waiver must be express, and a waiver of immunity from jurisdiction does not in itself amount to a waiver of immunity from execution, for which a separate waiver is necessary (compare the similar position for State immunity, Chapter 9, paragraph 9.17). By s. 2(3) the waiver may be made by the head of the Mission or his deputy.

The immunity is granted to the sending State in respect of its agents, and it is only the State that can waive it. Waiver without authority is ineffective and cannot be retrospective (see *R.* v. *Madan*[26]). An undertaking by State or agent that immunity will be waived if dispute arises, e.g. in a lease, is of no legal effect, as is the position at common law for sovereign immunity (see above at 8.1, and *Empson* v. *Smith*[27]).

As an example of the process of waiver, we may note that the Foreign and Commonwealth Office recently asked Zambia to waive immunity in respect of a diplomat in whose residence a substantial quanity of heroin was found, and waiver was accordingly made.

Where a person initiates proceedings he submits to any counterclaim directly connected with the principal claim (*cf.* the State Immunity Act, s. 2(6)). In *High Commissioner for India* v. *Ghosh*[28] a claim for money due or damages was held not to compel submission to a counterclaim for defamation.

14.23   Period of immunity

This begins when the person entitled enters the United Kingdom to take up his post, or, if he is already here, when his

26. [1961] 2 Q.B. 1; 33 I.L.R. 368 (1961).
27. [1966] 1 Q.B. 426; 41 I.L.R. 407 (1965) *per* Diplock, L.J.
28. [1960] 1 Q.B. 134; 28 I.L.R. 150 (1959).

appointment is notified to the Foreign and Commonwealth Office (Article 39(1), s. 2(2)).

In *R. v. Governor of Pentonville Prison, ex parte Teja*,[29] where a non-accredited commercial agent of the Costa Rican Government argued that he was entitled to immunity as a person on a diplomatic mission, Lord Parker said that to gain immunity an agent must have been "in some form accepted or received by this country". The condition of acceptance does not however seem to accord with the words of the Article.

In *R. v. Lambeth Justices, ex parte Yusufu*[30] the Divisional Court said that this provision was merely procedural and did not serve to confer immunity on a person not otherwise entitled to it (which is clearly correct).

Article 40 provides for the according of immunity to a diplomat passing through a third State on the way between his post and his home country. This provision has been considered in the above case and in *R. v. Governor of Pentonville Prison, ex parte Teja*[31]; in both cases it was held that there was no basis of fact for concluding that the conditions for according immunity in this context were satisfied.

Proceedings pending against a person when he becomes first entitled to immunity cannot be pursued further without a waiver being made after that date (see *Ghosh* v. *d'Rozario*[32]).

When his functions end, his immunity ceases when he leaves the United Kingdom, or after a reasonable period in which to do so, but immunity continues in respect of any acts he performs in the exercise of his functions as a member of the Mission (Article 39(2)).

The customary rule, embodied in the Convention, meant that in respect of non-official acts done during the period he enjoyed immunity a diplomat could be sued here after a reasonable time had elapsed since the termination of his appointment (see *Magdalena Steam Navigation Co.* v. *Martin*,[33] *Musurus Bey* v. *Gadban*[34] and *In re Suarez*).[35] In

---

29. [1971] 2 Q.B. 274.
30. *The Times*, 20 February 1985.
31. *Supra*, fn. 29.
32. [1962] 2 All E.R. 640; 33 I.L.R. 361 (1962).
33. (1859) 2 El. & El. 94.
34. [1894] 2 Q.B. 352.
35. [1918] 1 Ch. 176.

Empson v. *Smith*[36] the Court of Appeal made it clear that, on termination of diplomatic status for whatever reason, any subsisting action that had had to be stayed on the ground of the defendant's immunity could be revived (*cf*. the approach of the French court in *Foucault de Mondion* v. *Tcheng-Ki-Tong*).[37]

"A reasonable period": this has varied from court to court and case to case. It will obviously depend on the particular facts of the case. In *In re Suarez* (*supra*) one month was allowed, and that is the period laid down for United Kingdom fiscal purposes.

The agent cannot be sued at any time in respect of official acts because that would be tantamount to suing his Government (see *Zoernsch* v. *Waldock*[38]).

On his death his family retain their privileges until the expiry of a reasonable period in which to leave the country (Article 39(3)).

14.24 Certain of the foregoing privileges and immunities may be conferred on organizations by Orders in Council made pursuant to the International Organizations Act 1968. Such organizations must be declared by Order in Council to have as members the United Kingdom or its Government and one or more foreign sovereign poweres. The privileges that may be conferred are immunity from suit and legal process, inviolability of archives and premises, and certain fiscal privileges. Representatives of such organizations may, under the Act, have conferred on them by Order in Council similar privileges to those enjoyed by the diplomatic agent (for a full account of these matters, the reader is referred to *Halsbury's Laws of England* (4th Edn.) Vol. 18, page 819, *et seq*.).

---

36. *Supra*, fn. 18.
37. (1892) 19 *Journal de Droit International Prive* 429.
38. [1964] 2 All E.R. 256, *per* Diplock, L.J.

CHAPTER 15

THE CONSULAR RELATIONS
ACT 1968

15.1 This Act gives the force of law to certain provisions of the
Vienna Convention on Consular Relations 1963 (Cmnd.
2113). It applies to all consular posts in the United Kingdom,
whether or not the sending State is a party to the Convention.

15.2 Consular agents, unlike diplomatic agents, do not
represent States in all their international relations and are not
accredited to the receiving State. A consul renders only
non-political and technical services for the sending State and
for nationals of both States.

15.3 The Convention's provisions not embodied in the Act
cover such matters as the establishment of consular relations
and consular posts and the exercise of consular functions.
Heads of consular posts are divided into four classes,
consuls-general, consuls, vice-consuls and consular agents.
The Convention also contains, *inter alia*, provisions regarding
precedence of consular posts, the appointment of members of
consular staffs and precedence between members of the staff.

15.4 The privileges accorded by the Act may be curtailed by
Order in Council on the principle of reciprocity (s. 2); and
there is power under s. 3 to give statutory force to agreements
curtailing or extending consular privileges, e.g. by applying to
consular premises, members of a consular post, their families
and residences, some of the privileges accorded under the
Diplomatic Privileges Act (see Sched. 2, Act of 1968).

15.5 The relevant Articles of the Vienna Convention are found
in the First Schedule to the Act.
  Consular officers are of two categories, career consular
officers and honorary consular officers (Article 1(2)). The

distinction is not defined in the Act. As an honorary consular officer may be paid for his work (this is clear from Article 66) the test is probably whether he is full-time employed or not and whether it is a post normally held for the purpose of prestige. Except where specifically noted, the following privileges apply only to posts held by career consular officers.

15.6 Definitions (Article 1)

"Consular post" means any consulate-general, consulate, vice-consulate or consular agency.

"Head of consular post" means the person charged with the duty of acting in that capacity.

"Consular premises" means the buildings or parts of buildings and the land ancillary thereto, irrespective of ownership, used exclusively for the purposes of the consular post.

15.7 Consular premises

The consular premises enjoy a limited inviolability. The United Kingdom authorities (which by s. 1(2) includes any constable and any person exercising a power of entry under any enactment) may not enter that part of the premises used exclusively for the work of the consular post without consent (consent may be assumed in case of fire or other emergency). In view of the definition of consular premises given above, the limiting clause for exclusive use seems tautological.

The consular premises, their furnishings, the property of the consular post and its means of transport shall be immune from any form of requisition for purposes of national defence or public utility; and if expropriation for such purposes is necessary, all possible steps must be taken to avoid impeding the performance of consular functions and property compensation must be paid (Article 31).

The premises (this includes under Article 60 the premises of an honorary consular post) and the residence of the head of the post are exempt from all dues and taxes (other than such as represent payment for specific services rendered (Article 32(1)).

15.8   Archives

The consular archives and documents are inviolable at all times and wherever they may be (Article 33). By Article 1 the archives include all the papers, documents, correspondence, books, films, tapes and registers of the consular post, together with the ciphers and codes, the card-indexes and any article of furniture intended for their protection or safe-keeping.

By Article 61, the consular archives and documents of a consular post headed by an honorary consular officer shall be inviolable at all times and wherever they may be, provided that they are kept separate from other papers and documents and, in particular from the private correspondence of the head of the consular post and of any person working with him, and from the materials, books or documents relating to their profession or trade.

15.9   Communications (Article 35)

The United Kingdom must permit and protect the free communication of the consular post for all official purposes. The post may use all appropriate means of communication, including diplomatic or consular couriers or bags, code and cipher, but the use of a wireless transmitter needs the United Kingdom's consent.

All correspondence relating to the post and its functions is inviolable.

The consular bag must be clearly marked and must contain only official correspondence and documents or articles intended exclusively for official use. It must not be opened or detained, but if there is serious reason to believe it contains unauthorized articles, the State's agent may be asked to open it, and if he refuses it may be returned to its place of origin.

Article 35 also applies to consular posts headed by an honorary consular officer (Article 58).

15.10   Fees

Consular fees and charges may be levied under the laws of the sending State for consular acts and are exempt from the United Kingdom dues and taxes (Article 39).

Article 39 also applies to consular posts headed by an honorary consular officer (Article 58).

15.11   Immunities of Career Consular Officers

Personal inviolability

Consular officers (which means by Article 1 persons, including the head of a consular post, entrusted in that capacity with the exercise of consular functions) are not liable to arrest or detention pending trial, except in the case of a grave crime and pursuant to a decision of the competent judicial authority (by s. 1(2) a grave crime means an offence punishable on a first conviction with a term that may extend to five years or with a more severe sentence). Apart from this exception, consular officers may not be committed to prison nor are they liable to any other form of restriction on their personal freedom save in execution of a judicial decision of final effect.

15.12

Immunity from jurisdiction

(i) Consular officers, as defined above, and consular employees (which means by Article 1 persons employed in the administrative or technical service of a consular post) are immune from jurisdiction "in respect of acts performed in the exercise of consular functions", subject to an exception in respect of a civil action

  (a) on a contract made by such a person not as his State's agent, or
  (b) by a third party for damage arising from an accident in

the United Kingdom caused by a vehicle, vessel or aircraft. This Article, Article 43, also applies to honorary consular officers (Article 58).

"Consular functions" are lengthily defined by Article 5. They include, in summary (items numbered as in the Act):

(a) protecting the interests of the sending State and its nationals within the limits of international law;
(b) promoting commercial, economic, cultural, scientific and, generally, friendly relations between the States;
(d) issuing travel documents;
(e) helping and assisting nationals of the sending State;
(f) acting as notary and civil registrar;
(h) safeguarding the interests of minors of the sending State, and persons under a disability;
(i) protecting where necessary the interests of nationals of the sending State before United Kingdom tribunals;
(j) taking evidence on behalf of the sending State;
(k) supervising, inspecting and assisting vessels and aircraft of the sending State, and
(m) performing any other proper functions entrusted to a consular post by the sending State.

15.13

Compellability as witness

(ii) Members of a consular post may be called upon as witnesses. "Members of a consular post" means by Article 1 consular officers, consular employees and members of the service staff, which last means persons employed in the domestic service of a consular post.

A consular officer may decline to give evidence, in which case no coercive measure or penalty may be applied to him. The taking of his evidence must not interfere with the performance of his functions.

A consular employee or member of the service staff must not decline to give evidence, with this exception: no member of a consular post, including, by Article 58, an honorary consular officer, need give evidence on matters connected with the exercise of their functions or produce official correspondence and documents or give expert evidence on the law of the sending State (Article 44).

15.14

Social Security (Article 48)

Members of a consular post with respect to services rendered by them for the sending State, and members of their families forming part of their households, are exempt from United Kingdom social security provisions. So also are members of the private staff (i.e. persons who are employed exclusively in the private service of a member of the consular post) provided they are not United Kingdom nationals or permanently resident here and are covered by the social security provisions of another State.

By s. 1(6) this exemption does not apply in respect of insurable employment or where contributions are required under the National Insurance Acts.

15.15

Taxation (Article 49)

Consular officers and employees and members of their families forming part of their households are exempt from all dues and taxes, except

(a) indirect taxes normally incorporated in the price of goods or services;

(b) taxes on land (but see above Article 32);

(c) estate, succession or inheritance duties, and duties on transfers (save on death—see Article 51 below);

(d) taxes on private income, including capital gains, having its source in the United Kingdom, and capital taxes on commercial investments made here;

(e) charges levied for specific services rendered;

(f) court fees, mortgage dues, stamp duties.

Members of the service staff are exempt from tax on the wages they receive for their services.

Under Article 66, an honorary consular officer is exempt only from all dues and taxes on the remuneration and emoluments which he receives from the sending State in respect of the exercise of consular functions.

15.16

Public services (Article 52)

Members of the consular post and members of their families forming part of their households, and, under Article 67, honorary consular officers, are exempt from all personal services, all public service of any kind, and from military obligations such as those connected with requisitioning, military contributions and billeting.

15.17

Baggage (Article 50)

The United Kingdom must permit entry free of Customs duty, taxes and related charges (other than charges for storage, cartage and similar services) to

(a) articles for the official use of the consular post
(b) articles for the personal use of a consular officer or members of his family forming part of his household, including articles intended for his establishment, but the articles intended for consumption shall not exceed the quantities necessary for direct utilisation by the persons concerned.

Consular employees enjoy the same privilege but only in respect of articles imported at the time of first installation.

Under Article 62 such free entry must be allowed, in respect of a consular post headed by an honorary consular officer, to certain articles, provided they are for the official use of the post. The articles are coats-of-arms, flags, signboards, seals and stamps, books, official printed matter, office furniture, office equipment and similar articles supplied to the post by or at the instance of the sending State.

The personal baggage of a (career) consular officer and any member of his family forming part of his household may not be inspected unless there is serious reason to believe it contains articles other than those referred to in paragraph (b) above or illegal articles or articles subject to quarantine. Any inspection must be carried out in the presence of the person concerned.

15.18

Death (Article 51)

On the death of a member of the consular post or a member of his family forming part of his household, the United Kingdom must

(a) permit the export of his movable property, except property acquired in the United Kingdom which is prohibited from exportation;

(b) not levy any estate, succession, inheritance or transfer duties on movable property which is in the United Kingdom solely due to the member's presence here.

15.19   Exceptions

Gainful occupation

By Article 57 the privileges and immunities relating to consular posts headed by career consular officers are not accorded

(a) to consular employees or to members of the service staff who carry on any private gainful occupation in the United Kingdom;

(b) to members of the families of such persons or members of his private staff;

(c) to members of the family of a member of a consular post who themselves carry on any private gainful occupation in the United Kingdom.

15.20

United Kingdom nationals

By Article 71, which applies to all posts, career and honorary, consular officers who are nationals of or permanently resident in the United Kingdom need be granted only immunity from jurisdiction and personal inviolability in respect of official acts performed in the exercise of their functions, and the right under Article 44(3) not to give evidence, or produce official documents, relating to the exercise of their functions, nor give expert evidence on the law of the sending State. No other person who is a United Kingdom national or permanently resident here need be granted any privileges or immunities.

"United Kingdom national" means, by s. 1(2), a citizen of the United Kingdom or colonies, a person who is a British subject by virtue of ss. 2, 13, or 16 of the British Nationality Act 1948 or the British Nationality Act 1965, or a British protected person within the meaning of the Act of 1948.

"Permanently resident" is not defined. Du Parcq, L.J., said in *Henriksen* v. *Grafton Hotel Ltd.*[1] that "permanent"

"is indeed a relative term and is not synonymous with 'everlasting'".

In this context the term probably means a person not resident here merely through his employment.

15.21

Family of honorary consular officer

"Privileges and immunities provided in the present Convention shall not be accorded to members of the family of an honorary consular officer or of a consular employee employed at a consular post headed by an honorary consular officer". (Article 58(3).)

15.22   Waiver

Under Article 45, which applies also to privileges in respect of an honorary consular officer, the sending State may, by express

1. [1942] 2 K.B. 184, 196.

waiver in writing, waive, with regard to a member of a consular post any of the privileges set out above under "personal inviolability" and "immunity from jurisdiction". The waiver of immunity in respect of civil proceedings is not a submission to execution; for that a separate waiver is necessary. (See also Chapter 9, paragraph 9.17; Chapter 14, paragraph 14.22.)

If a consular officer or employee himself institutes proceedings he cannot gain immunity on any counterclaim "directly connected with the principal claim". In *High Commissioner for India* v. *Ghosh*[2] a counterclaim for slander was held to be independent of a claim for debt or damages and accordingly a proper subject for immunity.

15.23   Period of immunity (Article 53)

This Article applies also to honorary consular officers.

The period begins when the member of the consular post enters the United Kingdom to take up his post, or, if here already, when he enters on his duties with the post.

His family and private staff enjoy their privileges from the same moment as he does, or from the date they enter the United Kingdom, or from the date they qualify as family or staff, whichever is the latest.

When his consular functions have ended, his privileges, and those of his dependents, cease when he leaves the United Kingdom or after a reasonable time in which to do so. The dependents' privileges also end up when they cease to qualify as family or staff, or, if they intend to leave the United Kingdom within a reasonable time, until their departure.

However, there is no limitation of time for the immunity enjoyed by a consular officer or employee with respect to acts performed in the exercise of his functions.

If a member of the consular post dies, his family enjoy their privileges until they leave the United Kingdom or a reasonable time in which to leave has expired.

2. [1960] 1 Q.B. 134; 28 I.L.R. 150 (1959).

15.24   **Definitions**

The statutory definitions have been given above as the relevant phrases have occurred in the text, but it may be helpful to set out here the provisions of Article 1, which define terms used in the English text of the Convention.

"Consular post" means any consulate-general, consulate, vice-consulate or consular agency.

"Consular district" means the area assigned to a consular post for the exercise of consular functions.

"Head of a consular post" means the person charged with the duty of acting in that capacity.

"Consular officer" means any person, including the head of a consular post, entrusted in that capacity with the exercise of consular functions.

"Consular employee" means any person employed in the administrative or technical service of a consular post.

"Member of the consular post" means consular officers, consular employees and members of the service staff.

"Members of the consular staff" means consular officers, other than the head of a consular post, consular employees and members of the service staff.

"Members of the private staff" means a person who is employed exclusively in the private service of a member of the consular post.

"Consular premises" means the buildings or parts of buildings and the land ancillary thereto, irrespective of ownership, used exclusively for the purposes of the consular post.

"Consular archives" includes all the papers, documents, correspondence, books, films, tapes and registers of the consular post, together with the ciphers and codes, the card-indexes and any article of furniture intended for their protection or safekeeping.

APPENDICES

APPENDIX 1

STATE IMMUNITY ACT 1978

CHAPTER 33

ARRANGEMENT OF SECTIONS

PART I

PROCEEDINGS IN UNITED KINGDOM BY OR AGAINST
OTHER STATES

Immunity from jurisdiction

209

APPENDICES

An Act to make new provision with respect to proceedings in the
    United Kingdom by or against other States; to provide for the
    effect of judgments given against the United Kingdom in the courts
    of States parties to the European Convention on State Immunity;
    to make new provision with respect to the immunities and
    privileges of heads of State; and for connected purposes.
                                                    [20th July 1978]

PART I

PROCEEDINGS IN UNITED KINGDOM BY OR AGAINST OTHER STATES

Immunity from jurisdiction

General immunity from jurisdiction

1.—(1) A State is immune from the jurisdiction of the courts of the
United Kingdom except as provided in the following provisions of
this Part of this Act.

(2) A court shall give effect to the immunity conferred by this
section even though the State does not appear in the proceedings in
question.

Exceptions from immunity

Submission to jurisdiction

2.—(1) A State is not immune as respects proceedings in respect of which it has submitted to the jurisdiction of the courts of the United Kingdom.

(2) A State may submit after the dispute giving rise to the proceedings has arisen or by a prior written agreement; but a provision in any agreement that it is to be governed by the law of the United Kingdom is not to be regarded as a submission.

(3) A State is deemed to have submitted—

(*a*) if it has instituted the proceedings; or

(*b*) subject to subsections (4) and (5) below, if it has intervened or taken any step in the proceedings.

(4) Subsection (3)(*b*) above does not apply to intervention or any step taken for the purpose only of—

(*a*) claiming immunity; or

(*b*) asserting an interest in property in circumstances such that the State would have been entitled to immunity if the proceedings had been brought against it.

(5) Subsection (3)(*b*) above does not apply to any step taken by the State in ignorance of facts entitling it to immunity if those facts could not reasonably have been ascertained and immunity is claimed as soon as reasonably practicable.

(6) A submission in respect of any proceedings extends to any appeal but not to any counter-claim unless it arises out of the same legal relationship or facts as the claim.

(7) The head of a State's diplomatic mission in the United Kingdom, or the person for the time being performing his functions, shall be deemed to have authority to submit on behalf of the State in respect of any proceedings; and any person who has entered into a contract on behalf of and with the authority of a State shall be deemed to have authority to submit on its behalf in respect of proceedings arising out of the contract.

Commercial transactions and contracts to be performed in United Kingdom

3.—(1) A State is not immune as respects proceedings relating to—

(*a*) a commercial transaction entered into by the State; or

(*b*) an obligation of the State which by virtue of a contract (whether a commercial transaction or not) falls to be performed wholly or partly in the United Kingdom.

(2) This section does not apply if the parties to the dispute are States or have otherwise agreed in writing; and subsection (1)(*b*) above does not apply if the contract (not being a commercial transaction) was made in the territory of the State concerned and the obligation in question is governed by its administrative law.

(3) In this section "commercial transaction" means—

(*a*) any contract for the supply of goods or services;

(*b*) any loan or other transaction for the provision of finance and any guarantee or indemnity in respect of any such transaction or of any other financial obligation; and

(*c*) any other transaction or activity (whether of a commercial, industrial, financial, professional or other similar character) into which a State enters or in which it engages otherwise than in the exercise of sovereign authority;

but neither paragraph of subsection (1) above applies to a contract of employment between a State and an individual.

Contracts of employment

4.—(1) A State is not immune as respects proceedings relating to a contract of employment between the State and an individual where the contract was made in the United Kingdom or the work is to be wholly or partly performed there.

(2) Subject to subsections (3) and (4) below, this section does not apply if—

(*a*) at the time when the proceedings are brought the individual is a national of the State concerned; or

(*b*) at the time when the contract was made the individual was neither a national of the United Kingdom nor habitually resident there; or

(*c*) the parties to the contract have otherwise agreed in writing.

(3) Where the work is for an office, agency or establishment maintained by the State in the United Kingdom for commercial purposes, subsection (2)(*a*) and (*b*) above do not exclude the application of this section unless the individual was, at the time when the contract was made, habitually resident in that State.

(4) Subsection (2)(*c*) above does not exclude the application of this section where the law of the United Kingdom requires the proceedings to be brought before a court of the United Kingdom.

(5) In subsection (2)(*b*) above "national of the United Kingdom" means a citizen of the United Kingdom and Colonies, a person who is a British subject by virtue of section 2, 13 or 16 of the British

Nationality Act 1948 or by virtue of the British Nationality Act 1965, a British protected person within the meaning of the said Act of 1948 or a citizen of Southern Rhodesia.

(6) In this section "proceedings relating to a contract of employment" includes proceedings between the parties to such a contract in respect of any statutory rights or duties to which they are entitled or subject as employer or employee.

Personal injuries and damage to property

5. A State is not immune as respects proceedings in respect of—
   (*a*) death or personal injury; or
   (*b*) damage to or loss of tangible property.
caused by an act or ommission in the United Kingdom.

Ownership, possession and use of property

6.—(1) A State is not immune as respects proceedings relating to—
   (*a*) any interest of the State in, or its possession or use of, immovable property in the United Kingdom; or
   (*b*) any obligation of the State arising out of its interest in, or its possession or use of, any such property.

(2) A State is not immune as respects proceedings relating to any interest of the State in movable or immovable property, being an interest arising by way of succession, gift or bona vacantia.

(3) The fact that a State has or claims an interest in any property shall not preclude any court from exercising in respect of it any jurisdiction relating to the estates of deceased persons or persons of unsound mind or to insolvency, the winding up of companies or the administration of trusts.

(4) A court may entertain proceedings against a person other than a State notwithstanding that the proceedings relate to property—
   (*a*) which is in the possession or control of a State; or
   (*b*) in which a State claims an interest,
if the State would not have been immune had the proceedings been brought against it or, in a case within paragraph (*b*) above, if the claim is neither admitted nor supported by prima facie evidence.

Patents, trade-marks etc.

7. A State is not immune as respects proceedings relating to—
   (*a*) any patent, trade-mark, design or plant breeders' rights belonging to the State and registered or protected in the United Kingdom or for which the State has applied in the United Kingdom;

(*b*) an alleged infringement by the State in the United Kingdom of any patent, trade-mark, design, plant breeders' rights or copyright; or

(*c*) the right to use a trade or business name in the United Kingdom.

Membership of bodies corporate etc.

8.—(1) A State is not immune as respects proceedings relating to its membership of a body corporate, an unincorporated body or a partnership which—

(*a*) has members other than States; and

(*b*) is incorporated or constituted under the law of the United Kingdom or is controlled from or has its principal place of business in the United Kingdom,

being proceedings arising between the State and the body or its other members or, as the case may be, between the State and the other partners.

(2) This section does not apply if provision to the contrary has been made by an agreement in writing between the parties to the dispute or by the constitution or other instrument establishing or regulating the body or partnership in question.

Arbitrations

9.—(1) Where a State has agreed in writing to submit a dispute which has arisen, or may arise, to arbitration, the State is not immune as respects proceedings in the courts of the United Kingdom which relate to the arbitration.

(2) This section has effect subject to any contrary provision in the arbitration agreement and does not apply to any arbitration agreement between States.

Ships used for commercial purposes

10.—(1) This section applies to—

(*a*) Admiralty proceedings; and

(*b*) proceedings on any claim which could be made the subject of Admiralty proceedings.

(2) A State is not immune as respects—

(*a* an action in rem against a ship belonging to that State; or

(*b*) an action in personam for enforcing a claim in connection with such a ship,

if, at the time when the cause of action arose, the ship was in use or intended for use for commercial purposes.

(3) Where an action in rem is brought against a ship belonging to a State for enforcing a claim in connection with another ship belonging to that State, subsection (2)(*a*) above does not apply as respects the first-mentioned ship unless, at the time when the cause of action relating to the other ship arose, both ships were in use or intended for use for commercial purposes.

(4) A State is not immune as respects—

    (*a*) an action in rem against a cargo belonging to that State if both the cargo and the ship carrying it were, at the time when the cause of action arose, in use or intended for use for commercial purposes; or

    (*b*) an action in personam for enforcing a claim in connection with such a cargo if the ship carrying it was then in use or intended for use as aforesaid.

(5) In the foregoing provisions references to a ship or cargo belonging to a State include references to a ship or cargo in its possession or control or in which it claims an interest; and, subject to subsection (4) above, subsection (2) above applies to property other than a ship as it applies to a ship.

(6) Sections 3 to 5 above do not apply to proceedings of the kind described in subsection (1) above if the State in question is a party to the Brussels Convention and the claim relates to the operation of a ship owned or operated by that State, the carriage of cargo or passengers on any such ship or the carriage of cargo owned by that State on any other ship.

Value added tax, customs duties etc.

11. A State is not immune as respects proceedings relating to its liability for—

    (*a*) value added tax, any duty of customs or excise or any agricultural levy; or

    (*b*) rates in respect of premises occupied by it for commercial purposes.

Procedure

Service of process and judgments in default of appearance

12.—(1) Any writ or other document required to be served for instituting proceedings against a State shall be served by being transmitted through the Foreign and Commonwealth Office to the Ministry of Foreign Affairs of the State and service shall be deemed to have been effected when the writ or document is received at the Ministry.

(2) Any time for entering an appearance (whether prescribed by rules of court or otherwise) shall begin to run two months after the date on which the writ or document is received as aforesaid.

(3) A State which appears in proceedings cannot thereafter object that subsection (1) above has not been compiled with in the case of those proceedings.

(4) No judgment in default of appearance shall be given against a State except on proof that subsection (1) above has been complied with and that the time for entering an appearance as extended by subsection (2) above has expired.

(5) A copy of any judgment given against a State in default of appearance shall be transmitted through the Foreign and Commonwealth Office to the Ministry of Foreign Affairs of that State and any time for applying to have the judgment set aside (whether prescribed by rules of court or otherwise) shall begin to run two months after the date on which the copy of the judgment is received at the Ministry.

(6) Subsection (1) above does not prevent the service of a writ or other document in any manner to which the State has agreed and subsections (2) and (4) above do not apply where service is effected in any such manner.

(7) This section shall not be construed as applying to proceedings against a State by way of counter-claim or to an action in rem; and subsection (1) above shall not be construed as affecting any rules of court whereby leave is required for the service of process outside the jurisdiction.

Other procedural privileges

13.—(1) No penalty by way of committal or fine shall be imposed in respect of any failure or refusal by or on behalf of a State to disclose or produce any document or other information for the purposes of proceedings to which it is a party.

(2) Subject to subsections (3) and (4) below—
  - (*a*) relief shall not be given against a State by way of injunction or order for specific performance or for the recovery of land or other property; and
  - (*b*) the property of a State shall not be subject to any process for the enforcement of a judgment or arbitration award or, in an action in rem, for its arrest, detention or sale.

(3) Subsection (2) above does not prevent the giving of any relief or the issue of any process with the written consent of the State concerned; and any such consent (which may be contained in a prior agreement) may be expressed so as to apply to a limited extent or

generally; but a provision merely submitting to the jurisdiction of the courts is not to be regarded as a consent for the purposes of this subsection.

(4) Subsection (2)(*b*) above does not prevent the issue of any process in respect of property which is for the time being in use or intended for use for commercial purposes; but, in a case not falling within section 10 above, this subsection applies to property of a State party to the European Convention on State Immunity only if—

(*a*) the process is for enforcing a judgment which is final within the meaning of section 18(1)(*b*) below and the State has made a declaration under Article 24 of the Convention; or

(*b*) the process is for enforcing an arbitration award.

(5) The head of a State's diplomatic mission in the United Kingdom, or the person for the time being performing his functions, shall be deemed to have authority to give on behalf of the State any such consent as is mentioned in subsection (3) above and, for the purposes of subsection (4) above, his certificate to the effect that any property is not in use or intended for use by or on behalf of the State for commercial purposes shall be accepted as sufficient evidence of that fact unless the contrary is proved.

(6) In the application of this section to Scotland—

(*a*) the reference to "injunction" shall be construed as a reference to "interdict";

(*b*) for paragraph (*b*) of subsection (2) above there shall be substituted the following paragraph—

"(*b*) the property of a State shall not be subject to any diligence for enforcing a judgment or order of a court or a decree arbitral or, in an action in rem, to arrestment or sale."; and

(*c*) any reference to "process" shall be construed as a reference to "diligence", any reference to "the issue or any process" as a reference to "the doing of diligence" and the reference in subsection (4)(*b*) above to "an arbitration award" as a reference to "a decree arbitral".

Supplementary provisions

States entitled to immunities and privileges

14.—(1) The immunities and privileges conferred by this Part of this Act apply to any foreign or commonwealth State other than the United Kingdom; and references to a State include references to—

(*a*) the sovereign or other head of that State in his public capacity;

(*b*) the government of that State; and

(*c*) any department of that government,

but not to any entity (hereafter referred to as a "separate entity") which is distinct from the executive organs of the government of the State and capable of suing or being sued.

(2) A separate entity is immune from the jurisdiction of the courts of the United Kingdom if, and only if—

(*a*) the proceedings relate to anything done by it in the exercise of sovereign authority; and

(*b*) the circumstances are such that a State (or, in the case of proceedings to which section 10 above applies, a State which is not a party to the Brussels Convention) would have been so immune.

(3) If a separate entity (not being a State's central bank or other monetary authority) submits to the jurisdiction in respect of proceedings in the case of which it is entitled to immunity by virtue of subsection (2) above, subsections (1) to (4) of section 13 above shall apply to it in respect of those proceedings as if references to a State were references to that entity.

(4) Property of a State's central bank or other monetary authority shall not be regarded for the purposes of subsection (4) of section 13 above as in use or intended for use for commercial purposes; and where any such bank or authority is a separate entity subsections (1) to (3) of that section shall apply to it as if references to a State were references to the bank or authority.

(5) Section 12 above applies to proceedings against the constitutent territories of a federal State; and Her Majesty may by Order in Council provide for the other provisions of this Part of this Act to apply to any such constituent territory specified in the Order as they apply to a State.

(6) Where the provisions of this Part of this Act do not apply to constituent territory by virtue of any such Order subsections (2) and (3) above shall apply to it as if it were a separate entity.

Restriction and extension of immunities and privileges

15.—(1) If it appears to Her Majesty that the immunities and privileges conferred by this Part of this Act in relation to any State—

(*a*) exceed those accorded by the law of that State in relation to the United Kingdom; or

(*b*) are less than those required by any treaty, convention or other international agreement to which that State and the United Kingdom are parties,

Her Majesty may by Order in Council provide for restricting or, as the case may be, extending those immunities and privileges to such extent as appears to Her Majesty to be apropriate.

(2) Any statutory instrument containing an Order under this section shall be subject to annulment in pursuance of a resolution of either House of Parliament.

Excluded matters

16.—(1) This Part of this Act does not affect any immunity or privilege conferred by the Diplomatic Privileges Act 1964 or the Consular Relations Act 1968; and—

(a) section 4 above does not apply to proceedings concerning the employment of the members of a mission within the meaning of the Convention scheduled to the said Act of 1964 or of the members of a consular post within the meaning of the Convention scheduled to the said Act of 1968;

(b) section 6(1) above does not apply to proceedings concerning a State's title to or its possession of property used for the purposes of a diplomatic mission.

(2) This Part of this Act does not apply to proceedings relating to anything done by or in relation to the armed forces of a State while present in the United Kingdom and, in particular, has effect subject to the Visiting Forces Act 1952.

(3) This Part of this Act does not apply to proceedings to which section 17(6) of the Nuclear Installations Act 1965 applies.

(4) This Part of this Act does not apply to criminal proceedings.

(5) This Part of this Act does not apply to any proceedings relating to taxation other than those mentioned in section 11 above.

Interpretation of Part I

17.—(1) In this Part of this Act—

"the Brussels Convention" means the International Convention for the Unification of Certain Rules Concerning the Immunity of State-owned Ships signed in Brussels on 10th April 1926;

"commercial purposes" means purposes of such transactions or activities as are mentioned in section 3(3) above;

"ship" includes hovercraft.

(2) In sections 2(2) and 13(3) above references to an agreement include references to a treaty, convention or other international agreement.

219

(3) For the purposes of sections 3 to 8 above the territory of the United Kingdom shall be deemed to include any dependent territory in respect of which the United Kingdom is a party to the European Convention on State Immunity.

(4) In sections 3(1), 4(1), 5 and 16(2) above references to the United Kingdom include references to its territorial waters and any area designated under section 1(7) of the Continental Shelf Act 1964.

(5) In relation to Scotland in this Part of this Act "action in rem" means such an action only in relation to Admiralty proceedings.

PART II

JUDGMENTS AGAINST UNITED KINGDOM IN
CONVENTION STATES

Recognition of judgments against United Kingdom

18.—(1) This section applies to any judgment given against the United Kingdom by a court in another State party to the European Convention on State Immunity, being a judgment—

(a) given in proceedings in which the United Kingdom was not entitled to immunity by virtue of provisions corresponding to those of sections 2 to 11 above; and

(b) which is final, that is to say, which is not or is no longer subject to appeal or, if given in default of appearance, liable to be set aside.

(2) Subject to section 19 below, a judgment to which this section applies shall be recognized in any court in the United Kingdom as conclusive between the parties thereto in all proceedings founded on the same cause of action and may be relied on by way of defence or counter-claim in such proceedings.

(3) Subsection (2) above (but not section 19 below) shall have effect also in relation to any settlement entered into by the United Kingdom before a court in another State party to the Convention which under the law of that State is treated as equivalent to a judgment.

(4) In this section references to a court in a State party to the Convention include references to a court in any territory in respect of which it is a party.

Exceptions to recognition

19.—(1) A court need not give effect to section 18 above in the case of a judgment—

(a) if to do so would be manifestly contrary to public policy or if any party to the proceedings in which the judgment was given had no adequate opportunity to present his case; or

(*b*) if the judgment was given without provisions corresponding to those of section 12 above having been complied with and the United Kingdom has not entered an appearance or applied to have the judgment set aside.

(2) A court need not give effect to section 18 above in the case of a judgment—

(*a*) if proceedings between the same parties, based on the same facts and having the same purpose—

(i) are pending before a court in the United Kingdom and were the first to be instituted; or

(ii) are pending before a court in another State party to the Convention, were the first to be instituted and may result in a judgment to which that section will apply; or

(*b*) if the result of the judgment is inconsistent with the result of another judgment given in proceedings between the same parties and—

(i) the other judgment is by a court in the United Kingdom and either those proceedings were the first to be instituted or the judgment of that court was given before the first-mentioned judgment became final within the meaning of subsection (1)(*b*) of section 18 above; or

(ii) the other judgment is by a court in another State party to the Convention and that section has already become applicable to it.

(3) Where the judgment was given against the United Kingdom in proceedings in respect of which the United Kingdom was not entitled to immunity by virtue of a provision corresponding to section 6(2) above, a court need not give effect to section 18 above in respect of the judgment if the court that gave the judgment—

(*a*) would not have had jurisdiction in the matter if it had applied rules of jurisdiction corresponding to those applicable to such matters in the United Kingdom; or

(*b*) applied a law other than that indicated by the United Kingdom rules of private international law and would have reached a different conclusion if it had applied the law so indicated.

(4) In subsection (2) above references to a court in the United Kingdom include references to a court in any dependent territory in respect of which the United Kingdom is a party to the Convention, and references to a court in another State party to the Convention include references to a court in any territory in respect of which it is a party.

PART III

MISCELLANEOUS AND SUPPLEMENTARY

Heads of State

20.—(1) Subject to the provisions of this section and to any necessary modifications, the Diplomatic Privileges Act 1964 shall apply to—

(*a*) a sovereign or other head of State;

(*b*) members of his family forming part of his household; and

(*c*) his private servants.

as it applies to the head of a diplomatic mission, to members of his family forming part of his household and to his private servants.

(2) The immunities and privileges conferred by virtue of subsection (1)(*a*) and (*b*) above shall not be subject to the restrictions by reference to nationality or residence mentioned in Article 37(1) or 38 in Schedule 1 to the said Act of 1964.

(3) Subject to any direction to the contrary by the Secretary of State, a person on whom immunities and privileges are conferred by virtue of subsection (1) above shall be entitled to the exemption conferred by section 8(3) of the Immigration Act 1971.

(4) Except as respects value added tax and duties of customs or excise, this section does not affect any question whether a person is exempt from, or immune as respects proceedings relating to, taxation.

(5) This section applies to the sovereign or other head of any State on which immunities and privileges are conferred by Part I of this Act and is without prejudice to the application of that Part to any such sovereign or head of State in his public capacity.

Evidence by certificate

21. A certificate by or on behalf of the Secretary of State shall be conclusive evidence on any question—

(*a*) whether any country is a State for the purposes of Part I of this Act, whether any territory is a constituent territory of a federal State for those purposes or as to the person or persons to be regarded for those purposes as the head or government of a State;

(*b*) whether a State is a party to the Brussels Convention mentioned in Part I of this Act;

(*c*) whether a State is a party to the European Convention on State Immunity, whether it has made a declaration under Article 24 of that Convention or as to the territories in respect of which the United Kingdom or any other State is a party;

(d) whether, and if so when, a document has been served or received as mentioned in section 12(1) or (5) above.

General interpretation

22.—(1) In this Act "court" includes any tribunal or body exercising judicial functions; and references to the courts or law of the United Kingdom include references to the courts or law of any part of the United Kingdom.

(2) In this Act references to entry of appearance and judgments in default of appearance include references to any corresponding procedures.

(3) In this Act "the European Convention on State Immunity" means the Convention of that name signed in Basle on 16th May 1972.

(4) In this Act "dependent territory" means—

(a) any of the Channel Islands;

(b) the Isle of Man;

(c) any colony other than one for whose external relations a country other than the United Kingdom is responsible; or

(d) any country or territory outside Her Majesty's dominions in which Her Majesty has jurisdiction in right of the government of the United Kingdom.

(5) Any power conferred by this Act to make an Order in Council includes power to vary or revoke a previous Order.

Short title, repeals, commencement and extent

23.—(1) This Act may be cited as the State Immunity Act 1978.

(2) Section 13 of the Administration of Justice (Miscellaneous Provisions) Act 1938 and section 7 of the Law Reform (Miscellaneous Provisions) (Scotland) Act 1940 (which become unnecessary in consequence of Part I of this Act) are hereby repealed.

(3) Subject to subsection (4) below, Parts I and II of this Act do not apply to proceedings in respect of matters that occurred before the date of the coming into force of this Act and, in particular—

(a) sections 2(2) and 13(3) do not apply to any prior agreement, and

(b) sections 3, 4 and 9 do not apply to any transaction, contract or arbitration agreement,

entered into before that date.

(4) Section 12 above applies to any proceedings instituted after the coming into force of this Act.

223

(5) This Act shall come into force on such date as may be specified by an order made by the Lord Chancellor by statutory instrument.

(6) This Act extends to Northern Ireland.

(7) Her Majesty may by Order in Council extend any of the provisions of this Act, with or without modification, to any dependent territory.

DIPLOMATIC PRIVILEGES ACT 1964

CHAPTER 81

ARRANGEMENT OF SECTIONS

An Act to amend the law on diplomatic privileges and immunities by giving effect to the Vienna Convention on Diplomatic Relations; and for purposes connected therewith.   [31st July, 1964]

Replacement of existing law

1. The following provisions of this Act shall, with respect to the matters dealt with therein, have effect in substitution for any previous enactment or rule of law.

Application of Vienna Convention

2.—(1) Subject to section 3 of this Act, the Articles set out in Schedule 1 to this Act (being Articles of the Vienna Convention on Diplomatic Relations signed in 1961) shall have the force of law in the United Kingdom and shall for that purpose be construed in accordance with the following provisions of this section.

(2) In those Articles—

"agents of the receiving State" shall be construed as including any constable and any person exercising a power of entry to any premises under any enactment (including any enactment of the Parliament of Northern Ireland);

"national of the receiving State" shall be construed as meaning citizen of the United Kingdom and Colonies;

"Ministry for Foreign Affairs or such other ministry as may be agreed" shall be construed as meaning the department of the Secretary of State concerned;

and, in the application of those Articles to Scotland, any reference to attachment or execution shall be construed as a reference to the execution of diligence, and any reference to the execution of a judgment as a reference to the enforcement of a decree by diligence.

(3) For the purposes of Article 32 a waiver by the head of the mission of any State or any person for the time being performing his functions shall be deemed to be a waiver by that State.

(4) The exemption granted by Article 33 with respect to any services shall be deemed to except those services from any class of employment which is insurable employment, or in respect of which contributions are required to be paid, under the National (Industrial Injuries) Acts, 1946 to 1964, the National Insurance Acts, 1946 to 1964, any enactment for the time being in force amending any of those Acts, or any corresponding enactment of the Parliament of Northern Ireland, but not so as to render any person liable to any contribution which he would not be required to pay if those services were not so excepted.

(5) Articles 35, 36 and 40 shall be construed as granting any privilege or immunity which they require to be granted.

(6) The references in Articles 37 and 38 to the extent to which any privileges and immunities are admitted by the receiving State and to additional privileges and immunities that may be granted by the receiving State shall be construed as referring respectively to the extent to which any privileges and immunities may be specified by Her Majesty by Order in Council and to any additional privileges and immunities that may be so specified.

Restriction of privileges and immunities

3.—(1) If it appears to Her Majesty that the privileges and immunities accorded to a mission of Her Majesty in the territory of any State, or to persons connected with that mission, are less than those conferred by this Act on the mission of that State or on persons connected with that mission, Her Majesty may by an Order in Council withdraw such of the privileges and immunities so conferred from the mission of that State or from such persons connected with it as appears to Her Majesty to be proper.

(2) An Order in Council under this section shall be disregarded for the purposes of paragraph (a) of the proviso to section 4 of the British Nationality Act, 1948 (citizenship of children of certain persons possessing diplomatic immunity).

Evidence

4. If in any proceedings any question arises whether or not any person is entitled to any privilege or immunity under this Act a certificate issued by or under the authority of the Secretary of State stating any fact relating to that question shall be conclusive evidence of that fact.

Consequential amendments

5.—(1) In section 14 (1) of the Aliens Restriction (Amendment) Act, 1919 (saving for diplomatic persons), for the words "head of a foreign diplomatic mission or any member of his official staff or household" there shall be substituted the words "member of a mission (within the meaning of the Diplomatic Privileges Act, 1964) or any person who is a member of the family and forms part of the household of such a member."

(2) In paragraph (a) of the proviso to section 4 of the British Nationality Act, 1948, for the words from "possesses such immunity" to "His Majesty" there shall be substituted the words "is a person on whom any immunity from jurisdiction is conferred by or under the Diplomatic Privileges Act, 1964, or on whom such immunity from jurisdiction as is conferred by that Act on a diplomatic agent is conferred by or under any other Act."

Orders in Council

6.—(1) No recommendation shall be made to Her Majesty in Council to make an Order under section 2 of this Act unless a draft thereof has been laid before Parliament and approved by resolution of each House of Parliament; and any statutory instrument containing an Order under section 3 of this Act shall be subject to annulment in pursuance of a resolution of either House of Parliament.

(2) Any power to make an Order conferred by the foregoing provisions of this Act includes power to vary or revoke an Order by a subsequent Order.

Saving for certain bilateral arrangements

7.—(1) Where any special agreement or arrangement between the Government of any State and the Government of the United Kingdom in force at the commencement of this Act provides for extending—

(*a*) such immunity from jurisdiction and from arrest or detention, and such inviolability of residence, as are conferred by this Act on a diplomatic agent; or

(*b*) such exemption from customs duties, taxes and related charges as is conferred by this Act in respect of articles for the personal use of a diplomatic agent;

to any class of person, or to articles for the personal use of any class of person, connected with the mission of that State, that immunity and inviolability or exemption shall so extend, so long as that agreement or arrangement continues in force.

(2) The Secretary of State shall publish in the London, Edinburgh and Belfast Gazettes a notice specifying the States with which and the classes of person with respect to which such an agreement or arrangement as is mentioned in subsection (1) of this section is in force and whether its effect is as mentioned in paragraph (*a*) or paragraph (*b*) of that subsection, and shall whenever necessary amend the notice by a further such notice; and the notice shall be conclusive evidence of the agreement or arrangement and the classes of person with respect to which it is in force.

Short title, interpretation, commencement, repeal and saving

8.—(1) This Act may be cited as the Diplomatic Privileges Act, 1964.

(2) This Act shall be construed as if Southern Rhodesia were a State.

(3) This Act shall come into force on such day as Her Majesty may by Order in Council appoint.

(4) The enactments mentioned in Schedule 2 to this Act are hereby repealed to the extent specified in column 3 of that Schedule.

(5) Any Order in Council under the Diplomatic Immunities Restriction Act, 1955, which is in force immediately before the commencement of this Act shall, so far as it could have been made under section 3 of this Act, have effect as if so made.

SCHEDULES

Section 2   SCHEDULE 1

ARTICLES OF VIENNA CONVENTIONS HAVING THE FORCE OF LAW
IN THE UNITED KINGDOM

See Appendix 3, page 230.

ARTICLES OF THE VIENNA CONVENTION (1961) HAVING THE FORCE OF LAW IN THE UNITED KINGDOM

ARTICLE 1

For the purpose of the present Convention, the following expressions shall have the meanings hereunder assigned to them:

(a) the "head of the mission" is the person charged by the sending State with the duty of acting in that capacity;

(b) the "members of the mission" are the head of the mission and the members of the staff of the mission;

(c) the "members of the staff of the mission" are the members of the diplomatic staff, of the administrative and technical staff and of the service staff of the mission;

(d) the "members of the diplomatic staff" are the members of the staff of the mission having diplomatic rank;

(e) a "diplomatic agent" is the head of the mission or a member of the diplomatic staff of the mission;

(f) the "members of the administrative and technical staff" are the members of the staff of the mission employed in the administrative and technical service of the mission;

(g) the "members of the service staff" are the members of the staff of the mission in the domestic service of the mission;

(h) a "private servant" is a person who is in the domestic service of a member of the mission and who is not an employee of the sending State;

(i) the "premises of the mission" are the buildings or parts of buildings and the land ancillary thereto, irrespective of ownership, used for the purposes of the mission including the residence of the head of the mission.

ARTICLE 22

1. The premises of the mission shall be inviolable. The agents of the receiving State may not enter them, except with the consent of the head of the mission.

2. The receiving State is under a special duty to take all appropriate steps to protect the premises of the mission against any intrusion or damage and to prevent any disturbance of the peace of the mission or impairment of its dignity.

3. The premises of the mission, their furnishings and other property thereon and the means of transport of the mission shall be immune from search, requisition, attachment or execution.

ARTICLE 23

1. The sending State and the head of the mission shall be exempt from all national, regional or municipal dues and taxes in respect of the premises of the mission, whether owned or leased, other than such as represent payment for specific services rendered.

2. The exemption from taxation referred to in this Article shall not apply to such dues and taxes payable under the law of the receiving State by persons contracting with the sending State or the head of the mission.

ARTICLE 24

The archives and documents of the mission shall be inviolable at any time and wherever they may be.

ARTICLE 27

1. The receiving State shall permit and protect free communication on the part of the mission for all official purposes. In communicating with the Government and other missions and consulates of the sending State, wherever situated, the mission may employ all appropriate means, including diplomatic couriers and messages in code or cipher. However, the mission may install and use a wireless transmitter only with the consent of the receiving State.

2. The official correspondence of the mission shall be inviolable. Official correspondence means all correspondence relating to the mission and its functions.

3. The diplomatic bag shall not be opened or detained.

4. The packages constituting the diplomatic bag must bear visible external marks of their character and may contain only diplomatic documents or articles intended for official use.

5. The diplomatic courier, who shall be provided with an official document indicating his status and the number of packages constituting the diplomatic bag, shall be protected by the receiving

State in the performance of his functions. He shall enjoy personal inviolability and shall not be liable to any form of arrest or detention.

6. The sending State or the mission may designate diplomatic couriers *ad hoc*. In such cases the provisions of paragraph 5 of this Article shall also apply, except that the immunities therein mentioned shall cease to apply when such a courier has delivered to the consignee the diplomatic bag in his charge.

7. A diplomatic bag may be entrusted to the captain of a commercial aircraft scheduled to land at an authorised port of entry. He shall be provided with an official document indicating the number of packages constituting the bag but he shall not be considered to be a diplomatic courier. This mission may send one of its members to take possession of the diplomatic bag directly and freely from the captain of the aircraft.

ARTICLE 28

The fees and charges levied by the mission in the course of its official duties shall be exempt from all dues and taxes.

ARTICLE 29

The person of a diplomatic agent shall be inviolable. He shall not be liable to any form of arrest or detention. The receiving State shall treat him with due respect and shall take all appropriate steps to prevent any attack on his person, freedom or dignity.

ARTICLE 30

1. The private residence of a diplomatic agent shall enjoy the same inviolability and protection as the premises of the mission.

2. His papers, correspondence land, except as provided in paragraph 3 of Article 31, his property, shall likewise enjoy inviolability.

ARTICLE 31

1. A diplomatic agent shall enjoy immunity from the criminal jurisdiction of the receiving State. He shall also enjoy immunity from its civil and administrative jurisdiction, except in the case of:
   (*a*) a real action relating to private immovable property situated in the territory of the receiving State, unless he holds it on behalf of the sending State for the purposes of the mission;

(*b*) an action relating to succession in which the diplomatic agent is involved as executor, administrator, heir or legatee as a private person and not on behalf of the sending State;

(*c*) an action relating to any professional or commercial activity exercised by the diplomatic agent in the receiving State outside his official functions.

2. A diplomatic agent is not obliged to give evidence as a witness.

3. No measures of execution may be taken in respect of a diplomatic agent except in the cases coming under sub-paragraphs (*a*), (*b*) and (*c*) of paragraph 1 of this Article and provided that the measures concerned can be taken without infringing the inviolability of his person or of his residence.

4. The immunity of a diplomatic agent from the jurisdiction of the receiving State does not exempt him from the jurisdiction of the sending State.

ARTICLE 32

1. The immunity from jurisdiction of diplomatic agents and of persons enjoying immunity under Article 37 may be waived by the sending State.

2. The waiver must always be express.

3. The initiation of proceedings by a diplomatic agent or by a person enjoying immunity from jurisdiction under Article 37 shall preclude him from invoking immunity from jurisdiction in respect of any counter-claim directly connected with the principal claim.

4. Waiver of immunity from jurisdiction in respect of civil or administrative proceedings shall not be held to imply waiver of immunity in respect of the execution of the judgment, for which a separate waiver shall be necessary.

ARTICLE 33

1. Subject to the provisions of paragraph 3 of this Article, a diplomatic agent shall with respect to services rendered for the sending State be exempt from social security provisions which may be in force in the receiving State.

2. The exemption provided for in paragraph 1 of this Article shall also apply to private servants who are in the sole employ of a diplomatic agent, on condition:

(*a*) that they are not nationals of or permanently resident in the receiving State; and

(*b*) that they are covered by the social security provisions which may be in force in the sending State or a third State.

3. A diplomatic agent who employs persons to whom the exemption provided for in paragraph 2 of this Article does not apply shall observe the obligations which the social security provisions of the receiving State impose upon employers.

4. The exemption provided for in paragraphs 1 and 2 of this Article shall not preclude voluntary participation in the social security system of the receiving State provided that such participation is permitted by that State.

5. The provisions of this Article shall not affect bilateral or multilateral agreements concerning social security concluded previously and shall not prevent the conclusion of such agreements in the future.

ARTICLE 34

A diplomatic agent shall be exempt from all dues and taxes, personal or real, national, regional or municipal, except:

- (a) indirect taxes of a kind which are normally incorporated in the price of goods or services;
- (b) dues and taxes on private immovable property situated in the territory of the receiving State, unless he holds it on behalf of the sending State for the purposes of the mission;
- (c) estate, succession or inheritance duties levied by the receiving State, subject to the provisions of paragraph 4 of Article 39;
- (d) dues and taxes on private income having its source in the receiving State and capital taxes on investments made in commercial undertakings in the receiving State;
- (e) charges levied for specific services rendered;
- (f) registration, court or record fees, mortgage dues and stamp duty, with respect to immovable property, subject to the provisions of Article 23.

ARTICLE 35

The receiving State shall exempt diplomatic agents from all personal services, from all public service of any kind whatsoever, and from military obligations such as those connected with requisitioning, military contributions and billeting.

ARTICLE 36

1. The receiving State shall, in accordance with such laws and regulations as it may adopt, permit entry of and grant exemption

from all customs duties, taxes, and related charges other than charges for storage, cartage and similar services, on:

(*a*) articles for the official use of the mission;

(*b*) articles for the personal use of a diplomatic agent or members of his family forming part of his household, including articles intended for his establishment.

2. The personal baggage of a diplomatic agent shall be exempt from inspection, unless there are serious grounds for presuming that it contains articles not covered by the exemptions mentioned in paragraph 1 of the Article, or articles the import or export of which is prohibited by the law or controlled by the quarantine regulations of the receiving State. Such inspection shall be conducted only in the presence of the diplomatic agent or of his authorised representative.

ARTICLE 37

1. The members of the family of a diplomatic agent forming part of his household shall, if they are not nationals of the receiving State, enjoy the privileges and immunities specified in Articles 29 to 36.

2. Members of the administrative and technical staff of the mission, together with members of their families forming part of their respective households, shall, if they are not nationals of or permanently resident in the receiving State, enjoy the privileges and immunities specified in Articles 29 to 35, except that the immunity from civil and administrative jurisdiction of the receiving State specified in paragraph 1 of Article 31 shall not extend to acts performed outside the course of their duties. They shall also enjoy the privileges specified in Article 36, paragraph 1, in respect of articles imported at the time of first installation.

3. Members of the service staff of the mission who are not nationals of or permanently resident in the receiving State shall enjoy immunity in respect of acts performed in the course of their duties, exemption from dues and taxes on the emoluments they receive by reason of their employment and the exemption contained in Article 33.

4. Private servants of members of the mission shall, if they are not nationals of or permanently resident in the receiving State, be exempt from dues and taxes on the emoluments they receive by reason of their employment. In other respects, they may enjoy privileges and immunities only to the extent admitted by the receiving State. However, the receiving State must exercise its jurisdiction over those persons in such a manner as not to interfere unduly with the performance of the functions of the mission.

ARTICLE 38

1. Except in so far as additional privileges and immunities may be granted by the receiving State, a diplomatic agent who is a national of or permanently resident in that State shall enjoy only immunity from jurisdiction, and inviolability, in respect of official acts performed in the exercise of his functions.

2. Other members of the staff of the mission and private servants who are nationals of or permanently resident in the receiving State shall enjoy privileges and immunities only to the extent admitted by the receiving State. However, the receiving State must exercise its jurisdiction over those persons in such a manner as not to interfere unduly with the performance of the functions of the mission.

ARTICLE 39

1. Every person entitled to privileges and immunities shall enjoy them from the moment he enters the territory of the receiving State on proceeding to take up his post or, if already in its territory, from the moment when his appointment is notified to the Ministry for Foreign Affairs or such other ministry as may be agreed.

2. When the functions of a person enjoying privileges and immunities have come to an end, such privileges and immunities shall normally cease at the moment when he leaves the country, or on expiry of a reasonable period in which to do so, but shall subsist until that time, even in case of armed conflict. However, with respect to acts performed by such a person in the exercise of his functions as a member of the mission, immunity shall continue to subsist.

3. In case of the death of a member of the mission, the members of his family shall continue to enjoy the privileges and immunities to which they are entitled until the expiry of a reasonable period in which to leave the country.

4. In the event of the death of a member of the mission not a national of or permanently resident in the receiving State or a member of his family forming part of his household, the receiving State shall permit the withdrawal of the movable property of the deceased, with the exception of any property acquired in the country the export of which was prohibited at the time of his death. Estate, succession and inheritance duties shall not be levied on movable property the presence of which in the receiving State was due solely to the presence there of the deceased as a member of the mission or as a member of the family of a member of the mission.

ARTICLE 40

1. If a diplomatic agent passes through or is in the territory of a third State, which has granted him a passport visa if such visa was necessary, while proceeding to take up or to return to his post, or when returning to his own country, the third State shall accord him inviolability and such other immunities as may be required to ensure his transit or return. The same shall apply in the case of any members of his family enjoying privileges or immunities who are accompanying the diplomatic agent, or travelling separately to join him or to return to their country.

2. In circumstances similar to those specified in paragraph 1 of this Article, third States shall not hinder the passage of members of the administrative and technical or service staff of a mission, and of members of their families, through their territories.

3. Third States shall accord to official correspondence and other official communications in transit, including messages in code or cipher, the same freedom and protection as is accorded by the receiving State. They shall accord to diplomatic couriers, who have been granted a passport visa if such visa was necessary, and diplomatic bags in transit the same inviolability and protection as the receiving State is bound to accord.

4. The obligations of third States under paragraphs 1, 2 and 3 of this Article shall also apply to the persons mentioned respectively in those paragraphs, and to official communications and diplomatic bags, whose presence in the territory of the third State is due to *force majeure*.

RECENT MATERIAL

This appendix contains material that came in too late for inclusion in the main body of the text.

A.   R. v. Secretary of State for Foreign and Commonwealth Affairs, ex parte Trawnik and another.

The applicants were German citizens, living in West Berlin, who sought to defeat a proposal by H.M. Government to establish a machine-gun range at Gatow for use by British troops stationed there. In the course of their action for a *quia timet* injunction on the ground of apprehended nuisance as a result of the noise of the firing, the Foreign Secretary issued a certificate under s. 21 of the State Immunity Act 1978 certifying that Germany was a State for the purposes of s. 1 of the Act and that the persons to be regarded for the purposes of Part 1 of the Act as the Government of Germany included members of the Allied Kommandatura of Berlin, including Major-General Lennox. If this certificate, along with similar certificates issued under the Crown Proceedings Act 1947, were conclusive the applicants' main action would fail.

Forbes, J., in the Divisional Court, said that the position at common law was that questions concerning the identity and recognition of foreign States were matters of which the courts would take judicial notice and thus were strictly not matters to be proved by evidence at all. Once given, such certificates were conclusive of the facts stated therein and no evidence could be adduced by parties to contradict them. Reference was made to *Duff Development Co. Ltd.* v. *Kelantan Government*[2] and *Carl Zeiss Stiftung* v. *Rayner & Keeler Ltd. (No. 2)*[3]. In order to succeed in an application for judicial review of the certificate the applicants would have to establish that the facts were contrary to those stated by the Secretary of State. But no evidence could be called to rebut or contradict the facts. The certificate was only reviewable by the courts to see whether, in the

1. *The Times*, 18 April 1985.
2. [1924] A.C. 797, 808; 2 I.L.R. 124 (1924).
3. [1967] 1 A.C. 852, 901, 956.

first place, it was what it purported to be, namely a certificate issued by the Secretary of State or someone authorized to issue it on his behalf: if there was evidence to show that it was not a genuine certificate at all then it was a complete nullity and the court could say so. Neither the statutory provision nor the common law prevented the admission of evidence which contradicted the genuineness of the certificate itself.

Further, the court could compare the matter which was certified with the words of the statute to see whether or not the certificate on its face fell within the sphere allotted by the statute to the Secretary of State. Kennedy, J., said that the statutory provision meant the content of a certificate, provided that it was a certificate, could not be challenged. In a proper case the court might be prepared to consider whether a purported certificate was genuine or a nullity, but once it was clear that the document was what it purported to be, namely a certificate given under the Act by an appropriate authority, dealing with matters which the Act enabled that person to certify, any possibility of judicial review was at an end. If there was an abuse of power in its issue the court could give no redress.

B. White Paper, April 1985 (Cmnd. 9497)

H.M. Government's reply to the Foreign Affairs Committee's report, *The Abuse of Diplomatic Immunities and Privileges*, was contained in their April 1985 White Paper (Cmnd. 9497). Their conclusions may be summarized as follows:

They agree that amendment of the Vienna Convention is not a viable proposition and that the solution to abuse should be sought in a firmer policy towards the application of the Convention. They have already revised and strengthened their requirements and procedures on the notification of staff of diplomatic missions, and intend to take all practical steps to ensure that they have appropriate information at as early a stage as possible on all staff newly appointed to missions in London. They have already in the past year used their discretion to limit the size of individual missions and intend to continue to do so on an *ad hoc* basis.

Administrative measures have been taken to deal with abuse of diplomatic premises and to limit the extent of mission premises in accordance with international law and practice. Proposals for legislation to control in exceptional circumstances the acquisition and disposal of premises are under consideration. The Government regards as incompatible with the functions of a mission trading or other activities conducted for financial gain, such as selling tickets for airlines or holidays, or charging fees for language classes or public lectures, and educational activities, such as schools or students' hostels; and diplomatic status is now to be withdrawn from separate Tourist Offices.

Demonstrations outside missions will continue to be allowed so long as they do not imperil the safety or efficient working of the mission. Consultation by the police with the Home Office and the Foreign and Commonwealth Office on any change of policy over the policing of demonstrations will be improved (this last is largely as a result of the changing of policy with regard to demonstrations outside South Africa House implemented by the police without consulting the F.C.O.).

As to the diplomatic bag, the Government reiterate their willingness to take any necessary action on the basis of the overriding right of self-defence or the duty to protect human life (they would have acted as they did in the case of Mr Dikko even if the crate in which he was found had in fact constituted a diplomatic bag). They do not think that it would be practical to seek to change the legal rules on the diplomatic bag, but they are ready to scan a bag electronically on specific occasions where the grounds for suspicion are sufficiently strong. In October 1984 missions in London as well as H.M. Customs and Excise were given revised clarification of the rules on the identification (including labels and seals) and the handling of foreign diplomatic bags, and these rules will be rigorously applied. Records of the size and weight of bags will not be made as a matter of routine but will be undertaken where there are specific grounds for doing so.

Guidelines on breaches of the criminal law by diplomats and their families and the criteria for dealing with them have been clarified and more stringent standards are being applied. In August 1984 Heads of Missions were informed of the Foreign Secretary's statement to the Foreign Affairs Committee in July that "it would be right in future to expect and to apply more stringent standards". They were in particular asked for cooperation in waiving immunity or arranging for the withdrawal of any members of staff who might be responsible for serious offences. Specific guidance is now being issued to all diplomats newly appointed to London on the attitude likely to be taken in the event of any breach of United Kingdom laws and regulations, including driving and shop-lifting offences, and they are asked to ensure that dependant members of their families are also aware of this guidance. It has also been brought to the attention of existing staff of diplomatic missions.

INDEX

References are to paragraph numbers

Central banks—*cont.*
  funds not for commercial purposes, 9.20
  immunity of funds, 3.22
  injunctions against, 9.20
  separate entity test, 4.12
  U.S. law, 9.20
Channel Islands, 10.6
Collisions between ships, 7.25, 7.26
Colonies, 10.6
Commercial activities, 5.1–5.3
  and State immunity, 2.10
  definition, 6.2, 7.19
    in U.S. law, 6.2.1
  engaged in by ambassador, 14.8
  exception to unavailability of processes against property, 9.18
  non-immune, 13.3
    non-retrospection, 11.2
  State involvement, 3.5–3.12, 4.5
  statutory exceptions, 6.1–6.4, 9.10
  treaty obligations, 6.4
  see also Acta gestionis; Acta imperii: distinguished from *acta gestionis*
Common law
  incorporation into international law, 3.18
  shipping, 7.1–7.17
  sovereign status, 4.1–4.7
  State immunity, 2.2–2.9, 3.1–3.27
    exceptions, 5.1–5.4
  submissions to the jurisdiction, 8.1–8.2
Commonwealth countries
  conference attendance, 14.2
  immunity of members of missions, 14.15
Communications
  consular, 15.9
  diplomatic missions, 14.21
Computerized records, 14.20.11
Conference attendance, 14.2
Conscription, 14.13
Consular agents
  classes, 15.3
  status, 15.2
Consular bags, 15.9
Consular district, definition, 15.24
Consular employee, definition, 15.24
Consular functions, definition, 15.12
Consular officers
  categories, 15.5
  compellability of witnesses, 15.13

Consular officers—*cont.*
  definition, 15.24
    "permanently resident", 15.20
  exemption from public service, 15.16
  honorary, 15.21
  immunities following death, 15.18
    for families, 15.23
  immunity
    from jurisdiction, 15.12
    of baggage, 15.17
  period of immunity, 15.23
  personal inviolability, 15.11
  social security exemptions, 15.14
  tax exemptions, 15.15
  U.K. nationals, 15.20
Consular posts
  communications, 15.9
  definition, 15.6, 15.24
    head, 15.6, 15.24
    member, 15.24
    members of private staff, 15.24
    staff members, 15.24
  exceptions to immunities, 15.19
  waivers, 15.22
Consular premises
  definition, 15.6, 15.24
  exemption from taxes, 15.7
  immunity from requisition, 15.7
  limited inviolability, 15.7
Consular privileges, 13.12
  reciprocity principle, 15.4
  scope of 1968 Act, 15.1
Consumer legislation, 2.5
Contracts
  made at Embassies, 6.7
  made in U.K., 6.7
  to be performed in U.K., statutory exceptions, 6.5–6.7
Contracts of employment
  common law, 6.8
  statute, 6.9–6.12
    non-retrospection, 11.2
  treaty, 6.13
Copyright, 6.32
Council of Europe
  immunities, 13.12
  State immunity concerns, 2.14
Criminal proceedings, immunity from, 10.2
Customs duty liability, 6.34
Cyprus, ratification of European Convention, 2.9

INDEX

243

State immunity—*cont.*
  development, 1.1
  doctrine of absolute immunity, 3.28
    limited exceptions, 3.11
  exceptions, 9.8
  excluded matters, 10.1–10.6
  from execution, 9.16.1
  from jurisdiction and execution,
    differences in national laws, 9.16
  from pre-judgement attachment,
    8.4.2
  from processes issued against
    property, 9.18
  included matters, 10.6
  limited rights to execute treaty
    obligations, 9.19
  nineteenth century enlargement, 3.5
  post-war phase, 3.14
  procedural privileges
    common law, 9.1–9.4
    statute, 9.5–9.22
  proscribed reliefs, 9.17–9.18
  scope, 1.2, 1.3
  statute, 2.10–2.13, 3.28
    exceptions, 5.5, 6.1–6.35
    non-retrospection, 11.1–11.2
  treaty, 2.14–2.15, 3.29
    non-retrospection, 11.3
  U.K.'s isolated position, 3.13
  waivers, 8.1, 8.4
    by prior treaty in U.S., 8.4.2
  see also Submission to jurisdiction
  see also Sovereign immunity
States
  sovereign status, 4.1
  submission to jurisdiction, 8.4
Statute law
  shipping, 7.18–7.22
  sovereign status, 4.8–4.12
  State immunity, 2.10–2.13, 3.28
    exceptions, 5.5, 6.1–6.35
  submission to jurisdiction, 8.3–8.7
Submission to jurisdiction
  and consents, 9.17, 9.18
  common law, 8.1–8.2
  in cases of claim and counterclaim,
    8.10
  non-restrospection, 11.2
  persons who may make, 8.6
  procedures, 8.12
  recognition of judgments of foreign
    courts, 9.21
  scope, 8.5

Submission to jurisdiction—*cont.*
  statute law, 8.3–8.7
  tests, 8.4.2
  treaty, 8.8–8.13
Sucharitkul, Sompong, 2.16
Switzerland
  cases relating to *acta imperii/acta
    gestionis* dichotomy, 12.21
  ratification of European Convention,
    2.9

Tate, J. B., 3.12
Taxation, 2.5, 10.5
  exemption
    and exceptions of diplomatic
      agents, 14.11
    of consular fees and charges, 15.10
    of consular staff and families, 15.15
    of fees and charges of diplomatic
      missions, 13.10 14.20.12
    of private servants of mission staff,
      14.18
  immunities of mission staff, 14.17
  immunity of consular premises, 15.7
  statute, 6.34
Territorial waters, 6.5, 6.12, 10.6
Territories, constituent
  status, 4.13
  see also Federated States
Tort
  common law, 6.14
  statute law, 6.15–6.22
  treaty, 6.21
Towage claims, 7.18
Trade names, 6.33
  statute, 6.32
Trademarks
  statute, 6.32
  treaty, 6.33
Treaty obligations, 2.9
  definition of State, 4.15
  shipping, 7.23–7.27
  State immunity, 2.14–2.15, 3.29
Trust funds, 5.4, 6.22, 6.26
  no immunity for foreign sovereigns,
    3.11

Unfair dismissal claims, 3.26
United Kingdom
  definition
    of "territory", 10.6
    of "U.K. national", 6.12, 15.20